CCNP™ Exam Notes™: Cisco® LAN Switch Configuration

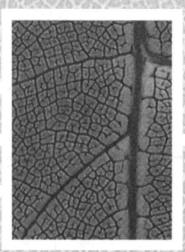

Todd Lammle
Robert Padjen

San Francisco • Paris • Düsseldorf • Soest • London

Associate Publisher: Neil Edde
Contracts and Licensing Manager: Kristine O'Callaghan
Acquisitions & Developmental Editor: Neil Edde
Editor: Ronn Jost
Project Editor: Donna Crossman
Technical Editor: James D. Taylor
Book Designer: Bill Gibson
Graphic Illustrator: Tony Jonick
Electronic Publishing Specialist: Rhonda Ries
Project Team Leader: Jennifer Durning
Proofreaders: Maryka Trent Baraka, Patty Brewer, Al Davis, Phil Hamer, Rob Siedenburg
Indexer: Marilyn Smith
Cover Designer: Archer Design
Cover Photographer: The Image Bank

SYBEX, Network Press, and the Network Press logo are registered trademarks of SYBEX Inc.

Exam Notes is a trademark of SYBEX Inc.

Screen reproductions produced with Collage Complete.

Collage Complete is a trademark of Inner Media Inc.

This study guide and/or material is not sponsored by, endorsed by or affiliated with Cisco Systems, Inc. Cisco®, Cisco Systems®, CCDA™, CCNA™, CCDP™, CCNP™, CCIE™, CCSI™, the Cisco Systems logo and the CCIE logo are trademarks or registered trademarks of Cisco Systems, Inc. in the United States and certain other countries. All other trademarks are trademarks of their respective owners.

TRADEMARKS: SYBEX has attempted throughout this book to distinguish proprietary trademarks from descriptive terms by following the capitalization style used by the manufacturer.

The author and publisher have made their best efforts to prepare this book, and the content is based upon final release software whenever possible. Portions of the manuscript may be based upon pre-release versions supplied by software manufacturer(s). The author and the publisher make no representation or warranties of any kind with regard to the completeness or accuracy of the contents herein and accept no liability of any kind including but not limited to performance, merchantability, fitness for any particular purpose, or any losses or damages of any kind caused or alleged to be caused directly or indirectly from this book.

Copyright ©2000 SYBEX Inc., 1151 Marina Village Parkway, Alameda, CA 94501. World rights reserved. No part of this publication may be stored in a retrieval system, transmitted, or reproduced in any way, including but not limited to photocopy, photograph, magnetic or other record, without the prior agreement and written permission of the publisher.

Library of Congress Card Number: 99-66410

ISBN: 0-7821-2542-5

Manufactured in the United States of America
10 9 8 7 6 5 4 3 2 1

Acknowledgments

Many thanks to those who helped us complete yet another Sybex book. From development through production, your hard work and dedication to this project are recognized and appreciated.

We would like to acknowledge Neil Edde, who developed and oversaw the project to the end with patience and insight.

Many thanks also to the editing team for their attention to details large and small (but all equally important): Editor Ronn Jost, who kept the flow with his careful editing; Technical Editor Jim Taylor, who kept things technically honest; and Project Editor Donna Crossman, who stayed busy keeping us all on schedule.

Much appreciation goes to the production team for taking the words and making them look great on the page: Project Team Leader Jennifer Durning, who motivated and organized the production side of the project with gusto and energy; and Jan Fisher and her talented team of proofreaders and electronic publishing specialists at Publication Services.

Thanks to everyone for contributing their hard work, energy, and motivation.

Table of Contents

Introduction

This book is intended to start you out on an exciting new path toward obtaining your CCNP certification. It reaches beyond popular certifications such as the MCSE and CNE to provide you with an indispensable factor in understanding today's network—insight into the Cisco world of internetworking.

If you've purchased this book, you are probably chasing one of the Cisco professional certifications: CCNA/CCNP, CCDA/CCDP, or CCIE. All of these are great goals, and they are also great career builders. Glance through any newspaper and you'll find employment opportunities for people with these certifications—these ads are there because finding qualified network administrators is a challenge in today's market. The certification means you know something about the product, but, more importantly, it means you have the ability, determination, and focus to learn—the greatest skills any employee can have!

You've probably also heard all the rumors about how hard the Cisco tests are—believe us, the rumors are true! Cisco has designed a series of exams that truly challenge your knowledge of their products. Each test not only covers the materials presented in a particular class, it also covers the prerequisite knowledge for that course.

Is This Book for You?

This book covers everything you need to know to pass the Cisco CLSC exam. It will teach you how to perform basic configurations on Cisco switches using both the command line interface (CLI) and the menu systems of the different Catalyst switches. Each chapter begins with a list of the CLSC test objectives covered in it; make sure you read them over before working through the chapter.

The Sybex Exam Notes books were designed to be succinct, portable exam review guides. They can be used either in conjunction with a more complete study program—supplemented by books, CBT courseware, or practice in a classroom/lab environment—or as an exam review for those who don't feel the need for more extensive test preparation. It isn't our goal to "give the answers away," but rather to identify those topics on which you can expect to be tested and to provide sufficient coverage of these topics.

Perhaps you've been working with Cisco internetworking technologies for years now. The thought of paying lots of money for a specialized Cisco exam preparation course probably doesn't sound too appealing. What can they teach you that you don't already know, right? Be careful, though. Many experienced network administrators, even CCIEs, have walked confidently into test centers only to walk sheepishly out of them after failing a Cisco exam. As they discovered, there's the Cisco of the real world and the Cisco of the Cisco certification exams. It's our goal with these Exam Notes books to show you where the two converge and where they diverge. After you've finished reading through this book, you should have a clear idea of how your understanding of the technologies involved matches up with the expectations of the Cisco test makers.

Or perhaps you're relatively new to the world of Cisco internetworking, drawn to it by the promise of challenging work and higher salaries. You've just waded through an 800-page Cisco CLSC study guide or taken a class at a local training center. Lots of information to keep track of, isn't it? Well, by organizing the Exam Notes books according to the Cisco exam objectives, and by breaking up the information into concise, manageable pieces, we've created what we think is the handiest exam review guide available. Throw it in your briefcase and carry it to work with you. As you read through the book, you'll be able to quickly identify those areas you know best and those that require more in-depth review.

SEE ALSO The goal of the Exam Notes series is to help Cisco certification candidates familiarize themselves with the subjects on which they can expect to be tested in the certification exams. For complete, in-depth coverage of the technologies and topics involved in Cisco networking, we recommend the Cisco Certification Study Guide series from Sybex.

How Is This Book Organized?

As mentioned above, this book is organized according to the official exam objectives list prepared by Cisco for the CLSC exam. Within each chapter, the individual exam objectives are addressed in turn. Each objective section is further divided according to the type of information presented.

Critical Information

This section presents the greatest level of detail on information that is relevant to the objective. This is the place to start if you're unfamiliar with or uncertain about the technical issues related to the objective.

Necessary Procedures

Here you'll find instructions for procedures that require a lab computer to be completed. From logging in to a switch to configuring IP, the information in these sections addresses the hands-on requirements for the CLSC exams.

NOTE   Not every objective has a hands-on procedure associated with it. For such objectives, the "Necessary Procedures" section has been left out.

Exam Essentials

In this section, we've put together a concise list of the most crucial topics of subject areas that you'll need to fully comprehend prior to taking the Cisco exam. This section can help you identify those topics that might require more study on your part.

Key Terms and Concepts

Here we've compiled a mini-glossary of the most important terms and concepts related to the specific objective. You'll understand what all those technical words mean within the context of the related subject matter.

Sample Questions

For each exam objective, we've included a selection of questions similar to those you'll encounter on the actual Cisco exam. Answers and explanations are provided so you can gain some insight into the test-taking process.

How Do You Become a CCNP?

The CCNP certification is the new, hot Cisco certifications program. With the new certification programs, Cisco has created a stepping-stone approach to CCIE (Cisco Certified Internetwork Engineer) certification. By taking four more exams after you pass your CCNA, you can achieve CCNP status. One of the required CCNP exams is the CLSC exam.

Why Become a CCNP?

Cisco has created a certification process, not unlike Microsoft's or Novell's, to give administrators a set of skills, and prospective employers an authenticated way to measure those skills. Becoming a CCNP can be the initial step of a successful journey toward a new or refreshed, highly rewarding, and sustainable career.

As you study for the CLSC exam, we can't stress this enough: it's critical that you have some hands-on experience with Cisco switches. If you can get your hands on some Catalyst switches, you're set! But if you can't, we've worked hard to provide dozens of configuration examples throughout this book to help network administrators (or people who want to become network administrators) learn what they need to know to pass the CLSC exam.

SEE ALSO   One way to get the hands-on router experience you'll need in the real world is to attend one of the seminars offered by Globalnet System Solutions, Inc. (`http://www.lammle.com`), produced by Todd Lammle.

SEE ALSO   Keystone Learning Systems is producing high-quality training through videos featuring Todd Lammle. Go to `http://www.klscorp.com` for more information about all Cisco certification videos.

SEE ALSO   Go to `www.routersim.com` for router training tools to help you with your Cisco certifications.

Where Do You Take the Exams?

You may take the exams at any one of the more than 800 Sylvan Prometric Authorized Testing Centers around the world. For the location of a testing center near you, call 800-204-3926. Outside the United States and Canada, contact your local Sylvan Prometric Registration Center.

To register for a Cisco LAN Switch Configuration exam:

1. Determine the number of the exam you want to take. (The CLSC exam number is 640-404.)

2. Register with the Sylvan Prometric Registration Center nearest you. You will need to pay in advance for the exam. At this writing, registration costs $100 per exam, and the test must be taken within one year of payment. You can sign up for an exam up to six weeks in advance or as late as one working day prior to the day you wish to take it. If something comes up and you need to cancel or

reschedule your exam appointment, contact Sylvan Prometric at least 24 hours in advance. Same-day registration isn't available for the Cisco tests.

3. When you schedule the exam, you'll be provided with instructions regarding all appointment and cancellation procedures, the ID requirements, and the testing center location.

What the Cisco CLSC Exam Measures

The CLSC program was created to provide a solid introduction not only to the Cisco internetworking operating system (IOS) and to Cisco Catalyst hardware, but to internetworking in general, making it helpful to you in areas not exclusively associated with Cisco. It's hard to say at this point in the certification process, but it's not unrealistic to imagine that future network managers—even those without Cisco equipment—could easily require Cisco certifications of their job applicants.

To meet the CLSC certification skill level, you must be able to understand or do the following:

- Describe the major features of the Catalyst switches

- Describe the architecture and functions of the major components of the Catalyst switches

- Place Catalyst series switches in a network for optimal performance benefit

- Use the command line or menu-driven interface to configure the Catalyst series switches and their switching modules

- Use the command line or menu-driven interface to configure trunks, virtual LANs, and ATM LAN Emulation

- Maintain Catalyst series switches and perform basic troubleshooting

Tips for Taking Your Cisco CLSC Exam

The CLSC test contains 70 questions, which are to be answered in 90 minutes. You must schedule the test at least 24 hours in advance (unlike the Novell or Microsoft exams), and you aren't allowed to take more than one Cisco exam per day.

Many questions on the exam will have answer choices that at first glance look identical—especially the syntax questions! Remember to read through the choices carefully, because a "close" answer won't cut it. If you choose an answer in which the commands are in the wrong order or there is even one measly character missing, you'll get the question wrong. So to practice, take the sample quizzes at the end of each objective section over and over again until they feel natural to you. All of the exam questions are multiple choice, just like the examples in this book. Unlike Microsoft or Novell tests, the exam has answer choices that are really similar in syntax—some syntax will be dead wrong, but more than likely, it will just be very *subtly* wrong. Some other syntax choices may be almost right, except that the variables are shown in the wrong order.

Also, never forget that the right answer is the Cisco answer. In many cases, they'll present more than one correct answer, but the "correct" answer is the one Cisco recommends.

Here are some general tips for exam success:

- Arrive early at the exam center so you can relax and review your study materials—particularly IP tables and lists of exam-related information.

- Read the questions *carefully*. Don't jump to conclusions. Make sure you're clear on *exactly* what the question is asking.

- Don't leave any unanswered questions. These will be counted against you.

- When answering multiple-choice questions you're not sure about, use a process of elimination to get rid of the obviously incorrect answers first. Doing this will greatly improve your odds if you need to make an educated guess.

- Because the hard questions will eat up the most time, save them for last. You can move forward and backward through the exam.

- If you are unsure of the answer to a question, choose one of the answers anyway. Mark the question so that, if you have time, you can go back to it and double-check your answer. Remember, an unanswered question is as bad as a wrong one, so answer questions even if you're not certain of the correct choice; if you don't and you run out of time or forget to go back to the question, you'll get it wrong for sure.

Once you have completed an exam, you'll be given immediate online notification of your pass or fail status, plus a printed Examination Score Report indicating whether you passed or failed, along with your exam results by section. (The test administrator will give you the printed score report.) Test scores are automatically forwarded to Cisco within five working days after you take the test, so you don't need to send your score to them. If you pass the exam, you'll receive confirmation from Cisco, typically within two to four weeks.

There's one more thing you can do to prepare. Visit Brian Horakh's Web site—http://www.networkstudyguides.com—and go through the exercises and practice test questions he provides. This will really help you keep abreast of any changes made to the test.

How to Contact the Authors

Todd Lammle can be reached at his integration and consulting company located in Colorado at todd@lammle.com.

Robert Padjen can be reached at robert_padjen@yahoo.com.

How to Contact the Publisher

Sybex welcomes reader feedback on all of their titles. Visit the Sybex Web site at `http://www.sybex.com` for book updates and additional certification information. You'll also find online forms to submit comments or suggestions regarding this or any other Sybex book.

CHAPTER

1

Overall CLSC Course Objectives

Cisco Exam Objectives Covered in This Chapter

▶**Describe the major features of the Catalyst switches.** *(pages 3 – 7)*

▶**Describe the architecture and functions of the major components of the Catalyst switches.** *(pages 7 – 15)*

▶**Place Catalyst series switches in a network for optimal performance benefit.** *(pages 15 – 19)*

▶**Use the command line menu or menu-driven interface to configure the Catalyst series switches and their switching modules.** *(pages 19 – 27)*

▶**Use the command line menu or menu-driven interface to configure trunks, virtual LANs, and ATM LAN Emulation.** *(pages 27 – 37)*

▶**Maintain Catalyst series switches and perform basic troubleshooting.** *(pages 37 – 40)*

This chapter will introduce the Cisco Catalyst series of switches. The different types of Catalyst switches will be discussed, and an overview of the major features and architecture of the Catalyst switches will be provided.

This chapter will also discuss how to place Cisco Catalyst switches in a network for optimal performance, and describe the different command line and menu-driven interfaces of the different Catalyst switches. Within the command line and menu systems, the configuration of trunks, VLANs, and ATM LANE will also be introduced.

This is an important chapter, as it will give you an understanding of the different Catalyst switches and will also introduce the interfaces and menus available through the different switch menus.

Describe the major features of the Catalyst switches.

In this first objective, the different objectives covered in this book that describe the major features of the Catalyst switches will be discussed. An overview will be provided of the different Catalyst switches that Cisco provides, as well as of the major features of each type of switch.

This objective is important because the entire Cisco LAN Switch Configuration (CLSC) exam is based on the Cisco Catalyst series of switches.

Critical Information

The Cisco Catalyst switching technology is available in a wide variety of form factors to provide the needed port density in various installations. Table 1.1 describes the different chassis in the 5000 product line, in addition to the 2900, 4000, 6500, and 8500 product lines.

T A B L E 1.1: The Cisco Catalyst Chassis

Chassis	Features
1900	The 1900 series product is quite limited in configuration and performance; however, it offers a very low cost per port compared to the more advanced switches in the Cisco Catalyst product line. Given its limitations, it is suited for the wiring closet, or access layer, of the network for terminating workstations.
2820	The 2820 product is similar to the 1900 series; however, modules are available for ATM and FDDI. The 2820 is ideally suited for access services.

TABLE 1.1: The Cisco Catalyst Chassis *(cont.)*

2900	The 2900 series uses a fixed configuration and the Supervisor I engine from the Catalyst 5000 product. Although it's more expensive, many companies choose this product for workgroup deployment. This is one of many switches included in the current Cisco product line but not covered by the Cisco 640-404 exam and not presented in a formal manner in this book. It is included in this table for comparison with current (as of this writing) offerings. Fortunately, the use of the Supervisor I engine results in a switch that is similar to the 5000.
3000	The 3000 product line differs significantly from the 5000 product; however, Cisco has incorporated a number of features that make the 3000 a good choice for certain deployments. Incorporation of WAN links, stackability, and Catalyst features including ISL provide many services needed by administrators for remote locations.
3900	Not covered by the Cisco 640-404 exam, and not discussed in this book. The 3900 product is a fixed-configuration Token Ring switch. As an access-layer switch, it is designed to interconnect with a core Token Ring switch. The 5000/5500 is designed to address this role.
4000	The 4000 series includes the 4003 and 4912 models. They are positioned for the wiring closet and server-farm installations. This is a newer switch within Cisco's Catalyst product offerings. Not covered by the Cisco 640-404 exam, and not discussed further in this book.
5000	The Catalyst 5000 provides five slots, a 1.2Gbps backplane, and optional redundant power supplies.
5500	The Catalyst 5500 provides 13 slots for interface cards (although slot 13 is unavailable for frame switching) and is the largest of the 5000/5500 series switches. Fully populated, the switch weighs 176 pounds. It provides a 3.6Gbps backplane in crossbar configuration (three 1.2Gbps backplanes) for frame switching and a 5Gbps backplane for ATM cell switching. In addition, the platform provides for optional redundant Supervisor engines and optional redundant power supplies, and it includes dual backplane clocks.

T A B L E 1.1:   The Cisco Catalyst Chassis   *(cont.)*

5502	The 5502 is a two-slot, two-power-supply modular switch. It is well suited for the smaller network or the access layer.
5505	The 5505 is a five-slot Catalyst 5500 series switch capable of redundant Supervisor engines. It is frequently used in the distribution layer of the network, where the port density of the 5500 is unnecessary. It should be noted that the cost differential between the 5505, 5509, and 5500 chassis is very small, and administrators should review the cost differences before ordering to protect against "forklift upgrades" in the future.
5509	The 5509 is a nine-slot Catalyst 5500 series switch capable of redundant Supervisor engines. The release of the 5509 included provisions for greater gigabit port density in the 5500 series.
6500	The 6500 product line builds upon the 5500 series and provides additional gigabit performance. It was released in early 1999. Not covered by the Cisco 640-404 exam, and not discussed further in this book.
8500	The 8540 is designed for ATM and Gigabit Ethernet services in the network core, in addition to future voice services. It is well suited to the data center and network core. Not covered by the Cisco 640-404 exam, and not discussed further in this book.

NOTE   The 1900/2820 switch is covered in depth in Chapters 15–17 and 20. The 3000 series switch is covered in depth in Chapters 18, 19, and 21. The 5000 series switch is covered in depth in Chapters 4–11, 13, and 14.

Exam Essentials

Understand the features of the 1900 series switch.   It has either 12 or 24 ports and is suited for the wiring closet, or access layer, of the network for terminating workstations.

Understand the features of the 2820 series switch. The 2820 product is similar to the 1900 series; however, modules are available for ATM and FDDI. The 2820 is ideally suited for access services.

Understand the features of the 3000 series switch. Incorporation of WAN links, stackability, and Catalyst features including ISL provide many services needed by administrators for remote locations.

Remember the features of the 5000 series switch. The Catalyst 5000 provides five slots, a 1.2Gbps backplane, and optional redundant power supplies.

The Catalyst 5500 provides 13 slots for interface cards. It provides a 3.6Gbps backplane in crossbar configuration (three 1.2Gbps backplanes) for frame switching and a 5Gbps backplane for ATM cell switching.

Key Terms and Concepts

ISL: Inter-Switch Link can be used to trunk ports on a Catalyst switch. You want to trunk ports when you need a host in more than one VLAN at the same time; for example, in a server. Typically, ISLs are used between Catalyst switches.

Switch: In networking, a device responsible for multiple functions such as filtering, flooding, and sending frames. It works using the destination address of individual frames.

Trunk: Allows a port on a switch to be in one or more VLANs simultaneously. Used for multiple-link connection and also allows servers to be in multiple broadcast domains.

Virtual LAN: A group of devices on one or more logically segmented LANs (configured by use of management software), enabling devices to communicate as if attached to the same physical medium, when they are actually located on numerous different LAN segments.

Sample Questions

1. The Catalyst 5000 supports which of the following topologies?

   A. FDDI

   B. Ethernet

   C. FastEthernet

   D. Token Ring

   E. All of the above

   Answer: E. The Catalyst 5000 series supports FDDI, Ethernet, Token Ring, and ATM.

2. Which of the following describes the differences between the Catalyst 5000 and Catalyst 5500? (Choose all that apply.)

   A. The Catalyst 5000 supports redundant Supervisor engines.

   B. The Catalyst 5000 provides a 3.6Gbps backplane.

   C. The Catalyst 5500 supports redundant Supervisor engines.

   D. The Catalyst 5500 supports a 3.6Gbps backplane.

   E. The Catalyst 5500 provides LS1010 functionality.

   Answer: C, D, E. The 5500 is a larger, more flexible switch.

Describe the architecture and functions of the major components of the Catalyst switches.

In this objective, the Cisco Catalyst series of switches will continue to be described. The different architecture and functions of each Catalyst series switch will be described in this objective.

This is an important objective, as it will give you the understanding you need to troubleshoot the Cisco Catalyst series of switches, as well as needed information when studying for your CLSC exam.

Critical Information

In this section, the architecture and functions of the 1900/2820, 3000, and 5000 series switches will be described.

1900/2820 Series

Cisco's ClearChannel architecture, the heart of the Catalyst 1900 and 2820 series switches, consists of the packet exchange bus (X-bus), the forwarding engine, the embedded control unit (ECU), the management interface, and the shared buffer memory and switched ports. Figure 1.1 shows a simplified model of ClearChannel architecture.

FIGURE 1.1:   ClearChannel architecture

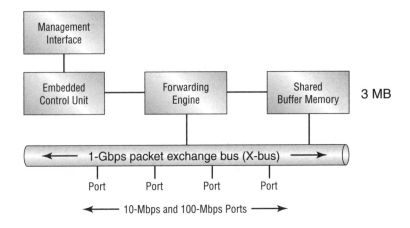

The switch uses a shared memory buffer with a 3MB capacity and a 1Gbps packet exchange bus.

Data enters the bus based on a priority system. Transaction priority and time of arrival determine the priority. A transaction priority is determined by a combination of time of arrival and port priority. Types of transactions include buffer memory requests, a packet transmission termination, etc. Port priority is based on the port origination of the packet, port 1 being the lowest and port 27 (a 100BaseT port) the highest.

ClearChannel architecture provides 27 switched ports using less than half (450Mbps) of the 1Gbps bandwidth.

3000 Series

All of the Catalyst 3000 switches have four main elements:

Cross-point switch matrix (AXIS bus):   This is used to connect between two network segments. Each connection lasts only as long as packets are being transmitted.

AUI connector: The Attachment Unit Interface is typically used to connect by way of a transceiver (transmitter/receiver) to dissimilar physical media, such as connecting thinnet to 10BaseT or 10BaseFL.

Expansion module: Two expansion slots are included in each Catalyst 3000 switch. You can add up to eight 10Mbps ports or two FastEthernet connections for connecting to servers or backbones. ATM and fiber-based LANs are also supported.

Stack ports: The 3000 switch supports up to eight Catalyst 3000 units connected together, forming one virtual unit.

This section discusses the architecture of the Catalyst 3000 switches, describing the AXIS bus, the LAN Module ASIC (LMA), and the Proprietary Fat Pipe ASIC (PFPA).

The 3000 switch uses the AXIS bus to facilitate frame switching. If you have a node at 10Mbps that has a destination node running 10Mbps, the switch will use the LAN Module ASIC (LMA) to perform the port switching. Any ports running above 10Mbps will use the Proprietary Fat Pipe ASIC (PFPA). Figure 1.2 shows the Catalyst 3000 architecture.

FIGURE 1.2: Catalyst 3000 architecture

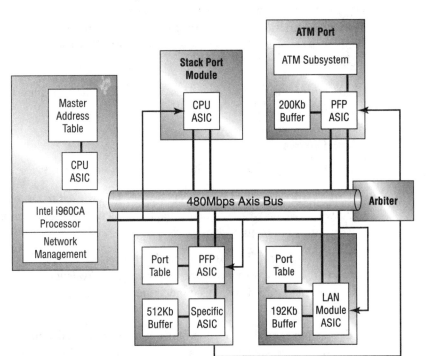

Notice in Figure 1.2 how all switching ASICs connect to the AXIS bus, and each ASIC has its own buffer to prevent congestion. 10Mbps ports have 192KB buffers, and 100Mbps ports have 512KB buffers.

5000 Series

The Catalyst 5000 series has five significant components, known as Application Specific Integrated Circuits (ASICs), in the Catalyst 5500 system that manage the switching functions. They're called the SAMBA, SAINT, SAGE, EARL, and Phoenix. These ASICs provide high-speed, hardware-based processing used in switching processes.

A clear understanding of these components is useful in overall troubleshooting and administration of the Catalyst system. This is especially true when evaluating different switches and options, such as the different Supervisor engines and the RSM and NetFlow (NFFC II) features. It is also beneficial when isolating hardware problems.

The Catalyst system uses a management bus to direct the switching process, while the actual data packets use a separate 1.2Gbps backplane. The management bus operates at 761Kbps. These buses interconnect various cards within the chassis for Ethernet, Token Ring, FDDI, and, in some cases, ATM.

NOTE This description of the Catalyst system is based on the original Catalyst 5000 and the Supervisor I. The 5500 and Supervisor III provide access to three 1.2Gbps backplanes, which are interconnected via the Phoenix ASICs.

SAMBA

The Synergy Advanced Multipurpose Bus Arbiter (SAMBA) ASIC is located on line modules and the supervisor modules. On the line cards, this chip is responsible for broadcast suppression based on thresholds established by the administrator. This ASIC also maintains statistics on packets.

The SAMBA operates in either master or slave mode. Master mode is used on the Supervisor engine, and slave mode is used on the line cards. The master is capable of addressing up to 13 line modules, while the slave is capable of serving up to 48 individual ports.

In the master/slave model, the slave SAMBA must wait for permission from the master before granting access to the port. This process is described in greater detail in the arbitration section of this chapter.

WARNING Cisco's SAMBA should not be confused with the SAMBA utility for providing SMB (Windows NT) services on Unix platforms.

SAINT

The SAINT (Synergy Advanced Interface and Network Termination) handles Ethernet switching on the Catalyst 5000 platform, and it also handles ISL encapsulation. Each Ethernet port has an independent 192KB buffer for inbound and outbound packets, which is divided to provide 168KB to outbound traffic and 24KB to inbound frames.

The buffer arrangement controlled by the SAINT has proven itself in hundreds of networks and rarely presents a troubleshooting issue—however, administrators must always consider buffer overflows and underpins as a factor. Again, capturing the appropriate counters with the show commands will provide the administrator with trouble-shooting tools.

SAGE

The SAGE (Synergy Advanced Gate-Array Engine) is similar to the SAINT, except that it is used for non-Ethernet applications, including FDDI, ATM LANE, Token Ring, and the Network Management Processor on the Supervisor engine.

EARL

No kingdom would be complete without an EARL, and building on the apparent pun, the Catalyst 5000 is no different. In switching, however, EARL refers to the Encoded Address Recognition Logic ASIC. This chip works with the bus arbitration system to control access to the data-switching bus. EARL also controls the destination ports of packet transfers.

More specifically, the EARL monitors frame flow and compiles the list of MAC addresses as related to port numbers and VLAN ID. In addition, the ASIC determines the destination port of frames and maintains the timer for aging entries out of the forwarding table. By default, entries are discarded after 300 seconds, although the administrator can change this value. Valid parameters are limited between 1 and 20 minutes. The EARL can maintain a table of up to 128,000 addresses. Because of this, the EARL handles forwarding and filtering decisions within the switch.

Administrators do not troubleshoot the EARL per se. Rather, issues with MAC address and port mappings controlled by EARL are a part of the diagnostic process. Understanding the significant function of the EARL in the Catalyst line, and its role in all switching, can assist in hardware-related debugging.

Phoenix

The Phoenix ASIC provides both a technical and an economical expansion of the Catalyst line. First, the gate array is responsible for interconnecting the three 1.2Gbps backplanes in the Catalyst 5500 chassis to create a crossbar fabric that bridges traffic between backplanes at gigabit speeds. Second, the architecture permits the use of legacy modules providing administrators with investment protection when upgrading from the Catalyst 5000. While the chassis needs replacement in such circumstances, some companies choose to defer trade-in or replacement of specific modules because of cost concerns.

The Phoenix ASIC includes a 384KB buffer to address congestion and is treated as a port by the bus arbiter and EARL modules.

Exam Essentials

Remember the architecture of the 1900 and 2820 switches.   The 1900/2820 ClearChannel architecture consists of the packet exchange bus (X-bus), the forwarding engine, the embedded control unit (ECU), the management interface, and the shared buffer memory and switched ports.

Understand the architecture used in the 3000 series of switches.   Cross-point switch matrix (AXIS bus) is used to connect between two network segments. Each connection lasts only as long as packets are being transmitted.

Remember the different types of architectures used in the 5000 series of switches.   The Catalyst 5000 series has five significant components, known as Application Specific Integrated Circuits (ASICs), in the Catalyst 5500 system that manage the switching functions. They're called the SAMBA, SAINT, SAGE, EARL, and Phoenix. These ASICs provide high-speed, hardware-based processing used in switching processes.

Key Terms and Concepts

ISL: Inter-Switch Link can be used to trunk ports on a Catalyst switch. You want to trunk ports when you need a host in more than one VLAN at the same time; for example, in a server. Typically, ISLs are used between Catalyst switches.

Switch: In networking, a device responsible for multiple functions such as filtering, flooding, and sending frames. It works using the destination address of individual frames.

Trunk: Allows a port on a switch to be in one or more VLANs simultaneously. Used for multiple-link connection and also allows servers to be in multiple broadcast domains.

Virtual LAN: A group of devices on one or more logically segmented LANs (configured by use of management software), enabling devices to communicate as if attached to the same physical medium, when they are actually located on numerous different LAN segments.

Sample Questions

1. Which ASIC provides a gigabit bridge between the backplanes in the Catalyst 5500?

   A. SAGE.

   B. SAINT.

   C. Phoenix.

   D. EARL.

   E. There is only one backplane in the Catalyst 5500.

   Answer: C.

2. Which component of the Catalyst system maintains the MAC address table for forwarding decisions?

   A. EARL.

   B. Phoenix.

   C. SAGE.

   D. The MAC Address Handling Processor.

   E. The Catalyst does not process MAC addresses.

Answer: A.

Place Catalyst series switches in a network for optimal performance benefit.

To place Cisco Catalyst switches in a network for optimal performance, you should create virtual LANs. A virtual local area network (VLAN) is a logical grouping of network users and resources connected to administratively defined ports on a switch.

By creating VLANs, you are able to create smaller broadcast domains within a switch by assigning different ports in the switch to different subnetworks. A VLAN is treated like its own subnet or broadcast domain. This means that frames broadcast are only switched between ports in the same VLAN.

This is an important objective, as it will give you an understanding of broadcast domains and how you can create broadcast domains within a switched internetwork. This section will also discuss how routers are used in this environment.

Critical Information

Using virtual LANs, you're no longer confined to physical locations. VLANs can be organized by location, function, department, or even the application or protocol used, regardless of where the resources or users are located.

Switches only read frames for filtering; they do not look at the Network layer protocol. This can cause a switch to forward all broadcasts. However, by creating VLANs, you are essentially creating broadcast domains. Broadcasts sent out from a node in one VLAN will not be forwarded to ports configured in a different VLAN. By assigning switch ports or users to VLAN groups on a switch or group of connected switches (called a *switch fabric*), you have the flexibility to add only the users you want in the broadcast domain regardless of their physical location. This can stop broadcast storms caused by a faulty network interface card (NIC) or an application from propagating throughout the entire internetwork.

When a VLAN gets too big, you can create more VLANs to keep the broadcasts from consuming too much bandwidth. The fewer users in a VLAN, the fewer affected by broadcasts.

To understand how a VLAN looks to a switch, it's helpful to begin by first looking at a traditional collapsed backbone. Figure 1.3 shows a collapsed backbone created by connecting physical LANs to a router.

F I G U R E 1.3:   Physical LANs connected to a router

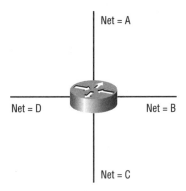

Net = A

Net = D   Net = B

Net = C

Each network is attached to the router, and each network has its own logical network number. Each node attached to a particular physical network must match that network number to be able to communicate on the internetwork. Now let's look at what a switch accomplishes. Figure 1.4 shows how switches remove the physical boundary.

F I G U R E 1.4: Switches remove the physical boundary.

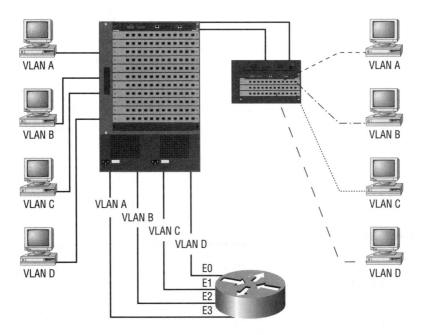

Switches create greater flexibility and scalability than routers can by themselves. You can group users into communities of interest, which are known as VLAN organizations.

Because of switches, you don't need routers anymore, right? Wrong. In Figure 1.4, notice that there are four VLANs or broadcast domains. The nodes within each VLAN can communicate with each other, but not with any other VLAN or node in another VLAN. When configured in a VLAN, the nodes think they are actually in a collapsed backbone as in Figure 1.3. What do these hosts in Figure 1.3 need to do to communicate to a node or host on a different network? They need to go through the router, just like when they are configured for VLAN communication as shown in Figure 1.4. Communication between VLANs, just as in physical networks, must go through the router.

Exam Essentials

Remember that routers are still used in a switched internetwork.   Routers break up the broadcast domains and are still used in a switched environment. However, router switch modules (RSMs) can be used in their place.

Understand how broadcast domains are created with switches.   Administrators assigning switch ports into a particular VLAN create broadcast domains. A router is used to connect the broadcast domains together.

Key Terms and Concepts

ISL: Inter-Switch Link can be used to trunk ports on a Catalyst switch. You want to trunk ports when you need a host in more than one VLAN at the same time; for example, in a server. Typically, ISLs are used between Catalyst switches.

Switch: In networking, a device responsible for multiple functions such as filtering, flooding, and sending frames. It works using the destination address of individual frames.

Trunk: Allows a port on a switch to be in one or more VLANs simultaneously. Used for multiple-link connection and also allows servers to be in multiple broadcast domains.

Virtual LAN: A group of devices on one or more logically segmented LANs (configured by use of management software), enabling devices to communicate as if attached to the same physical medium, when they are actually located on numerous different LAN segments.

Sample Questions

1. To process frames at layer 3, the Catalyst system, including external components, must include what? (Select all that apply.)

   A. A Supervisor III engine.

   B. Redundant Supervisor engines.

   C. An RSM module.

   D. A connection from each VLAN to a router, via either ISL/ 802.1q or direct connections to a port in each VLAN.

   E. It is not possible to process layer 3 in the Catalyst system.

   Answer: C, D. Routers break up broadcast domains. Switches work at layer 2 and need a router or RSM to create VLANs.

2. Switching is what kind of a process?

   A. Layer 1

   B. Layer 2

   C. Layer 3

   D. Layer 4

   Answer: B. Even though you have heard of layer 3 switches, the CLSC exam is interested in only layer 2 switching.

Use the command line menu or menu-driven interface to configure the Catalyst series switches and their switching modules.

In this objective, you will see the command line interface used on the Catalyst 5000 series switch, and also the menu-driven interface used by the 1900/2820 and 3000 series switches.

This objective is important because it will give you an introduction to each Catalyst switch interface. You must understand the different types of menu and command-line-interface commands used in the Catalyst series, and this objective will give you an introduction to that information.

Critical Information

In this section, you will read about the command line or menu-driven interface to configure the Catalyst series of switches.

1900/2820 Series

Choose the [M] option to enter the main menu, where you'll do all your other configurations. The main menu for the 1900 series is shown below:

```
Catalyst 1900 - Main Menu

[C] Console Settings
[S] System
[N] Network Management
[P] Port Configuration
[A] Port Addressing
[D] Port Statistics Detail
[M] Monitoring
[V] Virtual LAN
[R] Multicast Registration
[F] Firmware
[I] RS-232 Interface
[U] Usage Summaries
[H] Help


[X] Exit Management Console
```

The main menu of the Catalyst 2820 is shown below:

```
Catalyst 2820 - Main Menu
[C] Console Settings
[S] System
[N] Network Management
[P] Port Configuration
[A] Port Addressing
[D] Port Statistics Detail
[M] Monitoring
[B] Bridge Group
[R] Multicast Registration
[F] Firmware
[I] RS-232 Interface
[U] Usage Summaries
[H] Help
[X] Exit Management Console
Enter Selection:
```

Console Settings Menu

The Console Settings menu can be accessed by pressing **C** from the main menu. The settings on this menu allow you to change the switch password and implement other system security measures. The menu as it appears for both the Catalyst 1900 and the Catalyst 2820 switch is shown below:

```
Catalyst 1900 - Console Settings
-------------------Settings-----------------
[P] Password intrusion threshold              3 attempt(s)
[S] Silent time upon intrusion detection      None
[T] Management Console inactivity timeout     None
[D] Default mode of status LED                Port Status
-------------------Actions------------------
[M] Modify password
[X] Exit to Main Menu
Enter Selection:
```

The functions of the menu options are as follows:

[P] Password intrusion threshold: Controls the number of attempts at entering the correct password that will be allowed. After either the default of three attempts or the value you define, the console is disabled for the amount of time you define in the next option.

[S] Silent time upon intrusion detection: Controls the interval that must elapse after the password intrusion threshold has been violated before another attempt can be made. This control is defaulted to *no wait*, but can be any amount of time between 1 and 65,500 minutes.

[T] Management Console inactivity timeout: Controls the amount of time that the management console can remain inactive without timing out. After it has timed out, the user must reenter that password to activate the switch console.

[D] Default mode of status LED: Sets the default mode for the LED 30 seconds after setting the mode. The default mode setting is [1] Port Status. Other options available are [2] Utilization or [3] Duplex Status.

[M] Modify password: Allows you to change the password. The password may be four to eight characters long and any character on the keyboard. Remember, though, that the password is not case sensitive. If there is an existing password, the user must enter that password before a change will occur.

[X] Exit to Main Menu: Drops the user back one level to the main menu.

3000 Series

The Configuration menu enables you to view and set the Catalyst 3000 configuration parameters. As you can see in Figure 1.5, there are quite a few items you can configure.

FIGURE 1.5: The Configuration menu

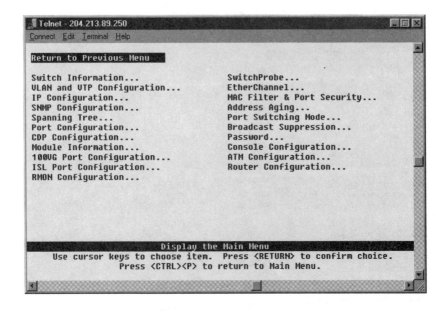

Switch Information

Figure 1.6 shows the Switch Information screen, where you enter the basic ID information about the switch and its location and role in your network.

System Description: The name and model of the switch unit

System ID: Assigned at the factory

MAC Address: The hardware address of the switch

Boot Description: The firmware revision

Interface Description: The type of switch

System Name: The name assigned by the administrator

System Location: Administratively assigned; optional

System Contact: The administratively assigned name for contact purposes

F I G U R E 1.6: 3000 Switch Information screen

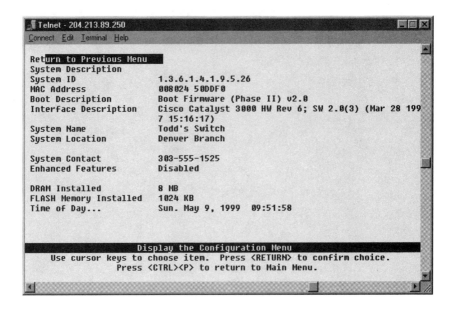

Enhanced Features: Indicates if advanced features are installed; for example, LANE and VLANs

DRAM Installed: The amount of RAM

FLASH Memory Installed: The amount of flash memory

Time of Day: The internal clock

NOTE If the unit is part of a stack, parameters for the entire stack will be displayed.

5000 Series

Unlike the router IOS, the Catalyst 5000/5500 uses set commands to define the switch settings. Because of this, there is no configure terminal command or mode. Let's take a look at the basic command to configure a Cisco Catalyst 5000 series switch.

Set Interface

```
set interface <sc0|s10> <up|down>
set interface sc0 [vlan] [ip_addr [netmask [broadcast]]]
set interface s10 <slip_addr> <dest_addr>
```

Usage

The set interface command is used to define an IP address and other configuration parameters for the SC0 and SL0 interfaces. The SC0 interface is usually configured and provides an in-band Telnet interface, in addition to SNMP. The SL0 interface is used for SLIP connections.

Example

```
Switch_A> (enable) set interface sc0 10.1.1.10 255.255.255.0
```

In this example, the SC0 interface will be assigned an IP address of 10.1.1.10 and a network mask of 255.255.255.0. The broadcast address will automatically be assigned as 10.1.1.255, and the virtual connection will remain bound to VLAN1.

Set IP Route

```
set ip route <destination> <gateway> [metric][primary]
```

Usage

The set ip route command is used to assign a default gateway or any static routes to the switch. The *destination* and *gateway* parameters are IP aliases or IP addresses in dot notation: *a.b.c.d.*

Example

```
Switch_A> (enable) set ip route 0.0.0.0 10.1.1.1
```

Here, the default route for the switch has been configured for the router at 10.1.1.1.

Exam Essentials

Remember how to change the 1900/2820 switch password.
The settings on the Console Settings menu will allow you to change the switch password and implement other system security measures.

Remember how to set an IP address on a Catalyst 5000 series switch. The set interface command is used to define an IP address and other configuration parameters for the SC0 and SL0 interfaces.

Key Terms and Concepts

ISL: Inter-Switch Link can be used to trunk ports on a Catalyst switch. You want to trunk ports when you need a host in more than one VLAN at the same time; for example, in a server. Typically, ISLs are used between Catalyst switches.

Switch: In networking, a device responsible for multiple functions such as filtering, flooding, and sending frames. It works using the destination address of individual frames.

Trunk: Allows a port on a switch to be in one or more VLANs simultaneously. Used for multiple-link connection and also allows servers to be in multiple broadcast domains.

Virtual LAN: A group of devices on one or more logically segmented LANs (configured by use of management software), enabling devices to communicate as if attached to the same physical medium, when they are actually located on numerous different LAN segments.

Sample Questions

1. Which of the following would need to be configured for a SLIP account?

   A. SC0.

   B. SL0.

   C. VLAN1.

   D. SLIP is not available on the Catalyst system.

   E. SLIP is available only with the RSM module.

   Answer: B. Configure the SL0 port for SLIP connectivity.

2. What command is used to set an IP route?

   A. ip route

   B. ip set route

   C. set ip route

   D. route set ip

   Answer: C. On the Catalyst 5000 series of switches, the command line uses the set command.

Use the command line menu or menu-driven interface to configure trunks, virtual LANs, and ATM LAN Emulation.

In this objective, you will continue to read about the menu-driven and command-line-interface commands used with the different Catalyst series switches. This section will show you the different ways to configure trunk links, VLANs, and ATM LANE on the 2820 and 5000 series switches.

This is an important objective to understand, as it will continue to describe the menu and command line interfaces used in the Catalyst switches, which is pertinent information when configuring switches and studying for your CLSC exam.

Critical Information

The critical information of this objective is found in the "Necessary Procedures" section just below.

Necessary Procedures

In this section, you will read about the command line menus and menu-driven interface to configure trunking, VLANs, and ATM LANE.

1900/2820 Series

To display the menu for configuring VLANs, select V. The Catalyst 1900 and Catalyst 2820 can be configured with up to four VLANs. The default configuration of a switch has all ports belonging to VLAN 1. The management domain is also contained within VLAN 1. A proper configuration will have at least one port that belongs to VLAN 1.

The opening menu for VLAN configuration on a 1900 looks like this:

```
Catalyst 1900 - Virtual LAN Configuration
------------------Information---------------
VTP version: 1
Configuration revision: 1
Maximum VLANs supported locally: 1005
Number of existing VLANs: 6
Configuration last modified by: 172.16.30.196 at 05-03-1999 18:35:56

-------------------Settings-----------------
[N] Domain name
[V] VTP mode control Server
[F] VTP pruning mode Disabled
[O] VTP traps Enabled

-------------------Actions------------------
[L] List VLANs           [A] Add VLAN
[M] Modify VLAN          [D] Delete VLAN
[E] VLAN Membership      [S] VLAN Membership Servers
[T] Trunk Configuration  [W] VTP password
[P] VTP Statistics       [X] Exit to Main Menu

Enter Selection:
```

The functions of the most important menu options are as follows:

[N] **Domain name:**   Allows you to assign a management domain to the switch before creating a VLAN. A Catalyst 1900 or Catalyst 2820 switch comes configured in a no-management domain state until a management domain is configured or the switch receives an advertisement for a management domain.

[V] **VTP mode control:**   May be set to either Transparent or Server. A Catalyst 1900 or Catalyst 2820 switch is configured as a VTP server by default, receiving advertisements on a configured trunk port. A switch automatically changes from VTP server mode to VTP client mode when it receives an advertisement with more than 128 VLANs.

[F] **VTP pruning mode:**   Controls whether to restrict the flood traffic of a VLAN to just those switches that have member ports. Each trunk is configured with its own pruning eligible list of VLANs.

[A] **Add VLAN:**   Adds a VLAN to the allowed list for the trunk. The default configuration allows all configured VLANs on a single trunk.

[M] **Modify VLAN:**   Allows you to modify an existing VLAN.

[D] **Delete VLAN:**   Allows you to delete an operating VLAN. The ports assigned to the VLAN will default back to VLAN 1.

[X] **Exit to Main Menu:**   Drops you back one level to the main menu.

Defining a VLAN

Defining a VLAN requires setting some attributes, including the VLAN number, name, IEEE 802.10 SAID value, and MTU size.

1. First access the VLAN Configuration menu by selecting V from the main menu. Then press A to select Add VLAN.

2. Next you must choose the type of VLAN. For Ethernet, enter 1.

3. Press **N** to configure the VLAN number, and enter the number of the VLAN to be added.

4. Define the VLAN name by pressing **V** and entering the name of the VLAN to be added.

5. To set the IEEE 802.10 SAID value, press **I** and enter the appropriate value. The SAID value must be within the range shown, and it cannot be the same as another IEEE 802.10 value.

6. To set the MTU size, press **M** and enter the MTU size.

7. Enable the VLAN by pressing **T** to select VLAN State, and select Enabled.

Configuring VLAN Trunks

A VLAN trunk is important because it allows a physical link between two VLAN-capable switches, or a VLAN-capable switch and a VLAN-capable router. A VLAN trunk can carry the traffic of multiple VLANs. This allows you to have VLANs extend into multiple Catalyst switches. VLAN trunking is supported only on the Enterprise versions of software.

1. Access the Virtual LAN menu by selecting **V** from the main menu.

2. Press **T** to access the Trunk Configuration menu. Select the appropriate trunk port by choosing either **A** or **B**, and press Enter.

3. To turn on trunking for the selected port, enter **T**, select **1**, and press Return or Enter.

Configuring VLAN Trunk Protocol

The VLAN Trunk Protocol (VTP) helps maintain the VLAN uniformity across the network as well as assisting with the alteration of VLANs. VTP allows VLAN changes to be communicated across the network to the other switches.

1. Access the Virtual LAN menu by selecting **V** from the main menu.

2. Confirm that a management domain name has been set.

3. Press **N** to access the Domain Name menu.

4. Confirm that the server has a VTP management domain, which ensures that VTP information can be exchanged with other VTP switches in the management domain.

5. Press Enter to view the Virtual LAN Configuration menu.

6. Open the VTP Mode Control menu by selecting V.

7. Choose the server mode by entering S at the prompt.

The switch can learn about other VTP-configured switches only by receiving their advertisements across the network. There must also be at least one trunk port configured on a switch.

3000 Series

The next menu is used to set up VLANs on the 3000 switch. From the Configuration menu, choose VLAN and VTP Configuration. Figure 1.7 displays the VLAN and VTP Configuration screen. It has the following options:

Local VLAN Port Configuration: Shows the current VLAN port assignments. You can change the assignment by using the cursor and then selecting Change. Only 14 ports are displayed at a time. Select the More option to see the other assigned ports.

VTP Administrative Configuration: Displays the domain name and the operation mode of the domain—server, client, or transparent. In server mode, changes can be made only from the local device. In client mode, you can make changes only from remote devices, and the transparent mode passes VTP packets.

VTP VLAN Configuration: Shows each VLAN administratively assigned and allows you to edit the assignments.

Local Preferred VLANs Configuration: Shows all configured VLANs.

Reassign Ports in Local VLAN: Used for moving a fully configured stack into an existing VTP administrative domain.

F I G U R E 1.7: The VLAN and VTP Configuration menu

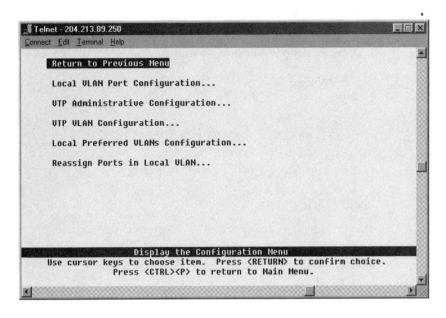

Configuring ISL Ports

Inter-Switch Link (ISL) can be used to trunk ports on a Catalyst 3000 switch. You want to trunk ports when you need a host in more than one VLAN at the same time; for example, in a server. The ISL menu is used to configure the ISL trunking mode for each ISL port. Typically, ISLs are used between Catalyst switches.

The ISL screen displays four menu headings:

Port: Shows the participating ISL ports on the switch

State: Gives the state of the port, either trunk or static

Note: A diagnostic message about the trunking states

Trunking Mode: Gives the status of the port—On, Off, Auto, or Desirable

Configuring ATM

Asynchronous Transfer Mode (ATM) can be used with the Catalyst family of switches, including the 3000 series. Local Area Network Emulation (LANE) is used on the switch to emulate a network broadcast environment such as Ethernet. See Chapter 12 for more information on ATM and LANE. The Catalyst 3000 uses the WS-X3006A ATM module for ATM support.

The ATM Configuration menu provides three options:

Operation Mode: Can be set to either client or server

Configuration Type: Sets the address for registration to the ATM switch

ATM SNAP Prefix: Sets the ATM prefix, LECS ESI address, and a selector byte value of FF to form the ATM address for the LECS (LAN Emulation Configuration Server)

5000 Series

The following router output will show you how to set VLANs and trunk ports.

Set VLAN

```
set vlan <vlan_num> <mod/ports...>
    (Note: An example of mod/ports is 1/1,2/1-12,3/1-2,4/1-12)

set vlan <vlan_num> [name <name>] [type <type>] [state <state>]
[said <said>] [mtu <mtu>] [ring <hex_ring_number>] [decring
<decimal_ring_number>]
    [bridge <bridge_number>] [parent <vlan_num>]
    [mode <bridge_mode>] [stp <stp_type>]
    [translation <vlan_num>] [backupcrf <off|on>]
    [aremaxhop <hopcount>] [stemaxhop <hopcount>]
```

Usage

The set vlan command serves multiple purposes. In most installations, the command is used to create VLANs and assign ports to particular VLANs. The parameters are as follows:

mod/port	The switch module and the port number within that module; for example, 1/1, 2/1-12, 3/1-2, 4/1-12
name	May be any length from 1 to 32 characters
state	May be either active or suspend
type	May be ethernet, fddi, fddinet, trcrf, or trbrf
said	May be any value from 1 to 4,294,967,294
mtu	May be any value from 576 to 18,190
hex_ring_number	May be any value from 0x1 to 0xfff, hex
decimal_ring_ number	May be any value from 1 to 4095
bridge_number	May be any value from 0x1 to 0xf
parent	May be any value from 2 to 1005
mode	May be either srt or srb
stp	May be ieee, ibm, or auto
translation	May be any value from 1 to 1005
hopcount	May be any value from 1 to 13

Example

```
Switch_A> (enable) set vlan 3 name Marketing
Switch_A> (enable) set vlan 3 3/1-4
```

In this example, the administrator has created VLAN 3 with the name Marketing, and ports 3/1-4 have been bound to the VLAN. Note that the 3/1-4 shorthand is available on some commands as an alternative to specifying each port individually (3/1, 3/2, 3/3, 3/4).

Set Trunk

```
set trunk <mod_num/port_num> [on|off|desirable|auto|nonegotiate]
[vlans] [trunk_type]
```

Usage

The set trunk command is used to establish a trunk between two switches or a switch and router. While ports can remain in auto mode (the default), at least one side of the connection must be set to on or desirable. Because of this, most administrators configure both sides of the trunk manually to avoid future problems that may arise when a trunk link cable is moved to another port.

vlans	May be any number from 1 to 1005; for example, 2-10,1005
trunk_type	May be isl, dot1q, dot10, lane, or negotiate

An ISL link requires the use of a FastEthernet port, although a Token Ring specification, TR-ISL, has been developed. FDDI uses the 802.10, or dot10, specification.

Example

```
Switch_A> (enable) set trunk 1/1 on isl
```

```
Port(s) 1/1 trunk mode set to on.
Port(s) 1/1 trunk type set to isl.
```

Port 1/1 has been manually configured for trunking using the ISL protocol.

Exam Essentials

Remember the difference between 1900 and 2820 VLAN configuration. The 2820 uses four bridge groups instead of VLANs. The 1900 has a VLAN option.

Remember how to set a trunk port on a 5000 series switch. The set trunk command is used to establish a trunk between two switches, a router, or a server.

Key Terms and Concepts

ISL: Inter-Switch Link can be used to trunk ports on a Catalyst switch. You want to trunk ports when you need a host in more than one VLAN at the same time; for example, in a server. Typically, ISLs are used between Catalyst switches.

Switch: In networking, a device responsible for multiple functions such as filtering, flooding, and sending frames. It works using the destination address of individual frames.

Trunk: Allows a port on a switch to be in one or more VLANs simultaneously. Used for multiple-link connection and also allows servers to be in multiple broadcast domains.

Virtual LAN: A group of devices on one or more logically segmented LANs (configured by use of management software), enabling devices to communicate as if attached to the same physical medium, when they are actually located on numerous different LAN segments.

Sample Questions

1. Which of the following commands will set ports 1 through 4 on card 3 to VLAN 3 for a 5000 series switch?

   A. set vlan 3 3/1-4

   B. vlan set 1-4 3

   C. set vlan 3/1-4

   D. set vlan 3/1-4 3

   Answer: A.

2. Which of the following commands will set port 1 on card 1 to trunk with ISL for a 5000 series switch?

   A. `trunk set 1/1`

   B. `set trunk 1/1 on isl`

   C. `set isl 1/1`

   D. `set trunk isl 1/1`

   Answer: B.

▶ Maintain Catalyst series switches and perform basic troubleshooting.

This objective will describe basic troubleshooting techniques that you can use when configuring and maintaining your Catalyst switch series.

This objective is important to understand, as troubleshooting is a large part of the internetworking experience. If you install a switch, you must be able to maintain it, as well as troubleshoot any problems.

This section will not discuss any particular Catalyst switch, but will show you the basic troubleshooting steps for all Catalyst switches.

Critical Information

Developing a troubleshooting approach for switches involves creating a flow process ending with a solution. This process uses questions and responses to work through to a solution. Once you determine there is a problem with a switch, a rough outline of the process might look like the following:

1. Determine the problem. What behavior is the switch demonstrating? Are the ATM module LEDs red? Are ports 4/1–24 inactive? Find out what the symptoms are. Ask the users what they were doing before the network went down. What does the Network Manager Station report? Query as many angles as possible and narrow down the problem's scope.

2. After discovering what has happened, begin to investigate what may have caused the problem by collecting facts from the switch. This information may involve interrogating the switch using CLI commands such as show or debug. A clearer definition of the problem can help you develop a solution quickly.

3. Now create the attack plan based on the information you've collected from the switch. The plan should limit changes to the switch in a controlled manner. One solution may seem obvious, but if too many changes are made at once, your "solution" may create new problems.

4. Now it's time to implement the attack plan, taking the steps you've just outlined. The steps created in the attack plan must be defined and carried out in sequence to provide a clearer picture of what happened that caused the problem and also to help create a solution to address the problem if it arises again.

5. Gather new data that results from changing the configuration of the switch. This again may mean using the CLI commands show and debug. The collected data can be used to narrow the attack plan. If a solution was found and the switch is fixed, you are the hero. If the problem has been narrowed down and the data points to a specific module or physical connection, you can begin again at step 1, eventually finding the solution and saving the day.

The five steps above can be graphically represented by the flow diagram found in Figure 1.8. Each of the main steps can be divided into further steps to provide more detail. In some cases, however, a solution may immediately become evident while you are collecting data regarding the initial problem situation.

FIGURE 1.8:   The five-step troubleshooting process

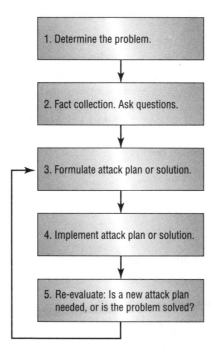

Exam Essentials

Remember to first determine the problem.   Collect facts from the switch. This information may involve interrogating the switch using CLI commands such as show or debug.

Understand that after the problem is determined, you need to create a plan of attack to solve the problem.   The steps created in the attack plan must be defined and carried out in sequence to provide a clearer picture of what happened that caused the problem and also to help create a solution to address the problem if it arises again.

Key Terms and Concepts

Switch: In networking, a device responsible for multiple functions such as filtering, flooding, and sending frames. It works using the destination address of individual frames.

Virtual LAN: A group of devices on one or more logically segmented LANs (configured by use of management software), enabling devices to communicate as if attached to the same physical medium, when they are actually located on numerous different LAN segments.

Sample Questions

1. When a problem occurs in your internetwork, what is the first thing you should do?

   A. Determine the problem.

   B. Create a plan of attack.

   C. Collect facts from the switch.

   D. Reload the switch.

   Answer: A. Try to determine the problem.

2. When a problem occurs in your internetwork, what is the second thing you should do?

   A. Determine the problem.

   B. Create a plan of attack.

   C. Collect facts from the switch.

   D. Reload the switch.

   Answer: C. After you have determined the problem, collect facts from the switch.

CHAPTER

2

Introduction to
Switching Concepts

Cisco Exam Objectives Covered in This Chapter

▶ **Describe the advantages of LAN segmentation.** *(pages 43 – 45)*

▶ **Describe LAN segmentation using bridges.** *(pages 46 – 49)*

▶ **Describe LAN segmentation using routers.** *(pages 49 – 51)*

▶ **Describe LAN segmentation using switches.** *(pages 52 – 54)*

▶ **Name and describe two switching methods.** *(pages 55 – 58)*

▶ **Describe full- and half-duplex Ethernet operation.** *(pages 59 – 63)*

▶ **Describe Token Ring switching concepts.** *(pages 63 – 66)*

In this chapter, the focus will be on understanding the major differences involved in segmenting a network with various devices. The devices used to segment a network include a bridge, a router, and a switch. The function and benefits of each device will be discussed.

The differences between half- and full-duplex devices and what is required to run each one will also be discussed. FastEthernet and its specifications, benefits, and distance limitations will also be covered. The discussion will then move on to the features and benefits of Token Ring LAN switching.

This is an extremely important chapter to comprehend for designing an internetwork. You must be able to understand LAN segmentation using various devices if you are going to succeed in an internetworking career. Everything you need to understand the concepts of LAN segmentation and switching will be covered.

Describe the advantages of LAN segmentation.

In this objective, segmentation of Ethernet networks will be examined. It is important to understand why Cisco recommends segmenting a network and how to do it with various devices.

This objective leads into this chapter well, as the next few objectives talk about how to segment your LAN with various devices and the benefits of each device. It is important to understand why you need to segment a network, and the various devices that are used to do just that.

Critical Information

You need to segment your network when it gets too large, or your business requirements will demand more bandwidth. You want to segment your network because of network congestion. Congestion "chokes" your bandwidth.

A way to solve congestion problems and increase the networking performance of your LAN is to divide a single Ethernet segment into multiple network segments. This maximizes available bandwidth, and your goal is to provide more bandwidth per user. Some of the technologies you can use to do that are as follows:

Physical segmentation: You can segment the network with bridges and routers, thereby breaking up the collision domains. This minimizes packet collisions by decreasing the number of workstations on the same physical segment.

Network switching technology (microsegmenting): Like a bridge or router, switches can also provide LAN segmentation capabilities. LAN switches (for example, the Cisco Catalyst 5000) provide dedicated, point-to-point, packet-switched connections between their ports. Since this provides simultaneous switching of packets between the ports in the switch, it increases the amount of bandwidth open to each workstation.

Full-duplex Ethernet devices: Full-duplex Ethernet can provide almost twice the bandwidth of traditional Ethernet networks. However, for this to work, the network interface cards (NICs) must be able to run in full-duplex mode.

FastEthernet: Using FastEthernet switches can provide 10 times the amount of bandwidth available from 10BaseT. The benefit of FastEthernet is that it is compatible with existing 10Mbps Ethernet networks.

FDDI: An older, solid technology that can provide 100Mbps bandwidth. By running dual rings, it has the capability of up to 200Mbps. It's typically used between closets or floors, or in a campus environment.

It should be no surprise that reducing the number of users per collision domain increases the bandwidth on your network segment. By keeping the traffic local to the network segment, users have more available bandwidth and enjoy a noticeably better response time than if you simply had one large backbone in place.

Exam Essentials

Remember why segmenting your network helps eliminate congestion problems. You need to understand the various devices available to do that (bridges, routers, and switches). The next few objectives will give you the information to eliminate the congestion.

Understand what causes congestion and how segmentation helps. By segmenting your network, you can effectively cut down on the amount of traffic on your network by making smaller networks.

Remember the different ways of improving bandwidth on a LAN. The basics ways of segmenting a network are as follows: physical segmentation, network switching technology (microsegmenting), full-duplex Ethernet devices, FastEthernet, and FDDI.

Key Terms and Concepts

Congestion: Network traffic in excess of network capacity.

Ethernet: LAN specification invented by Xerox Corporation. Uses the IEEE 802.3 series of standards

FDDI: Fiber Distributed Data Interface is a LAN token media access. It is a mature technology that can give you a solid 100Mbps bandwidth.

Segmentation: Section of a network that can be created by using bridges, routers, or switches.

Sample Questions

1. Which of the following is a solution for network congestion?

   A. 802.3

   B. Segmentation

   C. Ethernet

   D. CSMA/CD

   Answer: B. Segmenting your network is a good solution for networks with congestion problems.

2. Which of the following is an advantage of network segmentation?

   A. Ethernet

   B. Congestion

   C. Less congestion

   D. Video to the desktop

   Answer: C. If you were to segment your network correctly, you would have less congestion on your network links.

Describe LAN segmentation using bridges.

Bridges aren't used anymore—or are they? To fully understand how to segment an Ethernet network, it is important to understand the differences among all available devices.

In this objective, bridges and how they fit in an internetwork will be discussed. It is important to remember that switches are really multiport bridges that just have more functionality than regular bridges. Bridges have been around for a long time and were more popular in the 1980s when Cisco was still very young, and routers were considered very expensive.

Critical Information

A bridge can segment, or break up, your network into smaller, more manageable pieces. But if it's incorrectly placed in your network, it can cause more harm than good!

Bridges do their work at the MAC sublayer of the Data Link layer. They create both physical and logical separate network segments to reduce traffic load.

As Figure 2.1 shows, bridges work by examining the MAC or hardware addresses in each frame and forwarding the frame to the other physical segments—but only if necessary. These devices dynamically build a forwarding table of information comprised of each MAC address and the segment on which that address is located.

Now for the bad news.... A drawback to using bridges is that, if the destination MAC address is unknown to the bridge, the bridge will forward the frame to all segments except the port from which it received the frame. Also, a 20–30% latency period to process frames can occur. *Latency* is the time is takes for a frame to get from the source host to the destination host. This delay can increase

F I G U R E 2.1: Segmentation with a bridge

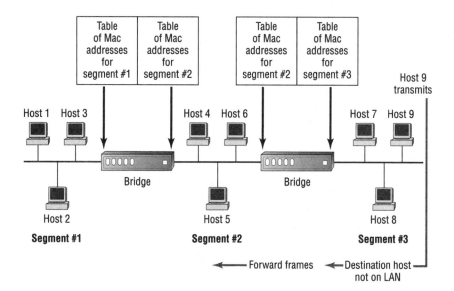

significantly if the frame cannot be immediately forwarded due to current activity on the destination segment.

Bridges will forward packets and multicast packets to all other segments to which the bridge is attached. Because the addresses from these broadcasts are never seen by the bridge, and therefore not filtered, broadcast storms can result. This same problem can happen with switches, as, theoretically, switch ports are bridge ports. A Cisco switch is really a multiport bridge that runs the Cisco IOS and performs the same (or more) functions as a bridge, but is much faster.

Exam Essentials

Understand how bridges segment a network. Bridges uses the hardware (MAC) address of a NIC card to build filter tables.

Remember how bridges filter a network. Bridges do not break up a network into smaller networks; they take a large network and filter it. It is still the same large broadcast network. Only routers can break up a large network into smaller networks.

Remember the benefit of using bridges in your internetwork. Bridges work only at the Data Link layer and have less overhead than a router. Also, protocols that cannot be routed can be bridged—for example, NetBEUI.

Key Terms and Concepts

Bridge: Device that filters a network by MAC or hardware address as defined at the Data Link layer.

Latency: Measured delay from the time a device receives a frame to the time it transmits it out another network segment.

Router: Device defined at the Network layer that creates inter-networks and does network addressing.

Switch: Device that filters by MAC or hardware address as defined at the Data Link layer.

Sample Questions

1. Which device would you use to segment your network if you were using a nonroutable protocol in your network?

   A. Repeater

   B. Bridge

   C. Router

   D. Switch

   Answer: B. A repeater does not segment a network; it only extends its distance. A bridge is protocol independent and can easily be used to segment a network with nonroutable protocols in use.

2. How does a bridge segment a network?

   A. By regenerating the digital signal

   B. By reading the logical address of a packet

   C. By creating a filter table of IP addresses

   D. By creating a filter table of MAC addresses

Answer: D. A bridge can filter your network by MAC or hardware addresses.

Describe LAN segmentation using routers.

Routers are a step up from bridges—literally. Bridges work at the Data Link layer and filter a network by MAC or hardware address. Routers work at the Network layer and create smaller networks called internetworks.

It is imperative that you understand the difference between how a bridge and a router segment a network. This is important because bridges filter by hardware addresses, which are used in a frame. Routers use logical addresses, which are found in a packet. By understanding the differences between a bridge and a router, you will be able to troubleshoot your internetwork more efficiently.

Critical Information

As you know, routers work at the Network layer and are used to route packets to destination networks. Routers, like bridges, use tables to make routing decisions. However, routers keep information on how to get only to remote networks in their tables, not to hosts; routers use this information to route packets through an internetwork. For example, routers use IP addresses instead of hardware addresses when making routing decisions.

Figure 2.2 shows how a router can break up a network. Notice that a router uses logical addresses to name the network and the host. Bridges only keep track of hardware addresses or hosts, not networks.

F I G U R E 2.2: Logical addressing

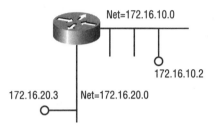

Exam Essentials

Understand how frames and packets are used in a network.
Frames are built at the Data Link layer and are used to send packets out on a local LAN only. Packets are built at the Network layer and can be routed through an internetwork.

Remember how routers segment a network.   Unlike bridges, routers actually create smaller networks and filter based on logical address, not MAC address.

Remember the advantage of routers over bridges.   Bridges create smaller collision domains, but the network is still one large broadcast domain. Routers create smaller collision domains *and* broadcast domains.

Key Terms and Concepts

Bridge: Device that filters a network by MAC or hardware address as defined at the Data Link layer.

Latency: Measured delay from the time a device receives a frame to the time it transmits it out another network segment.

MAC address: Also called a hardware address, this is used to address a host on a LAN.

Router: Device defined at the Network layer that creates internetworks and does network addressing.

Switch: Device that filters by MAC or hardware address as defined at the Data Link layer.

Sample Questions

1. If you want to segment your network and are using the IPX routed protocol, what device should you use?

   A. Repeater

   B. Bridge

   C. Router

   D. Segment

   Answer: C. A router can segment your network by logical address. IPX is an example of a protocol that uses a logical addressing scheme created by Novell.

2. If you want to segment your network, but you want to create smaller networks, not just filter your large network, what device should you use?

   A. Repeater

   B. Bridge

   C. Router

   D. Gateway

   Answer: C. A router can create smaller internetworks and name the networks.

Describe LAN segmentation using switches.

Y ou need to remember that a LAN switch filters by MAC address, just like a bridge. Of course, you have more functionality with a switch, but the theory is the same. Unlike with bridges, you can create smaller networks with a switch called virtual LAN (VLAN), but that will be covered later in this book. It is important to understand the fundamental differences in how a bridge, router, and switch work in an internetwork.

Critical Information

LAN switching is a great strategy for LAN segmentation. LAN switches improve performance by employing packet switching, which permits high-speed data exchanges. Just like bridges, switches use the destination MAC address to ensure that the packet is forwarded to the right outgoing port.

There are three different switching terms: port configuration switching, frame switching, and cell switching (ATM):

Port configuration switching: This allows a port to be assigned to a physical network segment under software control. It's the simplest form of switching.

Frame switching: This is used to increase available bandwidth on the network. It allows multiple transmissions to occur in parallel. This is the type of switching performed by all Catalyst switches.

Cell switching (ATM): This is similar to frame switching. ATM uses small, fixed-length cells that are switched on the network. It's the switching method used by all Cisco Lightstream switches.

A LAN switch bases the forwarding of frames on the frame's layer 2 address (layer 2 LAN switch) or on the frame's layer 3 address (multilayer LAN switch). LAN switches are sometimes referred to as frame switches because they generally forward layer 2 frames, in contrast to an ATM switch, which forwards cells.

As network use increases, more Token Ring and FDDI LAN switches are being seen, but Ethernet LAN switches are still the most common type.

Exam Essentials

Remember the differences among a bridge, a router, and a switch. Bridges and switches are similar, except that switches have more ports and more management. Routers work at the Network layer and use logical addressing, whereas bridges and switches use hardware addressing.

Remember how a switch works in an internetwork. Switches are really multiport bridges. By themselves, they do not create smaller internetworks as a router can. Also, they create a filter table of MAC address just as bridges do.

Remember the advantage of a switched network. Switches use layer 2 addressing to create a filter table, but allow one large broadcast domain. This is good if you want to create smaller collision domains and create point-to-point connections, but want to use nonroutable protocols. If you want to use routable protocols and break up your broadcast domains, you would create VLAN.

Key Terms and Concepts

Bridge: Device that filters a network by MAC or hardware address as defined at the Data Link layer.

Latency: Measured delay from the time a device receives a frame to the time it transmits it out another network segment.

MAC address: Also called a hardware address, this is used to address a host on a LAN.

Router: Device defined at the Network layer that creates internetworks and does network addressing.

Switch: Device that filters by MAC or hardware address as defined at the Data Link layer.

Sample Questions

1. Which of the following is true?

   A. Switches receive a frame and forward out to all segments.

   B. Routers receive a frame and forward out to all segments.

   C. Switches forward by hardware address.

   D. Switches filter by logical address.

   Answer: C. Switches receive a frame and forward it out only the port where the destination hardware address is located.

2. Which type of switching is used by the Cisco Catalyst series of switches?

   A. Port

   B. Fast

   C. Packet

   D. Frame

   Answer: D. Cisco Catalyst switches use frame switching.

Name and describe two switching methods.

Three switching methods (as covered in Cisco's curriculum) will actually be described: store-and-forward, cut-through, and fragment-free.

Even though three LAN switch types will be discussed, you really need to understand the difference between only two of them: cut-through and store-and-forward. This is important to understand when configuring Catalyst switches in an internetworking environment.

Critical Information

The latency for packet switching through the switch depends on the chosen switching mode. Options include store-and-forward, cut-through, and fragment-free.

Store-and-Forward Switching

Store-and-forward switching is one of two primary types of LAN switching. With this method, the LAN switch copies the entire frame into its onboard buffers and computes the cyclic redundancy check (CRC). The frame is discarded if it contains a CRC error, if it's a runt (less than 64 bytes, including the CRC), or if it's a giant (more than 1518 bytes, including the CRC). If the frame doesn't contain any errors, the LAN switch looks up the destination address in its forwarding, or switching, table and determines the outgoing interface. It then forwards the frame toward its destination. Because this type of switching copies the entire frame and runs a CRC, latency time can vary depending on frame length. This is the mode used by the Catalyst 5000 series switches.

Cut-Through (Real-Time) Switching

Cut-through switching is the other main type of LAN switching. With it, the LAN switch copies only the destination address (the first 6 bytes following the preamble) into its onboard buffers. It then looks up the destination address in its switching table, determines the outgoing interface, and forwards the frame toward its destination. A cut-through switch provides reduced latency because it begins to forward the frame as soon as it reads the destination address and determines the outgoing interface. Some switches can be configured to perform cut-through switching on a per-port basis until a user-defined error threshold is reached. At that point, they automatically change over to store-and-forward mode. When the error rate falls below the threshold, the port automatically changes back to cut-through mode.

Fragment-Free Switching

Fragment-free is a modified form of cut-through switching in which the switch waits for the collision windows, which are 64 bytes long, to pass before forwarding. If a packet has an error, it almost always occurs within the first 64 bytes. Fragment-free mode provides better error checking than the cut-through mode, with practically no increase in latency.

Figure 2.3 shows the different places at which the switching mode takes place in the frame.

F I G U R E 2.3: Different switching modes within a frame

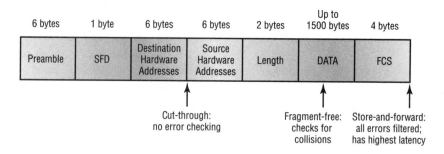

Exam Essentials

Remember the differences among the switching methods. Cut-through, fragment-free, and store-and-forward are the LAN switch types available.

Remember the difference between cut-through and store-and-forward. The cut-through method of LAN switching has a constant latency because the switch will read only the first 6 bytes of the frame after the preamble. Store-and-forward reads the entire frame; therefore latency will vary with frame length.

Remember the different names for the same LAN switch type. Cut-through can also be referred to as fast-forward. Fragment-free can also be referred to as modified cut-through.

Key Terms and Concepts

Cut-through: LAN switching method that looks only at the destination hardware address in a frame before making forwarding decisions.

Fragment-free: Modified form of cut-through switching in which the switch waits for the collision windows, which are 64 bytes long, to pass before forwarding.

Latency: Delay in time from when a port receives a frame and when it is forwarded out another port.

Store-and-forward: LAN switching method that copies the entire frame to its onboard buffers and runs a CRC before making forwarding decisions.

Sample Questions

1. Which type of LAN switching method reads only the first destination hardware address before forwarding the frame?

   A. Store-and-forward

   B. Port-switching

   C. Cut-through

   D. Fragment-free

   Answer: C. Cut-through switching reads only the first 6 bytes after the preamble in a frame.

2. Which switching method reads the first 64 bytes before choosing a switching method?

   A. Port-switching

   B. Store-and-forward

   C. Cut-through

   D. Fragment-free

   Answer: D. Fragment-free checks for fragmentation of the frames (collisions) before sending any frames out any ports.

3. Which type of switching method has the highest latency?

   A. Store-and-forward

   B. Port-switching

   C. Cut-through

   D. Fragment-free

   Answer: A. Store-and-forward has the highest latency of any switching method. Plus, latency will vary for each frame depending on its size.

Describe full- and half-duplex Ethernet operation.

In this objective, the difference between half- and full-duplex Ethernet networks and circuitry will be discussed. It is important to be able to describe the differences between the two and to understand the requirements for running full-duplex.

When the test requirements were written, you could run full-duplex only with a switch. This is no longer true, but the test has not been changed to reflect this change in technology.

Critical Information

According to Cisco, full-duplex Ethernet can both transmit and receive simultaneously, but it requires a switch port, not a hub, to be able to do so.

Full-duplex Ethernet uses point-to-point connections and is typically referred to as collision-free since it doesn't share bandwidth with any other devices. Frames sent by two nodes cannot collide because there are physically separate transmit and receive circuits between the nodes.

If you have a full-duplex 10Mbps Ethernet operating bidirectionally on the same switch port, you can theoretically have 20Mbps aggregate throughput. Full-duplex can now be used in 10BaseT, 100BaseT, and 100BaseFL media, but all devices (NIC cards, for example) must be able to support full-duplex transmission.

Half-Duplex Ethernet Design

Half-duplex Ethernet has been around a long time. Ethernet II came out in 1984 and is still the most popular of all LAN topologies.

Figure 2.4 shows the circuitry involved in half-duplex Ethernet. When a station is sending to another station, the transmitting circuitry is active at the transmitting station, and the receive circuitry is active at the receiving station. This uses a single cable similar to a narrow, one-way bridge.

Notice in this figure that loopback detection and collision detection are enabled.

FIGURE 2.4: Half-duplex circuitry

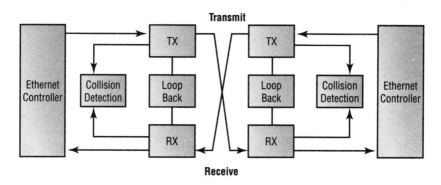

Full-Duplex Ethernet Design

Figure 2.5 shows full-duplex circuitry. Full-duplex Ethernet switch (FDES) technology provides a point-to-point connection between the transmitter of the transmitting station and the receiver of the receiving station. Half-duplex, standard Ethernet can usually provide 50–60% of the bandwidth available. In contrast, full-duplex Ethernet can provide a full 100%, because it can transmit and receive simultaneously, and because collisions don't occur.

To run full-duplex, you must have the following:

- Two 10Mbps or 100Mbps paths
- Full-duplex NIC cards
- Loopback and collision detection disabled

F I G U R E 2.5: Full-duplex circuitry

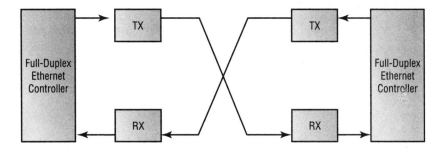

- Software drivers supporting two simultaneous data paths
- Adherence to Ethernet distance standards

Exam Essentials

Remember what is needed to run full-duplex Ethernet. You do not have to know the distance requirements, but it is important to understand what you need to run full-duplex. Do not take for granted that you know what you need. Remember what Cisco says you need: two 10 or 100Mbps paths and full-duplex network cards, and loop-back and collision detection must be disabled.

Understand the definitions of half- and full-duplex Ethernet. Half-duplex uses a single cable similar to a narrow, one-way bridge. Full-duplex provides a point-to-point connection between the trans-mitter of the transmitting station and the receiver of the receiving station.

Remember the benefits of full-duplex Ethernet. Supposedly, col-lisions do not occur because traffic in each direction in a full-duplex environment has its own set of wires (like a highway).

Key Terms and Concepts

Full-duplex Ethernet: Provides a point-to-point connection between the transmitter of the transmitting station and the receiver of the receiving station.

Half-duplex Ethernet: Uses a single cable similar to a narrow, one-way bridge.

Sample Questions

1. Which of the following are needed for running full-duplex?

   A. Two 10Mbps or 100Mbps paths

   B. SNMP

   C. Full-duplex NIC cards

   D. Loopback and collision detection disabled

   Answer: A, C, D. You need two physical paths and full-duplex NIC cards, and collision detection and loopback detection must be disabled.

2. Which of the following statements describes half-duplex?

   A. Provides a point-to-point connection between the transmitter of the transmitting station and the receiver of the receiving station

   B. Used in all Cisco switches

   C. Uses a single cable similar to a narrow, one-way bridge

   D. Is no longer supported

   Answer: C.

3. Which of the following statements describes full-duplex?

   A. It provides a point-to-point connection between the transmitter of the transmitting station and the receiver of the receiving station.

   B. It uses a single cable similar to a narrow, one-way bridge.

   C. It is used in all Cisco switches.

   D. When you upgrade your servers to full-duplex, all clients must be upgraded at the same time.

   Answer: A.

Describe Token Ring switching concepts.

IBM created Token Ring in the 1970s, and it became popular with true-blue customers needing to migrate from a mainframe environment. It lost to Ethernet in the popularity polls because it's expensive by comparison. Depending on what you're looking for, however, Token Ring may still be a good value. It is a more resilient network, especially under heavy loads. Sometimes you actually do get what you pay for.

To help meet the business requirement for more bandwidth, manufacturers designed higher-speed LANs as well as Token Ring switches. With higher-speed LANs, you still have the same limitations of a shared LAN: Traffic is subject to delay based on how busy the network segment is at any given time. This can be unacceptable in a multimedia environment.

This is an important objective to understand if you have more than one Token Ring network and need to run bridging protocols on your switches. You must understand how Token Ring frames are transmitted on the network. This objective will give you that information.

Critical Information

Each Token Ring switch port can have its own token, which can allow you to have more control over your internetwork environment. Unlike upgrading a shared LAN to a higher-speed LAN, which requires changing all the cabling and network interface cards (NICs), using switches allows media adaptation. This means that you can upgrade only a few NICs and their wiring where needed. Token Ring switches can be placed in the network without requiring changes to the clients or servers. You also will have better remote monitoring and management than if you used bridges, which create many physical and logical segments.

Cisco Switched Token Ring supports the following bridging protocols:

Source-route bridging (SRB): Uses the routing information field (RIF) in the frame to make forwarding decisions. The Cisco switch modifies the RIF field when it is an explorer packet.

Routing information field (RIF): Contains a single bit that defines the path direction of the frame or Token (left to right or right to left). It is also defined as part of a MAC header for source-routed frames, which contains path information. This bit is used in an explorer frame to notify computers that it is on its return path.

Transparent bridging (TB): Uses the hardware (MAC) address to make forwarding decisions.

Source-route transparent bridging (SRT): Can use either the MAC address or the RIF field when making forwarding decisions.

Source-route/transparent translational bridging (SR/TLB): The switch converts SRB frames to TB frames.

Source-route switching (SRS): Uses the RIF field to make forwarding decisions, but unlike SRB, does not modify the RIF field.

Verification

You can use several commands to verify and monitor operation of SRB. As always, show interface commands are useful for displaying interface operations. There are also several other helpful show and debug commands:

show rif: Displays the current contents of the RIF cache.

debug rif: Displays the routing information field data of Token Ring frames passing through the router.

show source bridge: Displays the current source bridge configuration and miscellaneous statistics.

Exam Essentials

Remember how source-route bridging works.   SRB uses the routing information field (RIF) in the frame to make forwarding decisions. The Cisco switch modifies the RIF field when it is an explorer packet.

Remember how transparent bridging works.   TB uses the hardware (MAC) address to make forwarding decisions.

Remember the debug command to see the RIF field.   The debug rif command will show you the RIF data as it passes through a router.

Remember the show command to see the RIF cache.   The show rif command will show you the RIF cache.

Key Terms and Concepts

RIF: The routing information field contains a single bit that defines the path direction of the frame or Token.

SRB: Uses the routing information field (RIF) in the frame to make forwarding decisions.

SRT: Source-route transparent bridging uses either the MAC address or the RIF field when making forwarding decisions.

TB: Transparent bridging uses the hardware (MAC) address to make forwarding decisions.

Sample Questions

1. What command will display the routing information field data of Token Ring frames passing through the router?

   A. show rif

   B. debug rif

   C. show token

   D. show source-bridge

   Answer: B.

2. Which statement is true about SRB?

   A. It can use either the MAC address or the RIF field when making forwarding decisions.

   B. It uses the hardware (MAC) address to make forwarding decisions.

   C. The Cisco switch modifies the RIF field when it is an explorer packet.

   D. It uses the RIF field to make forwarding decisions, but does not modify the RIF field.

   Answer: C. Source-route bridging modifies the RIF field in a frame as it traverses the LAN.

CHAPTER

3

Virtual LANs

Cisco Exam Objectives Covered in This Chapter

▶ **Define VLANs.** *(pages 69 – 71)*

▶ **Name seven reasons to create VLANs.** *(pages 72 – 76)*

▶ **Describe the role switches play in the creation of VLANs.**
(pages 76 – 80)

▶ **Describe VLAN frame filtering and VLAN frame tagging.**
(pages 80 – 83)

▶ **Describe how switches can be used with hubs.** *(pages 83 – 86)*

▶ **Name the five components of VLAN implementations.**
(pages 86 – 89)

▶ **Describe static and dynamic VLANs.** *(pages 89 – 94)*

▶ **Describe the VLAN technologies.** *(pages 94 – 98)*

▶ **Describe Token Ring VLANs.** *(pages 99 – 102)*

▶ **Describe Cisco's VLAN architecture.** *(pages 103 – 107)*

Th   his chapter discusses virtual LANs and how they
work in a Cisco switched environment. You'll learn why VLANs
are used in internetworking and why switches are the core equipment used in VLANs. When you create VLANs, you are essentially creating smaller broadcast domains within a switch.

This chapter also explains the VLAN technologies and the standards used in layer 2 switching. Finally, Cisco's VLAN technology and architecture, which includes both Ethernet and Token Ring internetworks, will be discussed.

This is an important chapter to understand before going on to the specific switch chapters in this book. You must have a basic understanding of switching concepts, and this chapter will give you just that.

Define VLANs.

A *virtual local area network* (VLAN) is a logical grouping of network users and resources connected to administratively defined ports on a switch. By creating VLANs, you are able to create smaller broadcast domains within a switch by assigning different ports in the switch to different subnetworks. A VLAN is treated like its own subnet or broadcast domain. This means that frames broadcast are switched between only ports in the same VLAN. To communicate between VLANs, a router must be used.

In this first objective, you will gain a basic understanding of VLANs. This section is important to understand before going on to the next objectives in this chapter.

Critical Information

Using virtual LANs, you're no longer confined to physical locations. VLANs can be organized by location, function, department, or even the application or protocol used, regardless of where the resources or users are located. As an administrator, you must make sure the network is properly segmented to keep problems on one segment from propagating through the internetwork. The most effective way of doing this is through switches and routers.

Since switches have become cost effective, a lot of companies are replacing the collapsed backbone with pure switched networks. This has also added a new chapter to network design, since broadcasts can propagate through the switched network. Routers, by default, send broadcasts only within the originating network, but switches forward broadcasts to all segments. This is called a *flat network* because it is one broadcast domain.

Routers, or route switch modules (RSMs), must be used in conjunction with switches to provide firewalls between networks (VLANs), which can stop broadcasts from propagating through the entire internetwork.

Various sources have noted that between 20 and 110% of the workforce changes or moves each year. Without VLANs, making these changes would be a full-time job for someone. However, with VLANs, the router configuration stays the same, which makes it easier for administrators and brings down administrative costs.

NOTE The maximum number of users that you can define per known network is 1000. However, Cisco recommends that a VLAN contain no more than 150 to 200 users.

Exam Essentials

Remember the best reason to create VLANs. VLANs break the physical barrier when creating internetworks. It no longer matters where a user is plugged in to a network.

Remember what a VLAN is. Virtual LANs are created with switches and break up broadcast domains.

Remember why a switch is better than a hub. Each switch port is its own collision domain. Think of each port as being a bridge port.

Key Terms and Concepts

Router: Device defined at the Network layer that creates internetworks and does network addressing.

Segmentation: Section of a network that can be created by using bridges, routers, or switches.

Switch: Device that filters by MAC or hardware address as defined at the Data Link layer.

Virtual LAN: A group of devices on one or more logically segmented LANs (configured by use of management software), enabling devices to communicate as if attached to the same physical medium, when they are actually located on numerous different LAN segments. VLANs are based on logical instead of physical connections, and thus, are tremendously flexible.

Sample Questions

1. Which of the following is true regarding VLANs? (Choose all that apply.)

   A. VLANs replace routers in an internetwork.

   B. VLANs are a group of ports or users in the same collision domain.

   C. VLANs are a group of ports or users in the same broadcast domain.

   D. VLANs are configured by physical location only.

   Answer: C.

2. Which of the following is true regarding VLANs? (Choose all that apply.)

   A. VLANs reduce administration costs.

   B. VLANs reduce server broadcasts.

   C. VLANs make security holes.

   D. VLANs reduce the propagation of broadcasts.

   Answer: A, D.

Name seven reasons to create VLANs.

In this objective, the seven reasons that Cisco has determined are good reasons for creating VLANs will be discussed. The seven reasons to create VLANs are as follows:

- Simplified administration
- Reduced administration costs
- Broadcast control
- Security
- Flexibility and scalability
- Distribution of traffic
- Distribution of network services

This is an important objective to understand. It is the largest in this chapter, and introduces a lot of information discussed in the other objectives throughout this chapter.

Critical Information

Let's discuss the different reasons for creating VLANs and how they can benefit your internetwork.

Administration Simplification and Cost Reduction

Some organizations have "roving users," who seem to be constantly moving from floor to floor or building to building. VLANs can help maintain a group of users regardless of their physical location. When users were attached to hubs, which were then connected to routers, administrators sometimes had to reconfigure the router or routers and workstations to help facilitate users every time they moved their physical location within a company.

Now as a user moves, an administrator just has to make sure the user's new switch port is part of their existing VLAN. Network addresses do not change, so administration is easier. Administrators no longer have to worry about security and the opening of resources into a network segment just because one user needs access to the resource.

Broadcast Control

Broadcasts occur in every protocol, but how often they occur depends upon the protocol, the application(s) running on the internetwork, and how these services are used.

Some older applications have been rewritten to reduce their bandwidth needs. However, there is a new generation of applications that are bandwidth-greedy—consuming all they can find. These are multimedia applications that use broadcasts and multicasts extensively. Faulty equipment, inadequate segmentation, and poorly designed firewalls can also add to the problems of broadcast-intensive applications. VLANs allow an administrator to create smaller broadcast domains within the switch fabric.

Security

The problem with the collapsed backbone internetwork was that security was created by connecting hubs with routers. Security was then maintained at the router, but anyone connecting to the physical network could have access to the network resources on that physical LAN. Also, a user could plug a network analyzer into the hub and see all the traffic in that network. Another problem was that users could join a workgroup by just plugging their workstation into the existing hub.

By using VLANs and creating multiple broadcast groups, administrators now have control over each port and user. Users no longer can just plug their workstation into any switch port and have access to network resources. The administrator controls each port and whatever resources it is allowed to use.

Flexibility and Scalability

Switches only read frames for filtering; they do not look at the Network-layer protocol. This can cause a switch to forward all broadcasts. However, by creating VLANs, you are essentially creating broadcast domains. Broadcasts sent out from a node in one VLAN will not be forwarded to ports configured in a different VLAN. By assigning switch ports or users to VLAN groups on a switch or group of connected switches (called a *switch fabric*), you have the flexibility to add only the users you want in the broadcast domain regardless of their physical location. This can stop broadcast storms caused by a faulty network interface card (NIC) or an application that propagates throughout the entire internetwork.

When a VLAN gets too big, you can create more VLANs to keep the broadcasts from consuming too much bandwidth. The fewer users in a VLAN, the fewer affected by broadcasts.

Traffic Distribution

When placing bridges in your network, a general rule of thumb to follow is the 80/20 rule. This means that 80% of the traffic should stay on the local broadcast domain, and 20% or less should be forwarded through the bridge. When creating VLANs, these rules still apply: 80% of the traffic flow should be local, or within the VLAN, and no more than 20% should flow between VLANs.

Network Service Distribution

To help keep traffic from having to traverse VLANs, servers can be trunked. This allows you to place a server into a switch and assign it as a member of all VLANs or just a selected few VLANs. This allows for all users to see the network services locally without creating inter-VLAN traffic.

The network administrator can assign a server to as many as 1005 VLANs. By default, all VLANs are included when you create a trunk, and the administrator must actually remove VLANs from the trunk.

Exam Essentials

Remember what Cisco describes as the seven reasons to create VLANs. These reasons are as follows:

- Simplified administration

- Reduced administration costs

- Broadcast control

- Security

- Flexibility and scalability

- Distribution of traffic

- Distribution of network services

Remember how VLANs allow administration simplification and cost reduction. Some organizations have "roving users," who seem to be constantly moving from floor to floor or building to building. VLANs can help maintain a group of users regardless of their physical location.

Understand how VLANs can create broadcast control. Administrators can use VLANs to create smaller broadcast domains.

Key Terms and Concepts

Latency: Measured delay from the time a device receives a frame to the time it transmits it out another network segment.

MAC address: Also called a hardware address, this is used to address a host on a LAN.

Virtual LAN: A group of devices on one or more logically segmented LANs (configured by use of management software), enabling devices to communicate as if attached to the same physical medium, when they are actually located on numerous different LAN segments. VLANs are based on logical instead of physical connections, and thus, are tremendously flexible.

Sample Questions

1. What is trunking?

    A. Sending of frames across a switch link

    B. Receiving of packets at a router interface

    C. 100Mbps, full-duplex server connection to a switch

    D. Allowing a switch port to be a member of more than one VLAN at the same time

Answer: D. Trunking allows you to place a server into a switch and assign it as a member of all VLANs or just a selected few VLANs.

2. When placing bridges in your network, what is a general rule of thumb that you should follow?

    A. The 20/80 rule.

    B. The 80/20 rule.

    C. Only one protocol per bridge segment.

    D. Replace your bridges with Cisco routers.

Answer: B. Even though D is a good answer, to have a good bridged segment, 80% of your traffic should stay local, and only 20% should cross the bridge.

Describe the role switches play in the creation of VLANs.

Each switch port is its own collision domain; however, by default, the switch creates one large broadcast domain. When a VLAN gets too big, you can create more VLANs to keep the broadcasts from consuming too much bandwidth. The fewer users in a VLAN, the fewer affected by broadcasts.

In this objective, you will learn how a switch works logically and physically within an internetwork, as well as how a network looks before and after switches, and how routers work with and without switches.

Critical Information

To understand how a VLAN looks to a switch, it's helpful to begin by first looking at a traditional collapsed backbone. Figure 3.1 shows a collapsed backbone created by connecting physical LANs to a router.

F I G U R E 3.1:   Physical LANs connected to a router

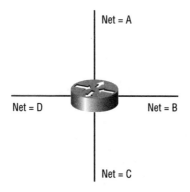

Each network is attached to the router, and each network has its own logical network number. Each node attached to a particular physical network must match that network number to be able to communicate on the internetwork. Now let's look at what a switch accomplishes. Figure 3.2 shows how switches remove the physical boundary.

Switches create greater flexibility and scalability than routers can by themselves. You can group users into communities of interest, which are known as *VLAN organizations*.

Because of switches, you don't need routers anymore, right? Wrong. In Figure 3.2, notice that there are four VLANs or broadcast

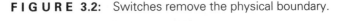

F I G U R E 3.2: Switches remove the physical boundary.

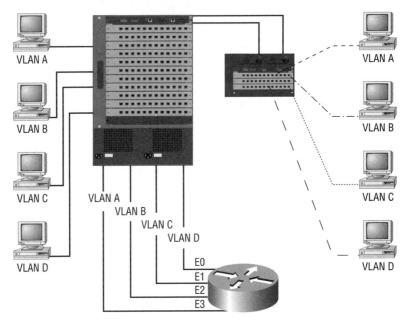

domains. The nodes within each VLAN can communicate with each other, but not with any other VLAN or node in another VLAN. When configured in a VLAN, the nodes think they are actually in a collapsed backbone as in Figure 3.1. What do these hosts in Figure 3.1 need to do to communicate to a node or host on a different network? They need to go through the router, just like when they are configured for VLAN communication as shown in Figure 3.2. Communication between VLANs, just as in physical networks, must go through the router.

Exam Essentials

Remember why you would want to use switches instead of hubs. Each switch port is its own collision domain. A hub creates one large collision domain.

Understand how a router works in a switched internetwork.   A router allows VLANs to communicate. If there's no router, there's no communication between VLANs. However, a route switch module (RSM) can be used instead of a router, but the RSM takes up a card slot in the switch and is limited to 400Mbps of throughput. However, it is more flexible when it comes to adding more VLANs than an external router.

Remember that VLANs create smaller broadcast domains.   An administrator can create VLANs in the switch fabric, which actually creates a broadcast domain.

Key Terms and Concepts

Broadcast domain: A group of devices receiving broadcast frames initiating from any device within the group. Because they do not forward broadcast frames, broadcast domains are generally surrounded by routers.

Collision domain: The network area in Ethernet over which frames that have collided will spread. Collisions are propagated by hubs and repeaters, but not by LAN switches, routers, or bridges.

Sample Questions

1. Which of the following is true?

   A. Switches allow you to replace your routers.

   B. Each switch port is its own broadcast domain.

   C. Each switch port is its own collision domain.

   D. Bridges are used to create smaller broadcast domains.

   Answer: C. Only routers can break up a broadcast domain. Each switch port is its own collision domain.

2. Which of the following is true?

   A. Virtual LANs allow you to break up broadcast domains.

   B. Virtual LANs allow you to break up collision domains.

   C. Routers propagate broadcasts throughout the internetwork.

   D. Routers create collision domains, not broadcast domains.

   Answer: A. Since switch ports create only smaller collision domains, VLANs are used to make smaller broadcast domains.

Describe VLAN frame filtering and VLAN frame tagging.

When creating VLANs, it is important to understand how the frame traverses the switch fabric. A *switch fabric* is a group of switches connected and under the same management domain.

In this objective, you will see what happens to a frame once it is received by a switch. It is important to understand frame filtering and frame tagging because they will help you in troubleshooting an internetworking environment.

Critical Information

How a frame is filtered and tagged as it traverses the switch fabric will be discussed in this section.

Frame Filtering

Switches build a table of known MAC (hardware) addresses and keep track of to which port each node is connected. This allows the switch to send a frame only to the destination and not to all other connected nodes.

Switches can synchronize this table with other switches, which can help locate nodes and cut down on broadcasts looking for destination hardware addresses. However, remember that frame filtering can affect latency and overall network performance.

Frame Tagging

When nodes or hosts need to communicate between VLANs, the packets need to go through a router. Since switches do not look at the packet information (layer 2 switches), the frame is sent to the router, and the router extracts the packet out of the frame and then discards the frame. When the router determines the correct exit interface, it puts the packet back into a frame to traverse the new VLAN.

The switch needs a way of keeping track of users and frames as they travel the switch fabric and VLANs. Frame identification (frame tagging)—a Cisco idea—uniquely assigns a user-defined ID to each frame. When a frame is received on a port, the switch places a unique identifier in each frame as it is forwarded through the switching fabric. This identifier defines the VLAN with which the frame is allowed to communicate.

When the frame goes from the switch to a router to be forwarded to a different VLAN, the switch will remove the identifier and then, when the frame reenters the switch to find the new VLAN, it will add a new identifier with the VLAN information it is now traversing.

If you are using NetFlow switching hardware on your Cisco switches, this will allow devices on different VLANs to communicate after taking just the first packet through the router. This means that communication can occur from port to port on a switch, rather than port to router to port when traversing VLANs. NetFlow switching hardware is also used on trunked ports.

VLAN Standardization

The IEEE 802.1Q committee has decided on frame tagging as the standardized solution for VLANs. Before frame tagging, each node was placed in a filter table, and each time the switch received a frame, it looked up the address in this filter table to decide the frame's fate.

With each frame tagged as it enters the switch, the frame contains all the information it needs to traverse the switch fabric, and no table is needed.

Exam Essentials

Understand how a switch uses frame filtering. Each switch builds a table of MAC (hardware) addresses of devices attached to the switch. If a hub is plugged into a switch port, it will remember every device plugged into that hub. It does this by reading the frames as they enter the switch.

Remember how frame tagging works. Each frame is tagged with VLAN information as it enters the switch. It identifies the user and the VLAN to which they belong. If they need to communicate with a device that is in a different VLAN, the switch sends the frame to a router or RSM.

Remember the frame-tagging standard. The IEEE 802.1Q committee has decided on frame tagging as the standardized solution for VLANs.

Key Terms and Concepts

802.1Q: IEEE standardization for frame tagging.

Frame: A logical unit of information sent by the Data Link layer over a transmission medium. The term often refers to the header and trailer, employed for synchronization and error control, that surround the data contained in the unit.

Frame filtering: Filter table built on each switch that keeps track of hardware addresses.

Frame tagging: Cisco proprietary solution for frames that traverse a multi-VLAN switch fabric.

Sample Questions

1. Which of the following is true regarding frame tagging? (Choose all that apply.)

   A. It is used by all Cisco switches.

   B. It is used by the Catalyst 5000 switches.

   C. It is used by all routers.

   D. It involves comparing frames with table entries.

   Answer: B. By default, the Catalyst 5000 series of switches uses frame tagging.

2. Which of the following is true regarding frame filtering? (Choose all that apply.)

   A. Cisco created frame filtering specifically for use with VLANs.

   B. Frame filtering compares frames with table entries.

   C. Frame filtering places a unique identifier in the header of each frame as it traverses the switch fabric.

   D. Frame filtering decreases administration costs.

   Answer: B. Each switch creates a filter table of hardware addresses.

Describe how switches can be used with hubs.

This is a small objective, but it is important. One of the greatest benefits of adding switches to your internetwork is the ability to have them work with your existing equipment. Plugging a hub into a switch port creates a collision domain for that hub. This is better than connecting a few hubs together, which creates one large collision domain.

In this objective, leveraging your existing equipment will be discussed. This is important to understand when upgrading your existing network, and when studying for the CLSC exam.

Critical Information

Network administrators have been installing active hubs for many years. Should these be replaced with switches? It would be nice to have 100Mbps switched connections to every desktop, but that is not always cost effective. However, 10 and 100Mbps shared hubs are rather inexpensive and can work within a switched fabric. You can also leverage your existing investment in shared hubs by connecting switches to the backplane of hubs. Backplane hub connections are defined as a connection into a backbone.

You can connect a hub into a switch port, and the switch will create a filter table of all hardware addresses connected to that port. You can make this port part of an existing VLAN or create a VLAN with just that one port. However, you cannot make individual nodes connected to that hub part of different VLANs.

It is best not to overload a switch port with a large number of users connected to a hub. A good example of how to use hubs and switches together is to use the hubs to connect printers to the switches. Generally, printers do not consume a large amount of bandwidth. However, connecting many CAD users (for example) to one switch port through a hub might not be a wise choice.

By using your legacy hubs, you can migrate your network slowly from a shared to a switched environment. Start by moving your servers to a switch port, and then find heavy network users and give them a dedicated port. This flexibility allows network managers to keep an existing environment and still build VLANs.

Exam Essentials

Remember the benefits of switches. You can leverage your existing investment in shared hubs by connecting switches to the backplane of hubs.

Remember when to connect hubs to switches. It is best not to overload a switch port with a large number of users connected to a hub. A good example of how to use hubs and switches together is to use the hubs to connect printers to the switches.

Key Terms and Concepts

Hub: The point where network devices connect. Hubs create one large collision domain and one large broadcast domain.

Switch: In networking, a device responsible for multiple functions such as filtering, flooding, and sending frames. It works using the destination address of individual frames. Switches operate at the Data Link layer of the OSI model. Each port is its own collision domain.

Sample Questions

1. Which is true when installing switches? (Choose all that apply.)

  A. You must replace all shared hubs when installing switches.

  B. Switches and shared hubs can be used together.

  C. Shared hubs can participate in multiple VLANs.

  D. You must use only 100Mbps network interface cards in servers.

  Answer: B. You can easily integrate your existing shared hubs into a switched environment.

2. Which of the following is true?

A. You can install only one 12-port hub in a switch port without oversubscribing the switch.

B. You can install only one 16-port hub in a switch port without oversubscribing the switch.

C. By using your legacy hubs, you can migrate your network slowly from a shared to a switched environment.

D. When connecting hubs to switches, the connection must be 100Mbps.

Answer: C. One of the greatest assets of using switches is that you can migrate slowly from your shared hubs to a switched internetwork.

Name the five components of VLAN implementations.

This is another small objective. However, the information presented in this objective is covered throughout this chapter. This information is an overview of what Cisco thinks you need to know before implementing VLANs in your internetwork.

This is important information to know. Since it is based on material that is presented throughout this chapter, consider reading the whole chapter and then memorizing the overview presented in this objective.

Critical Information

Cisco lists the five components of VLAN implementations as follows:

Switches: If you do not have any switches, you cannot have any VLANs. VLANs are created within a switch fabric so you can administratively cut the one large, default broadcast domain into smaller broadcast domains.

Routing: To be able to communicate between VLANs, you must have a router or route switch module (RSM). When a switch receives a frame with a destination hardware address located in a different VLAN than the frame originated from, the switch will forward the frame to a router. The router will strip the frame and then have only the packet. The router will determine the exit interface and then put the packet in a frame to be sent to the switch port that is configured to be in the destination VLAN. The switch will receive the frame and tag it with the new VLAN information.

VLAN transport protocols: In VLAN Trunk Protocol (VTP), all switches advertise their management domain on their trunk ports, their configuration revision number, and their known VLANs along with their individual boundaries. One or more interconnected devices that share the same VTP domain name make up a VTP domain. When configuring switches, remember that a switch can be assigned to only one VTP domain. Within the VTP domain, its servers and clients maintain all VLANs in the switch fabric, and a VTP domain sets the boundaries of individual VLANs. A VTP's servers and clients also send information through trunks to other attached switches and receive updates from those trunks.

VLAN management: Many network management programs can work within a Cisco switched fabric to add centralized control, switch configuration, and traffic management.

Interoperability: By using your legacy hubs, you can migrate your network slowly from a shared to a switched environment. Start by moving your servers to a switch port, and then find heavy network users and give them a dedicated port. This flexibility allows network managers to keep an existing environment and still build VLANs.

Exam Essentials

Remember the five components of VLANS. They are as follows: switches, routers, VTP, VLAN management, and interoperability.

Understand VTP. VLAN Trunk Protocol switches advertise their management domain on their trunk ports, their configuration revision number, and their known VLANs along with their individual boundaries.

Key Terms and Concepts

Router: A Network-layer mechanism, software or hardware, using one or more metrics to decide on the best path to use for transmission of network traffic. Sending packets between networks by routers is based on the information provided on Network layers.

Switch: In networking, a device responsible for multiple functions such as filtering, flooding, and sending frames. It works using the destination address of individual frames. Switches operate at the Data Link layer of the OSI model.

Sample Questions

1. Which of the following is true?

   A. Switches create smaller broadcast domains.

   B. Routers create smaller broadcast domains.

   C. Switches can be used with IP and IPX only.

   D. Routers can be used with IP and IPX only.

   Answer: B. Only routers can break up broadcast domains. Switches use VLANs to break up broadcast domains, but they must use a router to communicate between VLANs. The layer 3 protocol is irrelevant to a switch.

2. Which of the following is true?

   A. Switches create smaller collision domains.

   B. Routers create smaller collision domains.

   C. Switches replace routers in an internetwork.

   D. Switches should be used in an internetwork that uses multiple routing protocols.

   Answer: A, B. Both routers and switches create smaller collision domains. The layer 3 routing protocols are irrelevant to a switch.

Describe static and dynamic VLANs.

In this objective, a discussion of the two different ways of configuring VLANs will be presented. Typically, VLANs are created statically, or port by port. However, you can set up a dynamic list of users (hardware addresses) and use those to filter users from plugging into a switch and being part of a VLAN.

You will learn the differences between static and dynamic VLAN and how you would configure each type. This is important information to understand before implementing any VLANs in your internetwork.

Critical Information

In this section, two different ways of configuring VLANs will be presented.

Static VLANs

This is the typical way of creating VLANs, and it is the most secure. The switch port that you assign a VLAN association always maintains that association until an administrator changes the port assignment. This type of VLAN configuration is easy to set up and monitor, working well in a network where the movement of users within the network is controlled. Using network management software to configure the ports can be helpful, but is not mandatory.

To configure a static VLAN port, the administrator needs to connect to the switch either through the console cable and using the CLI (command line interface), or through a Cisco product called CWSI (Cisco Works for Switched Internetworks) from an NT or Unix device.

Let's take a look at how a static VLAN can be configured from a console port:

```
5000> (enable) set vlan 4 name Admin
Vlan 100 configuration successful
5000> (enable) set vlan 4 3/1-4
VLAN 100 modified.
VLAN 1 modified.
VLAN    Mod/Ports
----    ----------------------
4       3/1-4
        5000> (enable)
```

This dialog creates VLAN 4 and names it Admin. The name is optional; you set it so that you'll know which department VLAN 4 represents. The switch was then told to assign ports 1 through 4 on card 3 to this VLAN.

Dynamic VLANs

Dynamic VLANs determine a node's VLAN assignment automatically. Using intelligent management software, you can enable hardware (MAC) addresses, protocols, or even applications to create dynamic VLANs.

For example, suppose MAC addresses have been entered into a centralized VLAN management application. If a node is then attached to an unassigned switch port, the VLAN management database can look up the hardware address, and assign and configure the switch port to the correct VLAN. This can make management and configuration easier for the administrator. If a user moves, the switch will automatically assign them into the correct VLAN. However, more administration is needed initially to set up the database.

Cisco administrators can use the VMPS service to set up a database of MAC addresses that can be used for dynamic addressing of VLANs. VLAN Management Policy Server (VMPS) is a MAC-address-to-VLAN mapping database.

VLAN Management Policy Server (VMPS)

VMPS allows you to assign switch ports to VLANs dynamically. The hardware (MAC) address of the host is used to determine the VLAN assignment. This permits users to move their workstations or laptops without having to change VLAN assignments or configurations.

The VMPS database is stored on a TFTP host and is downloaded when the switch is loaded. VMPS uses UDP to communicate and listen for client requests. When a request is received on the switch, the VMPS checks the database for a match. VMPS will shut down the switch port if no match is found. You can create an explicit deny for any MAC address on any VLAN.

Dynamic Port VLAN Membership

You can assign a dynamic (nontrunking) port to only one VLAN at a time on a Catalyst series switch. A dynamic port is isolated from its static VLAN when the link comes up. In an attempt to match the MAC address to a VLAN in the VMPS database, the source MAC address from the first packet of a new host on the dynamic port is sent to VMPS. If there is no match, VMPS will deny the request or shut down the port, depending on the VMPS secure-mode setting. If there is a match, VMPS supplies the VLAN number to assign to the port.

NOTE Dynamic VLAN membership is not supported on the three-port Gigabit Ethernet module (WS-X5403).

If they are all in the same VLAN, multiple hosts—MAC addresses—can be active on a dynamic port. The port returns to an isolated state if the link goes down on a dynamic port. MAC addresses that come online through the port are checked again with VMPS before a port is assigned to a VLAN.

The following standards and limits apply to dynamic port VLAN membership:

- VMPS must be configured before you configure ports as dynamic.

- Spanning-tree PortFast is enabled automatically for any port you configure as dynamic, which prevents applications on the host from timing out and entering loops caused by incorrect configurations. If you wish, you can disable the spanning-tree PortFast mode.

- A port will connect immediately to the VLAN if you reconfigure it from static to dynamic. However, after a given period, VMPS will check the legality of the specific host on the dynamic port.

- Static secure ports cannot become dynamic ports unless you first turn off security on the static secure port.

- Static ports that are trunking cannot become dynamic ports unless you first turn off trunking on the trunk port.

NOTE   The VTP management domain, the management VLAN of VMPS clients, and the VMPS server must all be the same.

Exam Essentials

Remember what a static VLAN is.   With static VLANs, the switch port that you assign a VLAN association always maintains that association until an administrator changes the port assignment.

Remember what a dynamic VLAN is. Dynamic VLANs determine a node's VLAN assignment automatically. Using intelligent management software, you can enable hardware (MAC) addresses, protocols, or even applications to create dynamic VLANs.

Understand how to configure dynamic VLANs. Cisco administrators can use the VMPS service to set up a database of MAC addresses that can be used for dynamic addressing of VLANs. VLAN Management Policy Server (VMPS) is a MAC-address-to-VLAN mapping database.

Key Terms and Concepts

Dynamic VLAN: Dynamic VLANs determine a node's VLAN assignment automatically.

Static VLAN: With static VLANs, the switch port that you assign a VLAN association always maintains that association until an administrator changes the port assignment.

Sample Questions

1. If you are using dynamic VLANs, which of the following are true?

A. The administrator assigns VLAN by port.

B. A VLAN configuration server can be used.

C. Dynamic VLANs provide for automatic notification of a new network user.

D. Dynamic VLANs require more configurations in the wiring closet than static VLANs.

Answer: B, C. There is more work up front when using dynamic VLANs, but easier administration is provided in the long run.

2. If you are using static VLANs, which of the following are true?

   A. The administrator assigns VLAN by port.

   B. A VLAN configuration server can be used.

   C. Static VLANs provide for automatic notification of a new network user.

   D. Static VLANs require more configuration in the wiring closet then dynamic VLANs.

   Answer: A, D. More administration needs to be done on a day-to-day basis, but static VLANs are easier to set up than dynamic VLANs.

Describe the VLAN technologies.

Typically, when an administrator is talking about a fast backbone, they should be thinking FastEthernet, ATM, or even FDDI. Each of these is a transport protocol that can be used across a *trunked link*—a port or ports on a switch assigned to multiple VLANs.

In this objective, you will read about the different ways of trunking a backbone link. This is very important information that you must have both to implement a large switched internetwork and to be successful on the CLSC exam.

Critical Information

In VLAN Trunk Protocol (VTP), all switches advertise their management domain on their trunk ports, their configuration revision number, and their known VLANs along with their individual boundaries. One or more interconnected devices that share the same VTP domain name make up a VTP domain. When configuring switches, remember that a switch can be assigned to only one VTP domain.

Within the VTP domain, its servers and clients maintain all VLANs in the switch fabric, and a VTP domain sets the boundaries of individual VLANs. A VTP's servers and clients also send information through trunks to other attached switches and receive updates from those trunks.

VTP servers maintain information in one of two ways, either in the Trivial File Transfer Protocol (TFTP) or in nonvolatile random-access memory. VTP servers will enable you to modify the VLAN information by using the VTP Management Information Base (MIB) or the command line interface (CLI). This allows both servers and clients to be notified that they should be prepared to receive traffic on their trunk ports when VLANs are added and advertised. The VTP server also enables switches to delete VLANs and disable all ports assigned to them.

You configure a new VLAN on only one device in the management domain, because all other devices automatically learn the configured information through advertisement frames sent to a multicast address. These advertisement frames can be received by all neighboring devices, but are not forwarded by normal bridging procedures. This is how all devices in the same management domain learn about any new VLANs configured in the transmitting device. Because of this, VTP is sent on all trunk connections, including ISL, 802.1Q, and LANE.

VTP defines overall configuration values and publishes the following configuration information by using multicast advertisements:

- VTP domain name
- VTP Configuration revision number
- VLAN IDs (ISL)
- Emulated LAN names (ATM LAN Emulation)
- 802.10 SAID values (FDDI)
- Maximum transmission unit (MTU) size for a VLAN
- Frame format
- VLAN configuration

VLAN Transport Protocols across Backbones

Virtual LANs use communication protocols to communicate across trunked links. These VLAN protocols allow a single link to carry information from multiple VLANs. These protocols work with the VLAN Trunk Protocol (VTP) to automatically group VLAN trunk ports between switches. VTP is popular because it provides interoperability within the internetworking industry and is not network-resource intensive. It is also available for layer 2 and layer 3 VLANs.

VTP information can be distributed to all stations throughout the network, including servers, routers, and switches that participate as a VLAN configuration. VTP also provides auto-intelligence for configuring switches across the network.

The VLAN transport protocols include:

FastEthernet: Inter-Switch Link (ISL) is a VLAN transport protocol used across a FastEthernet trunked link.

FDDI: IEEE 802.10 is a VLAN transport protocol used across an FDDI trunked link. VLAN ID is a required field in the FDDI SAID header, which includes both a clear and a protected header. The 4-byte SAID field also allows for 4.29 billion distinct LANs. The 802.10 SAID field is used to identify the VLAN ID.

ATM: LAN Emulation (LANE) is a VLAN transport protocol used across an ATM trunked link.

Exam Essentials

Remember the FastEthernet VTP.   Inter-Switch Link (ISL) is a VLAN transport protocol used across a FastEthernet trunked link.

Remember the FDDI VTP.   IEEE 802.10 is a VLAN transport protocol used across an FDDI trunked link.

Remember the ATM VTP.   LAN Emulation (LANE) is a VLAN transport protocol used across an ATM trunked link.

Understand the SAID field in an FDDI header. VLAN ID is a required field in the FDDI SAID header, which includes both a clear and a protected header. The 802.10 SAID field is used to identify the VLAN ID.

Remember how many VLANs can be configured with 802.10. The 4-byte SAID field also allows for 4.29 billion distinct LANs.

Key Terms and Concepts

FDDI: Fiber Distributed Data Interface is a LAN standard, defined by ANSI X3T9.5. It can run at speeds up to 200Mbps and uses Token-passing media access on fiber-optic cable. For redundancy, FDDI can use a dual-ring architecture.

Virtual LAN: A group of devices on one or more logically segmented LANs (configured by use of management software), enabling devices to communicate as if attached to the same physical medium, when they are actually located on numerous different LAN segments. VLANs are based on logical instead of physical connections, and thus, are tremendously flexible.

VTP: VLAN Trunk Protocol (VTP) is used to automatically group VLAN trunk ports between switches.

Sample Questions

1. Which VLAN transport protocol does FastEthernet use?

   A. ISL

   B. 802.10

   C. LANE

   D. VTP

   Answer: A.

2. Which VLAN transport protocol is used with FDDI?

   A. ISL

   B. 802.10

   C. LANE

   D. VTP

   Answer: B.

3. If you are using FDDI, what field in the header is used as the VLAN ID and allows 4.29 billion distinct VLANs?

   A. T/RT

   B. VLAN

   C. SAID

   D. SIAD

   Answer: C.

4. Which statement is true regarding 802.10 VLANs?

   A. They define multiple protocol data units.

   B. A VLAN ID is required.

   C. The header includes a clear header and a protected header.

   D. The clear header replicates the source address contained in the MAC.

   Answer: B, C. In FDDI trunking, a VLAN ID is required, which includes both a clear and protected header.

5. Which of the following is true regarding 802.10?

   A. The 802.10 SAID identifies traffic as belonging to a particular VLAN.

   B. It is used with ATM and LANE.

   C. The FDDI 802.10 SAIDs are associated by the Catalyst 5000 Ethernet VLANs to create multiple broadcast domains.

   D. The 802.10 SAID field is used as a VLAN ID.

   Answer: D. FDDI uses a SAID field to identify the VLAN.

Describe Token Ring VLANs.

$\mathbf{E}$ssentially, a VLAN is a broadcast domain. There is only one type of broadcast frame in transparent bridging, and therefore, only one level of broadcast domain and one level of VLAN. However, you should know that in source routing, there are two kinds of broadcast frames:

- Those restricted to a single ring
- Those that traverse the entire bridged domain

In this objective, Token Ring VLAN fundamentals will be described. These fundamentals are important if you have an existing Token Ring network and you are installing Token Ring switches.

Critical Information

There are two levels of VLANs in a Token Ring switched network.

The first level is the Token Ring Concentrator Relay Function (TrCRF), where the VLAN is a logical ring assigned a ring number. The logical ring contains one or more physical ports on a Token Ring switch. Source-route switching (SRS) forwards frames within a TrCRF using the MAC address or route descriptor. On an RSM, you can define a logical ring (TrCRF) that does not contain any physical ports, but is used only to process source-routed traffic that terminates the RIF.

The Token Ring Bridge Relay Function (TrBRF) is the second level of VLAN, the parent VLAN to which TrCRF VLANs are assigned. Here the VLAN is a logical bridge and is assigned a bridge number (not a ring number), and forwards frames between groups of ports with the same ring number (TrCRF), employing SRB or SRT. In Figure 3.3, you can see the relationship between TrCRF and TrBRF VLANs.

F I G U R E 3.3: TrCRF and TrBRF VLANs

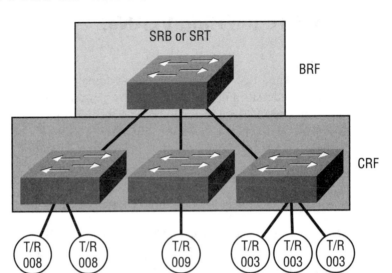

Token Ring VLAN Support on the RSM

Token Ring VLAN support on the RSM enables multiprotocol bridging and routing for Token Ring VLANs on the RSM. The RSM can function by itself, providing inter-VLAN routing. It also can be paired with a Catalyst VIP2 (Versatile Interface Processor), supplying external network connections with the identical port adapters used on Cisco 7500 series routers. The RSM/VIP2 coupling enables routing between Catalyst VIP2 port adapters and VLANs.

Token Ring VLAN support on the RSM enhances the Catalyst 5000 switch by supplying the following functions:

- IP and IPX routing for source-routed and nonsource-routed frames between Token Ring (TrBRF) VLANs and/or Ethernet VLANs and VIP2 interfaces

- Source-route bridging (SRB) that occurs between Token Ring (TrBRF) VLANs and VIP2 interfaces

- Source-route translational bridging (SR/TLB) that happens between Token Ring (TrBRF) VLANs and Ethernet VLANs and VIP2 interfaces

- Source-route transparent bridging (SRT), occurring between Token Ring (TrBRF) VLANs and SRT-capable VLANs and VIP2 interfaces

---

NOTE APPN and DLSw+ are supported for Token Ring VLANs on the RSM, but RSRB is not supported on the RSM.

The route switch module (RSM) is a card that plugs into a Catalyst switch and runs the Cisco IOS. The RSM is used in Token Ring networks to make it possible to route between Token Ring VLANs and Token Ring to Ethernet VLANs. The RSM interface is defined at the Token Ring bridged network (TrBRF) level.

You will need to create a logical ring on the RSM if you are running source-route bridging VLANs. This will allow the RSM to perform routing information field (RIF) processing.

Exam Essentials

Remember that in source routing, there are two kinds of broadcast frames. They are as follows:

- Those restricted to a single ring
- Those that traverse the entire bridged domain

Remember what an RSM is. The route switch module (RSM) is a card that plugs into a Catalyst switch and runs the Cisco IOS. It replaces a router.

Key Terms and Concepts

Token passing: A method used by network devices to access the physical medium in a systematic way based on possession of a small frame called a Token.

Token Ring: IBM's Token-passing LAN technology. It runs at 4 or 16Mbps over a ring topology. Defined formally by IEEE 802.5.

Transparent bridging: The bridging scheme used in Ethernet and IEEE 802.3 networks. It passes frames along one hop at a time, using routing information stored in tables that associate end nodes within bridge ports. This type of bridging is considered transparent because the source node doesn't need to know the entire route, as it does with source-route bridging.

Sample Questions

1. What are the two kinds of broadcast frames used in source routing?

   A. Those that are restricted to a single internetwork

   B. Those that are restricted to a single ring

   C. Those that traverse the entire bridged domain

   D. Those the traverse the entire internetwork

   Answer: B, C.

2. Which is true regarding the RSM with Token Ring?

   A. You cannot use the route switch module with Token Ring switches.

   B. The RSM enables multiprotocol bridging only for Token Ring VLANs.

   C. The RSM enables multiprotocol routing only for Token Ring VLANs.

   D. The RSM enables multiprotocol bridging and routing for Token Ring VLANs.

   Answer: D.

Describe Cisco's VLAN architecture.

This is another objective that has information found elsewhere in this chapter. However, this information will be compressed to give you a overview of what Cisco describes as their own VLAN architecture. Read this chapter, and then use this objective to study just the information presented in a compressed format.

This is a very important objective to understand when studying for your CLSC exam.

Critical Information

In this section, you will read about the basic VLAN technology available with Cisco switches. Cisco's VLAN technology includes:

VLANs across multiple backbones using FastEthernet, FDDI, and ATM: FastEthernet uses the Inter-Switch Link (ISL) as a VLAN transport protocol used across a FastEthernet trunked link. FDDI uses the IEEE 802.10 as a VLAN transport protocol across an FDDI trunked link. The VLAN ID is a required field in the FDDI SAID header, which includes both a clear and a protected header. The 4-byte SAID field also allows for 4.29 billion distinct LANs. The 802.10 SAID field is used to identify the VLAN ID. ATM uses LANE as a VLAN transport protocol used across an ATM trunked link.

Static VLANs: This is the typical way of creating VLANs, and it is the most secure way. The switch port that you assign a VLAN association always maintains that association until an administrator changes the port assignment.

Dynamic VLANs: Dynamic VLANs determine a node's VLAN assignment automatically. Using intelligent management software, you can enable hardware (MAC) addresses, protocols, or even applications to create dynamic VLANs.

Inter-Switch Link (ISL):   Intel and Xpoint Technologies have designed an Inter-Switch Link (ISL) network interface card that allows you place a node, or port, in more than one VLAN at a time. This is helpful for servers that need to communicate to all or most users, such as an e-mail server. On multi-VLAN (trunk) ports, each frame is tagged as it enters the switch. The ISL cards allow servers to send and receive frames tagged with multiple VLANs so the frame can traverse multiple VLANs without going though a router, which reduces latency. Some of the newer cards also support Fast EtherChannel.

Spanning-Tree Protocol: STP was developed by IBM to stop network loops in bridged environments. Since switches can be theoretically seen as multiport bridges, Spanning Tree is important to understand, especially in multi-VLAN organizations. If you connect more than one switch port to a destination switch or other network device, the ensuing network loop can bring the network down. Only one instance of STP per VLAN is allowed.

Frame filtering: Switches build a table of known MAC (hardware) addresses and keep track of to which port each node is connected. This allows the switch to send a frame only to the destination and not to all other connected nodes.

Frame tagging: The switch needs a way of keeping track of users and frames as they travel the switch fabric and VLANs. Frame identification (frame tagging)—a Cisco idea—uniquely assigns a user-defined ID to each frame. When a frame is received on a port, the switch places a unique identifier in each frame as it is forwarded through the switching fabric. This identifier defines the VLAN with which the frame is allowed to communicate. When the frame goes from the switch to a router to be forwarded to a different VLAN, the switch will remove the identifier and then, when the frame reenters the switch to find the new VLAN, it will add a new identifier with the VLAN information it is now traversing.

Exam Essentials

Remember the VTP protocols. FastEthernet uses ISL, FDDI uses 802.10, and ATM uses LANE.

Understand STP. STP was developed by IBM to stop network loops in bridged environments. Only one instance of STP per VLAN is allowed.

Remember how frame filtering is used. Switches build a table of known MAC (hardware) addresses and keep track of to which port each node is connected. This allows the switch to send a frame only to the destination and not to all other connected nodes.

Remember how frame tagging is used. Frame identification (frame tagging)—a Cisco idea—uniquely assigns a user-defined ID to each frame. When a frame is received on a port, the switch places a unique identifier in each frame as it is forwarded through the switching fabric.

Key Terms and Concepts

ATM (Asynchronous Transfer Mode): The international standard, identified by fixed-length 53-byte cells, for transmitting cells in multiple service systems such as voice, video, or data. Transit delays are reduced because the fixed-length cells permit processing to occur in the hardware. ATM is designed to maximize the benefits of high-speed transmission media such as SONET, E3, and T3.

FDDI: Fiber Distributed Data Interface is a LAN standard, defined by ANSI X3T9.5. It can run at speeds up to 200Mbps and uses Token-passing media access on fiber-optic cable. For redundancy, FDDI can use a dual-ring architecture.

Virtual LAN: A group of devices on one or more logically segmented LANs (configured by use of management software), enabling devices to communicate as if attached to the same physical medium, when they are actually located on numerous different

LAN segments. VLANs are based on logical instead of physical connections, and thus, are tremendously flexible.

VTP: VLAN Trunk Protocol is used to automatically group VLAN trunk ports between switches.

Sample Questions

1. Which statement regarding 802.10 VLANs is true?

   A. The 4-byte SAID allows for 4.29 billion distinct LANs.

   B. The 802.10 SAID identifies traffic as belonging to a particular VLAN.

   C. The 6-byte SAID allows for 4.29 billion distinct LANs.

   D. The FDDI 802.10 SAIDs are associated by the Catalyst 5000 Ethernet VLANs to create multiple broadcast domains.

   Answer: A. FDDI uses the SAID field to identify the VLAN ID. It is 4 bytes long.

2. Which statement is true regarding frame tagging?

   A. A filtering table is developed for each switch.

   B. Frame tagging is a technique used to identify frames based on user-defined offsets.

   C. Frame tagging assigns a unique user ID to each frame.

   D. Frame tagging is used on all Cisco routers and switches.

   Answer: C. As a frame enters a switch, a unique ID is placed in the header of each frame.

3. If you have multiple VLANs, which of the following is true regarding STP? (Choose all that apply.)

  A. Multiple instances of STP are allowed.

  B. Only 1 instance of STP per VLAN is allowed.

  C. Only 1 instance of STP is allowed per switch.

  D. You can have up to 64 instances of STP per VLAN.

Answer: B.

4. Which of the following is true regarding frame tagging? (Choose all that apply.)

  A. A unique identifier is placed in each frame as it is forwarded through the switching fabric.

  B. A filtering table is developed for each switch.

  C. Frame tagging is a technique used to identify frames based on user-defined offsets.

  D. Frame tagging is used on all Cisco routers and switches.

Answer: A. Switches place a VLAN ID on each frame as it enters a switch port.

CHAPTER

4

Placing Catalyst 5000 Series
Switches in Your Network

Cisco Exam Objectives Covered in This Chapter

> **Describe demand nodes and resource nodes.** *(pages 111 – 114)*

> **Describe configuration rules for demand nodes and resource nodes.** *(pages 114 – 118)*

> **Describe local resources and remote resources.** *(pages 118 – 121)*

> **Describe configuration rules for local resources and remote resources.** *(pages 121 – 125)*

> **Name five applications for Catalyst 5000 series switches.** *(pages 125 – 128)*

This chapter will address some of the generic concepts involved in designing and installing Catalyst systems in the network. These concepts include the definition of demand nodes and resource nodes, in addition to the positioning of local and remote resources in the network. A *demand node* is basically a user node that requests services from service providers. A *resource node* is a service provider and offers services to demand nodes. Lastly, this chapter will define five specific applications for Catalyst switches in the network.

This is a very important chapter to understand because placement of too many resource nodes and demand nodes on a network segment can cause bandwidth issues. Incorrect placement of service providers, or resource nodes, can cause major problems with latency, security, and scalability. It is important to understand how to place both resource nodes and demand nodes in an internetwork. This chapter will give you that information.

When studying for the CLSC exam, getting a firm grasp of the material presented here is essential. Each explanation of the objectives will give you a clear idea of what the objective is asking you to understand.

Describe demand nodes and resource nodes.

This objective will discuss the difference between demand nodes and resource nodes. You'll read about how resource nodes give network services to demand nodes. As you already know, resource nodes provide network services to demand nodes. The definition will be expanded in this objective.

This is an important objective to understand in this chapter. Before going on to the other objectives, make sure you have a firm understanding of the difference between demand nodes and resource nodes.

Critical Information

Networks, like companies, are broken into different functions. These functions are related to the needs of the corporation. Many parallels exist in the data-computing world. Client-server remains a model for database administration and design, in addition to file and print services.

In networking, two types of nodes are defined: demand nodes and resource nodes. Demand and resource nodes parallel clients and servers in the client-server model. Just as clients demand services, demand nodes demand services of their servers, or resource nodes.

Another way to view demand and resource nodes is to compare the network to the corporation itself. Human Resource (HR) departments are a resource when you need to find your vacation balance. You demand information, or a service, from the resource with that information. At the very least, the HR department could direct you to another resource—paralleling in a generic way the role of switches and other nonstorage network devices.

Demand Nodes

Demand nodes are resources that request information or services. If you wish, think of this as a demand for information from the Human Resources department. Much as you might want to learn the location of your paycheck, a workstation might demand to access a database or file on the server.

By definition, demand nodes request services from resource nodes. These services may be direct, as with a file server, or indirect, as with a switch or router. In addition, demand nodes are typically used and accessed by a single user.

Resource Nodes

Clearly, if a demand node is the client, a resource node must be the server. While this is true, the definition of a resource in the network is much broader than the server definition in client-server networking.

A resource in the company could be the Human Resources department, as presented previously, or it could be Shipping or Facilities. Basically, a resource defines those components that are used by one or more people.

This is true in networking as well. Demand nodes are workstations and other single-user devices. Resources are servers and databases, which are included in the historical client-server definition of computer systems. Routers, hubs, and switches are also considered resource nodes.

Exam Essentials

Understand what a demand node does in an internetwork.
Demand nodes typically are workstations and other end-user devices. They request network services from resource nodes.

Understand what a resource node provides in an internetwork.
Resource nodes include servers and printers, in addition to routers, hubs, and switches. Resource nodes provide services to demand nodes.

Key Terms and Concepts

Demand node: A demand node requests services from a resource node. Typically, a demand node is used by a single end user, and demand nodes include workstations.

Resource node: Resource nodes provide services to demand nodes. This may include file and print servers, databases, printers, and other directly requested services. However, resource nodes also include network resources, including routers, switches, and hubs.

Sample Questions

1. Which of the following would be included as a demand node?

   A. A router

   B. A server

   C. A mainframe

   D. A workstation

   E. A switch

   Answer: D. Workstations do not respond to requests for services from other devices.

2. A server is a resource node.

   A. True

   B. False

   Answer: A. Servers respond to demand nodes.

3. What are routers, switches, and hubs?

A. Demand nodes.

B. Resource nodes.

C. Neither. They are network devices.

D. Routers and switches are resource nodes, while hubs are neither.

Answer: B. All serve many users and respond to requests, albeit indirectly, for services.

Describe configuration rules for demand nodes and resource nodes.

This section will address the configuration rules that are targeted for the test. As with all networks, designers must consider the overall needs of the users and the applications that will contend for bandwidth.

Most administrators intuitively realize that servers (resource nodes) usually require substantially greater bandwidth than client workstations (demand nodes). Given this premise, it would be difficult to justify a design in which the workstations had 100Mbps full-duplex connections and the server was configured for 10Mbps half-duplex. Designers should also avoid shared media for resource nodes. These configuration rules will serve as a guide for deploying switches in production networks.

This is an important objective to understand because it can help you design your production network correctly the first time. Also, when studying for the CLSC exam, be sure you understand the rules discussed within this objective.

Critical Information

For a network designer, administrator, or test taker, the challenge of providing sufficient bandwidth to network resources can be formidable. Switches greatly simplify this problem by providing full-duplex connections and 100Mbps. (Gigabit and other technologies will be skipped here, but you should keep in mind that the fastest, noncontended connection should be used for resource nodes.) The test objective is geared toward understanding that resource nodes likely need greater performance than demand nodes.

Normally, resource nodes require substantially greater bandwidth than demand nodes. This is due to the disproportionate amount of data sent from demand nodes—resource nodes, as suppliers and receivers, typically handle a great deal of data. In addition, resource nodes serve numerous demand nodes, and because of this, the single connection from the resource node needs sufficient bandwidth to serve the numerous connections. Note that this does not necessarily require a direct relationship between clients and servers. For example, more than ten 10Mbps connections could call upon a resource node with a single 100Mbps connection. This is called over-subscription, and presumes that the demand nodes will not request resources concurrently or at full speed.

Demand Node Configuration Rules

Demand nodes should be given as much bandwidth as possible; however, many networks are constrained by budgets. Because of this, the configuration rules for demand nodes permit shared media (hubs) connected to the switch, as well as 10Mbps connections and half-duplex. However, it is recommended that demand nodes be placed near resource nodes, and that as much bandwidth be provided as the budget will allow.

NOTE Workstations are usually limited in their ability to use faster links—a slow 486 or Sparc 2 will probably not benefit from a high-speed connection, for example.

Resource Node Configuration Rules

Resource nodes are used by many users, particularly servers, and typi-cally they are equipped with higher-end hardware. So, Cisco has defined general guidelines as configuration rules for resource nodes, including:

- Position resources as close as practical to demand nodes.

- Configure resource nodes on dedicated links.

- Use 100Mbps connections where possible; however, be mindful of buffering and over-subscription issues.

- Use full-duplex connections where possible.

- Keep in mind the overall objective of these rules—provide the most performance and benefit from placing switches into the network.

Clearly, these rules will assist in achieving this goal. By using switches, each resource node and demand node will have its own collision domain. You can then use VLANs to create broadcast domains, and place the resource nodes and demand nodes in the same, small broadcast domains.

TIP Catalyst switches are frequently used to create server farms. These clusters of servers should have the fastest possible intercon-nections to the rest of the network.

Exam Essentials

Remember to design your network with resource nodes in mind. By using switches and VLANs, you can give each individual resource node and demand node its own collision domain. Then use the VLANs to create broadcast domains with the resource nodes and demand nodes in the same broadcast domain.

Remember that resource nodes should be near demand nodes. Recalling the caveats noted previously, place resource nodes as close to demand nodes as possible. Plan the network for efficiency, with fewer hop (layer 2 and layer 3) connections between high-utilization services.

Key Terms and Concepts

Full-duplex: The capacity to transmit information between a sending station and a receiving unit at the same time. This eliminates collisions on the link.

Half-duplex: The capacity to transfer data in only one direction at a time between a sending unit and a receiving unit.

Over-subscription: A network design concept where the designer predicts a reasonable proportion of potential demand on a particular connection. This may yield an *over-subscription rate* of 10%, for example. With this rate, a 100Mbps connection to the server could service ten 10Mbps connections from workstations. Some over-subscription calculations are based on the rated bandwidth versus the burst capability of the media—for example, frame-relay CIR compared to the physical bandwidth of the pipe. In this scenario, an over-subscribed connection may have 8 256Kbps PVCs serviced via a T-1. The presumption is that only some of the PVCs will operate at full speed at any given time.

Sample Questions

1. Which of the following is a reason for placing resource nodes on full-duplex links?

   A. Trunk utilization is reduced.

   B. Collisions are eliminated.

   C. Transmissions are encrypted.

   D. Resource nodes should use half-duplex.

   Answer: B. Full-duplex connections eliminate collisions, which improves performance.

2. Resource nodes should be placed on:

   A. A single, shared 10Mbps connection

   B. A single, shared 100Mbps connection

   C. Dedicated 100Mbps connections for each resource

   D. Connections equal to those used for demand nodes

   Answer: C. Of the choices, dedicated 100Mbps is the best solution. Full-duplex would be preferred as well.

Describe local resources and remote resources.

You may recall the 80/20 rule in network designs. For review, this rule stated that at least 80% of the traffic on the network should remain on the local wire, and that up to 20% of the traffic could leave the local network. This rule of thumb was designed as a basic guideline to address the limitations of routers and WAN circuits.

An understanding of this rule is significant in meeting the objective to correctly place local and remote devices in the network. This is important to understand when designing your internetwork as well as when troubleshooting and upgrading. When studying for your CLSC exam, understand everything you can about how servers and hosts should be placed in your internetwork.

Critical Information

In this section, the difference between local resources and remote resources will be described.

Local Resources

From a layer 3 perspective, local resources are on the same subnet as the node. Layer 2 adds differing definitions of local resources. For example, it is unlikely that performance across trunk links and multiple switches can compete with two stations connected to the same switch.

Think of local resources as being on the same switch and subnet (VLAN), with remote resources being on a different subnet (VLAN) and/or another switch. In actuality, this definition is slightly obsolete. It would be better to think of local and remote resources as being on a continuum. At one end, two resources connected to the same switch would be considered local resources. As the scale migrates toward remote resources, the nodes may be devices on different switches connected via a high-speed trunk. As you get closer to remote resources, the resources may be on the same switch, but attached to different VLANs, for example. Consider the bandwidth, processing, number of components, and protocols needed—as these parameters increase, it is more likely that the resources are not local.

Remote Resources

Remote resources are network services that can be used only by going through a router or layer 3 device. This can cause a problem with bandwidth because users will have to go to a remote network segment to do every task, which should not happen. However, if you had an e-mail server, DNS server, or WWW server, where traffic is light, you would be OK. However, a file and print server, for example, can cause major problems for the network if not properly installed in the correct location.

A solution for this problem is to create VLANs within a switched internetwork. This allows you to create broadcast domains regardless of the location of resources. For example, you can have an NT Server on one network segment into a switch, but with the port trunked so it will be part of all VLANs. This means that users will not have to go through a router to get to the network resources they need. This would require an ISL- or 802.1q-aware network adapter and the appropriate drivers for the operating system.

Exam Essentials

Understand the concept of local resources. Local resources are network services that are in the same broadcast domain as the demand nodes.

Understand the concept of remote resources. Remote resources are network services that are available only through a router and are not part of the same broadcast domain as the demand resources.

Key Terms and Concepts

Full-duplex: The capacity to transmit information between a sending station and a receiving unit at the same time. This eliminates collisions on the link.

Half-duplex: The capacity to transfer data in only one direction at a time between a sending unit and a receiving unit.

Local resources: Traditionally, local resources were those located on the same network; however, with the enhanced capabilities of switches, this definition must be broadened.

Remote resources: Remote resources include any device that is reachable only by traversing a link. If the demand node cannot connect to the resource via the backplane of the switch, it would be considered remote. Note that this definition is highly variable—it could be interpreted as resources on a different network as well.

Sample Questions

1. The demand node is connected to port 2/4 on the switch and has an IP address of 10.1.1.10/24. The resource node is on port 4/4 and has an IP address of 10.1.1.20/24. Assuming a standard installation, what is the relationship between these devices?

   A. Local resources

   B. Remote resources

   C. Both local and remote resources

   D. Cannot be determined

   Answer: A. The nodes are on the same switch and VLAN.

2. Which of the following would be a disadvantage to local resources?

   A. Improved performance

   B. Difficulty administrating resources at remote locations

   C. Collisions in the network

   D. Broadcast control

   Answer: B. It is unlikely that you'd see a question this confusing on the real test, but consider the answer and the tricky presentation. At a remote location, local resources would offer better performance, but would be harder to administer given the lack of physical access implied.

Describe configuration rules for local resources and remote resources.

As touched upon previously, local resources are preferred under most circumstances, as troubleshooting, trunk optimization, broadcast control, and network performance can be typically higher when the demand node is near the resource node.

As other considerations require the implementation and use of remote resources, it is important to consider the demands that may be placed on the network to access the remote resources.

This is an important objective in that it will help you understand how local and remote resources should be configured and installed in your internetwork. For the CLSC exam, this objective will give you information that will allow you to configure the switches to optimize performance on a theoretical level.

Critical Information

As in the real world, the test is best approached with an eye toward proper configuration of the network. As performance improves when bottlenecks are eliminated, the exam objectives include rules for local and remote resources. Now that the differences between local and remote have been covered, the rules should be straightforward.

Whenever possible, the network will provide more performance when bottlenecks and collisions are eliminated. So, the rules for local and remote resources include the use of full-duplex, 100Mbps connections whenever possible, in addition to placing resources near their demand nodes. A misplaced resource node, perhaps on the far end of a busy trunk link, is also discouraged. Lastly, dedicated links are preferred to shared media within the network.

NOTE Current network designs should limit the amount of layer 2 traffic crossing the network core. Services that route once and switch many times, such as MPOA or MLS, should be employed to limit broadcasts and control traffic.

To avoid the problems of putting too many network resources in the wrong place, you should follow the following rules:

- Place local resources with local demand nodes.

- Place remote resources on their own dedicated links and use full-duplex.

- Use FastEthernet if possible, or ATM, to help congestion problems. Gigabit Ethernet and EtherChannel technologies could also be used when possible.

Exam Essentials

Remember that misplaced resources hinder the advantages of switching. Remember that switching can yield substantial improvements in performance only if the network design permits these advantages.

Understand how to use dedicated links effectively. Understand that if the budget limits the number of switch ports available, you should reserve dedicated links for resource nodes and high end-user (demand) nodes.

Understand how to use FastEthernet where appropriate. Recall that trunk links should always be FastEthernet (however, administrators should also consider Fast EtherChannel). Gigabit technologies should also be considered.

Understand where to use full-duplex appropriately. Understand that collisions degrade the efficiency of the network. A dedicated half-duplex connection is still prone to collisions, and because of this, full-duplex is necessary to avoid this issue.

Understand how to place local resources near demand nodes. Recall that as addressed before, you shouldn't regard the network core and trunk links as having unlimited capacity. Keep services as close as is reasonable to their users. Security, support, and cost are all factors in this design consideration.

Key Terms and Concepts

FastEthernet: Any Ethernet specification with a speed of 100Mbps. FastEthernet is 10 times faster than 10BaseT, while retaining qualities such as MAC mechanisms, MTU, and frame format. These similarities make it possible for existing 10BaseT applications and management tools to be used on FastEthernet networks. FastEthernet is based on an extension of IEEE 802.3 specification.

Server cluster: A collection of servers in one grouping. Typically, clusters are used to enhance administration and support. Server clusters are also referred to as server farms.

Trunk: A connection between two switches. Typically, this connection interconnects multiple VLANs using ISL or 802.1q. Trunk links should always use the fastest link possible.

Sample Questions

1. An administrator would typically select which of the following for a link between an access switch for users and a distribution switch that connects the access switch to the server (access) switch?

   A. FastEthernet

   B. Half-duplex

   C. Full-duplex

   D. Ethernet

   E. ISL

   F. 802.1q

   Answer: A, C, E, F. This is a situation that calls for a trunk link accessing remote resources. So, FastEthernet and full-duplex are highly recommended. As a trunk, it is likely that more than one VLAN will require servicing—requiring a trunking protocol such as ISL or 802.1q.

2. Which of the following is not a configuration rule for local and remote resources?

   A. Use full-duplex.

   B. Use FastEthernet.

   C. Configure redundant links with 802.1d spanning tree.

   D. Place resources near demand nodes.

   Answer: C. While a good idea, redundancy is outside our scope for this objective.

Name five applications for Catalyst 5000 series switches.

This objective is geared toward understanding the ways to use the Catalyst 5000 system. Clearly, most administrators are interested in improving performance and reducing the Total Cost of Ownership (TCO). These goals are addressed with switched backbones serving 100Mbps connections and/or segmented 10/100Mbps workgroups. In addition, administration can be simplified with server clusters. These clusters consolidate UPS and environmental controls, in addition to placing the servers near administrators.

This is an important objective to understand when working in a production environment because it can give you the needed information when acquiring switches to meet your business requirements. Also, this objective can give you "big-picture" information when studying for the CLSC exam.

Critical Information

The five applications of Catalyst switches are as follows:

- To improve network performance

- To provide switched backbone
- To provide server clusters
- To provide 10/100Mbps to workgroups
- To provide FastEthernet

The details of each Catalyst 5000 switch service will now be discussed.

Improving Network Performance

By controlling the size of the collision domain and buffering traffic as necessary, the switch can greatly improve the efficiency of frame-based networks.

Providing Switched Backbone

Backbones have usually been provided by FDDI rings, which covered the needs of smaller networks. Scalability required additional FDDI interfaces connected to routers, and traffic was divided between rings based on protocol. This could be very inefficient and often included high costs. By designing a "backbone in a box," the switch can easily surpass the capabilities of other technologies.

Providing Server Clusters

An ideal network design would place resources as close to the users (demand nodes) as possible. However, this might distribute servers over a large area, adding complexity in support, power, and cooling requirements. It would be easier to locate all servers in a single room near the server support staff with battery and generator backups and heavy-duty air conditioning. The switch permits this functionality by allowing the servers to exist within the same VLAN (or multiple VLANs with ISL-aware NICs), while located far from the users.

Providing 10/100Mbps to Workgroups

Without fully understanding the implications of deploying 100Mbps to the workgroup or workstation, it would be dangerous to blindly create a situation that could lead to over-subscription. However,

100Mbps uplinks to downstream switches servicing workstations are rarely a bad idea, and some installations may yield themselves to segmentation with 10Mbps uplinks. The Catalyst 5000 is well positioned to function in this arena.

Providing FastEthernet to the Desktop

With higher-performance workstations, it has become practical to provide 100Mbps dedicated connections to enhance productivity and access to resources. However, installing FastEthernet to the workstations requires greater backbone and server performance, and designers must deploy such upgrades with an eye toward the impact on the entire network.

Exam Essentials

Remember that Catalyst switches provide five specific services. The services are as follows:

- Improving network performance

- Providing switched backbone

- Providing server clusters

- Providing 10/100Mbps to workgroups

- Providing FastEthernet

Key Terms and Concepts

FastEthernet: Any Ethernet specification with a speed of 100Mbps. FastEthernet is 10 times faster than 10BaseT, while retaining qualities such as MAC mechanisms, MTU, and frame format. These similarities make it possible for existing 10BaseT applications and management tools to be used on FastEthernet networks. FastEthernet is based on an extension of IEEE 802.3 specification.

Server cluster: A collection of servers in one grouping. Typically, clusters are used to enhance administration and support.

Total Cost of Ownership (TCO): To account for support and maintenance costs over the life of a device, TCO adds these costs to the initial acquisition (capital purchase) cost. Advanced TCO models include the costs of training and downtime.

UPS: Uninterruptible Power Supply. A battery connected to the main power supply to permit the graceful shutdown of equipment in the event of power failure.

Sample Questions

1. Which of the following is not a benefit of the Catalyst 5000 switch?

   A. FastEthernet to the desktop

   B. Server clusters

   C. Improved network performance

   D. High-speed x.25 switching

   E. Ethernet and FastEthernet workgroup support

   Answer: D. The Catalyst is not an x.25 switch.

2. Why are server clusters an indirect benefit of the Catalyst 5000?

   A. The Catalyst 5000 places a large number of resource nodes behind a single 100Mbps full-duplex trunk.

   B. Administration costs are increased, but the cost of the switches is reduced.

   C. Administration costs for support of the servers are reduced by providing high bandwidth while co-locating devices.

   D. They are the only method to configure 100Mbps full-duplex support to resource nodes.

   Answer: C. Clusters may reduce the costs associated with the administration of servers.

CHAPTER

5

Catalyst 5000 Series Switch

Cisco Exam Objectives Covered in This Chapter

▶ **Describe Catalyst 5000 series switch product evolution.**
(pages 131 – 134)

▶ **Describe Catalyst 5000 product features.** *(pages 134 – 137)*

▶ **Describe Catalyst 5002 product features.** *(pages 137 – 140)*

▶ **Describe Catalyst 5500 product features.** *(pages 140 – 144)*

Depending on the version of the Catalyst 5000/5500 series switch in use, the platform provides a significant number of features and functions. While the latest series offerings are beyond the scope of this exam guide and chapter, readers should visit the Cisco Web site—Cisco Connection Online (CCO)—at www.cisco.com for additional information regarding the newest systems, including the 6500 and 8500 series. While not on the current exam, these platforms build upon the 5000/5500 system and may be better solutions outside of exam considerations.

However, the remainder of this chapter will limit itself to the 5000, 5002, and 5500 platforms. The features and functions of these systems, in addition to the evolution of the platform, will be covered.

The Catalyst 5000 series of switches provides a 1.2Gbps backplane for the 5000, and a 3.6Gbps backplane for the 5500. These are not fast when compared to the new switches on the market, but may be sufficient for some time in most networks. The Supervisor engine supports separate hardware for the switching of frames and management, while the backplane is passive with no active components, which speeds the frames' progress through the switch.

This an important chapter in the CLSC book, as it provides the needed information on the 5000 series of switches. When studying for the CLSC exam, focus on the unique differences between the various platforms, in addition to the specific features of each system.

Describe Catalyst 5000 series switch product evolution.

The Catalyst 5000 series switch provides a good foundation for comparison to the other two 5000 platforms in the exam objectives. The product has evolved to support different port densities, higher bandwidth ports, improved performance, and new features.

With regard to the CLSC exam, this section will provide an understanding of the Catalyst 5000 series. Many of the features found in the 5000 have been enhanced in the newer product offerings; however, the 5000 uses the same frame forwarding process and line modules as the newer products. Understanding the Catalyst 5000 will greatly assist designers and administrators in learning the other switches in the 5000 series as well. For the exam, focus on each objective as it relates to the others in this chapter—considering the benefits of each system with regard to cost, scalability, functionality, and upgradability.

Critical Information

The original Catalyst 5000 provided five slots—four modular slots for user modules and one for the Supervisor engine. This product offers a single 1.2Gbps backplane and supports Ethernet, FastEthernet, Token Ring, FDDI/CDDI, and ATM LANE. With the 48-port, switched Ethernet module, the chassis could support 192 stations, not including ports on the Supervisor itself. The original product also supported SNMP and RMON, and included support for the online removal of modules. The chassis fits in a standard 19" rack.

The 5000 chassis was modified into the 5002, which offers a single slot for a user module. However, the chassis is capable of supporting all 5000 series line cards and comes with dual power supplies.

However, from an exam and usability perspective, the most significant change to the 5000 product line came with the 5500. In addition to adding ATM switching—integrating the LightStream (LS) 1010 back-plane—the chassis also provided for 3.6Gbps of frame switching and 13 total slots. Note that only 11 of these slots support frame mod-ules—the first slot is reserved for the Supervisor, and the 13th is reserved for the ASP, or the cell-switching engine of the LS1010. The 5500 also added redundancy to the system, with clock and Supervisor-engine redundancy added to the power supply system that was present in the 5002 and available in the 5000.

Most modules within the 5000 and 5500 system are interchangeable. The Supervisor III is needed to access the three 1.2Gbps backplanes in the 5500 chassis, and the ATM cell modules will work only in the LS1010 slots of the 5500, but the majority of the other modules are interchangeable between chassis without difficulty.

Table 5.1 outlines the differences between the three chassis.

T A B L E 5.1: The 5000, 5002, and 5500 Chassis

	5000	5002	5500
Backplane	1.2Gbps	1.2Gbps	3.6Gbps
Slots	5	2	13
Cell switching	No	No	Yes
Supervisor redundancy	No	No	Available
Power supplies	Modular	Built-in	Modular

Exam Essentials

Understand the evolution of the 5000 chassis and the compatibilities among systems. Remember the differences among the chassis in the Catalyst 5000 series, particularly the backplane capacities of each switch and the enhanced features of the 5500.

Remember that Cisco has designed the Catalyst platform for investment protection. Understand how Cisco views investment protection and designs the various modules within the 5000/5500 series to allow migration.

Key Terms and Concepts

Catalyst: Series of switches designed by Cisco to provide redundant backbone switching as well as workgroup switching and solutions.

Frame backplane: In the Catalyst 5000, the frame backplane operates at 1.2Gbps and supports frame-based technologies including Ethernet, Token Ring, and FDDI.

Gbps: Billion bits per second. The "G" stands for Giga.

PPS: Packets per second. This number represents the number of packets that the switch can process and forward in 1 second. PPS is more representative of performance, as it accounts for processor limitations and the varying size of the frames in the switch. While this section discusses the backplane capacity in terms of bits, the processor on the switch will usually include a rating for packets per second. This figure is calculated using 64-octet frames in most cases.

Sample Questions

1. Which of the following is an advantage of the 5000/5002/5500 product-line migration?

   A. Cell switching throughout the product line

   B. Interconnectivity via the HPPI protocol

   C. Support for the VIP2-50

   D. Investment protection

   Answer: D. Cisco provides investment protection between the platforms by allowing line modules to migrate from one chassis to another.

2. Which of the following is *not* true?

A. The 5002 provides only a single slot for a line module.

B. ATM cell switching is available on the 5500.

C. The 5000 supports dual power supplies.

D. The Supervisor engine in the 5002 may be placed in the 5000 chassis for fault-tolerance.

E. The 5500 provides three 1.2Gbps backplanes.

Answer: D. The 5000 does not support dual Supervisor engines. In addition, the Supervisor III must be used for redundancy.

Describe Catalyst 5000 product features.

While the Catalyst 5000 switch was a powerful tool for administrators when it first appeared on the market, the reality today is that greater backplane capacity and other benefits are needed for most networks. Restricted to a single 1.2Gbps backplane, the 5000 contains five slots and supports a single Supervisor engine. Dual power supplies provide limited fault tolerance.

This objective will give you the needed information to understand the Catalyst 5000 switch. You must have a firm understanding of this material to be successful on the CLSC exam as well as when designing your internetwork.

Critical Information

To design and administer networks, from both a consultant and employee perspective, it is important to be aware of the various products on the market and their features. This is especially true as your roles and responsibilities migrate toward design.

Cisco has included a significant number of objectives in the CLSC exam that relate to knowledge of their product line. This is augmented by knowledge of the 5000 (the next two sections will review the 5002 and 5500). However, it is vital that you review Cisco's documentation regarding all of their products on a regular basis when operating in the real world. Good designers would also benefit from researching other vendors' offerings and considering the use of multiple vendors in their network solutions.

In the "Exam Essentials" section, the key components of the 5000 chassis will be broken down; however, keep the items of this section in mind when moving on to the 5002, 5500, and other Catalyst products. Focus on the following benefits/features after the exam—a balance between future proofing, current needs, and cost usually influences purchasing decisions:

- The Catalyst 5000 provides for environmental monitoring and reporting.

- The fan trays, power supplies, and line modules may be removed or installed online (note that two power supplies are required).

- The Supervisor I supports two 100Mbps Ethernet connections.

- The 192-pin FutureBus connector is available in all slots of the chassis except the first, which is reserved for the Supervisor engine. The Supervisor connects with a 48-pin connector.

- The chassis has five slots.

- The top slot is always used by the Supervisor engine.

- The 5000 supports ATM LANE, Token Ring, Ethernet, FastEthernet, and FDDI/CDDI.

Exam Essentials

Remember the limitations of the 5000 chassis. Understand that the exam isn't focused on the negatives of the various products, but by concentrating on them, it will help you remember the material. The Catalyst 5000 is a large frame-based switch. There is no cell backplane (as appears in the 5500), and only one Supervisor engine is supported. The frame backplane supports only one 1.2Gbps backplane, and redundant Supervisor engines are not supported.

Remember the ports available on the Supervisor I engine. Be able to explain that the Supervisor I engine is available with two built-in RJ-45 100Mbps Ethernet ports, or fiber-based SC ports for multi mode or single mode. At full-duplex, the MM ports are capable of connections of 2000 meters, while the SM connectors are capable of 10,000-meter connections.

Understand that the 5000 is a good entry into the Catalyst system if backplane and slot limitations are not a factor. Remember that the 5000, with only 1.2Gbps backplane and four user slots, is well suited to smaller environments, including migration from FDDI to FastEthernet and other limited-scope implementations.

Key Terms and Concepts

Cell backplane: The cell backplane is for ATM cells only. In the 5500, it operates at 5Gbps.

Frame backplane: In the Catalyst 5000, the frame backplane operates at 1.2Gbps and supports frame-based technologies including Ethernet, Token Ring, and FDDI.

Meter: Unit of measure equal to roughly 1 yard. One thousand meters equals 1 kilometer.

Sample Questions

1. How many Supervisor engines are supported in the 5000 chassis (include redundant Supervisors)?

A. One.

B. Two.

C. The 5000 does not use a Supervisor.

D. The Supervisor is built-in.

Answer: A. The 5000 does not provide for redundant Supervisors.

2. The backplane in the 5000 chassis is capable of which of the following?

A. 761Kbps

B. 1.2Mbps

C. 3.6Gbps

D. 1.2Gbps

Answer: D. Make sure that you watch for the distinction between *Mbps* and *Gbps*. The 5000 backplane is 1.2Gbps.

Describe Catalyst 5002 product features.

The Catalyst 5002 is a fairly limited version of the Catalyst system; however, it is well suited for wiring closets and interconnects. The system contains two slots and supports two power supplies, and supports any module in the 5000 product line.

In this objective, the information needed to understand the Catalyst 5002 will be discussed. The 5002 was actually designed to meet the business requirements of McDonnell Douglas in southern California. After Cisco had designed the switch, they decided to actually go ahead and market the product to other customers. Since it has only two slots, one must be used for the Supervisor engine, which means it has very limited port density.

This is an important objective to understand since it provides needed information about additional Catalyst switches that can be used when designing an internetwork and when studying your Catalyst architecture for the CLSC exam.

Critical Information

The chassis on the Catalyst 5002 is capable of supporting a Supervisor engine and a single line module. As with the other 5000 products, the first slot is reserved for the Supervisor. The second slot may accommodate Ethernet, FastEthernet, FDDI/CDDI, Token Ring, ATM LANE, or the RSM module. The switch also provides for dual, built-in power supplies.

NOTE One limitation of the 5002 power supplies is that they are built into the chassis. Thus, power-supply failure will require swap-out of the entire chassis, not just the failed power supply.

For the exam, focus on the fact that while limited in slots, the chassis is capable of using any module from the 5000, including the ATM LANE and RSM modules. Also note that the 5002 chassis is capable of only 1.2Gbps in the backplane.

Recall that the Catalyst 5000 product operates as a store-and-forward switch, a function that remains in the 5002 and 5500 products as well. This contrasts with cut-through switching, which is not available in the 5000 product line.

Exam Essentials

Remember that the different components are interchangeable with the Catalyst 5000. Recall that while limited to two slots, the 5002 can use line modules from the 5000, including the Supervisor engine. The backplane of the 5002 is the same as with the 5000—1.2Gbps.

Remember that the Catalyst 5002 is a store-and-forward switch. Understand that as with the 5000 and 5500, the 5002 is a store-and-forward frame switch.

Understand how the limited number of slots is a significant issue with the 5002 chassis. While the 5002 is well suited to wiring closets, the cost differential between the 5000 and 5002 is worth researching before committing to the platform. Should the installation require more than one line module card, a fork-lift upgrade will be required. Advantages to the 5002 are its small size and built-in power supplies. As a side note, the cost difference between the chassis in the 5000 series (as of this writing) is very small.

Key Terms and Concepts

Cut-through packet switching: A packet-switching technique that flows data through a switch so that the leading edge exits the switch at the output port before the packet finishes entering the input port. Packets will be read, processed, and forwarded by devices that use cut-through packet switching as soon as the destination address is confirmed and the outgoing port is identified.

Fork-lift upgrade: An upgrade that requires complete removal of the old system. While the 5002's cards are interchangeable with 5000/5500, the chassis and built-in power supplies will need to be removed for expansion.

Store-and-forward packet switching: LAN switching technique in which every frame is copied into the switch's buffers, a CRC is performed, and if it is error free, the hardware destination address is looked up in the switch's filter table and an exit port is determined.

Sample Questions

1. Which of the following would be a useful application of the 5002?

   A. Workgroup switching

   B. Core switching

   C. Cell switching

   D. Highly redundant, fault-tolerant switching

   Answer: A. The small size of the switch severely limits it operation; however, it shares cards with the 5000 platform.

2. Which of the following is *not* true regarding the Catalyst 5002?

   A. Supports ATM LANE

   B. Supports ATM cell switching

   C. Supports Token Ring

   D. Supports FastEthernet

   E. Supports dual power supplies

   Answer: B. Only the 5500 provides a cell backplane of the 5000, 5002, and 5500 chassis.

Describe Catalyst 5500 product features.

Compared to the 5000, the Catalyst 5500 is a high-performance switch capable of supporting most organizations. Outfitted with three 1.2Gbps backplanes—for an aggregate backplane capacity of 3.6Gbps—the 5500 also supports redundant Supervisor engines and dual power supplies. In addition, the 5500 chassis is actually two switches in one. The first 12 slots are connected to the frame backplane, while the bottom 5 slots are connected to the cell backplane, depending on the module.

This objective is important in two regards: First, until recently, the 5500 was the flagship of the Catalyst line, and it remains the most capable in the 5000 series. Second, the features in the 5500 contrast greatly with those found in the 5000 and 5002. These differences provide a broad basis from which to ask questions regarding knowledge of the overall platform.

TIP   As of this writing, Cisco has released the 6500 and 8500 series of switches.

Critical Information

While the chassis provides 13 slots, only 11 may be used for frame-based services. The first slot must contain a Supervisor module, and the 13th slot is for the ASP LS1010 module only.

Table 5.2 represents the divisions between the three backplanes, and documents the backplane interface options (which are significant parts of the exam objectives for the 5500). Each letter (A, B, C) represents one of the three separate 1.2Gbps backplanes. Review of this breakdown is important in understanding the evolution from the 5000 to the 5500. Note that the 3.6Gbps of backplane capacity is actually three 1.2Gbps backplanes interconnected in a nonblocking fashion. These interconnects are provided via the Phoenix ASIC, which is described in the next chapter.

T A B L E 5.2: The Catalyst 5500 Backplane Configuration

Slot	Backplane and Use
1	Supervisor engine II or III (primary); A, B, C backplanes
2	Redundant Supervisor module or A, B, C backplanes
3	A, B, C backplane
4	A, B, C backplane
5	A, B, C backplane
6	B backplane
7	B backplane
8	B backplane
9	LS1010 module or B backplane
10	LS1010 module or C backplane
11	LS1010 module or C backplane
12	LS1010 module or C backplane
13	ATM switching engine (ASP module only)

Also, notice that the 5500 upgrades the fault-tolerance options compared to the 5000. In addition to providing more slots, slot 2 may be used for a second Supervisor engine, which operates in standby mode until failure of the primary Supervisor. Dual system clocks are also found on the 5500, and may be used in redundant configurations.

Exam Essentials

Remember that the 5500 chassis is capable of cell- and frame-based switching. Understand that unlike the 5000 platform and the other chassis in the 5000 product line, the Catalyst 5500 contains the LS1010 ATM cell switch backplane, permitting cell- and frame-based forwarding within the chassis. Note that an external connection is required to link the cell- and frame-based backplanes—there is no internal interconnect. The cell-based backplane operates at 5Gbps.

Remember that the redundant Supervisor engines are an option in the 5500 chassis. Remember that with the Supervisor II or III engine, administrators can place Supervisors in the first and second slots of the 5500 chassis and configure one to backup the other in the event of Supervisor engine failure. While not always transparent, this option is beneficial in higher-availability environments. Because the Supervisor III is required to access all three backplanes, few installations use the Supervisor II in redundant configurations.

TIP Many companies opt for redundant Catalyst systems; however, the redundant Supervisor option may augment the design.

Remember that the 5500 frame backplane provides 3.6Gbps of aggregate bandwidth. Recall that the backplane of the 5500 includes three 1.2Gbps backplanes that are interconnected via the Phoenix ASIC, which will be discussed later in this book. This addresses the greater bandwidth requirements of Gigabit Ethernet.

Key Terms and Concepts

Blocking: Older switches employed blocking techniques to control the flow of frames across the backplane. Most, including the Catalyst 5000 series switches, no longer employ this technique and are considered nonblocking.

Redundancy: In internetworking, the duplication of connections, devices, or services that can be used as a backup in case the primary connections, devices, or services fail.

Sample Questions

1. Which of the following are features of the 5500 chassis?

   A. 1.2Gbps backplane interconnectivity (frame)

   B. 3.6Gbps backplane interconnectivity (frame)

   C. 5Gbps backplane interconnectivity (frame)

   D. 5Gbps backplane interconnectivity (cell)

   E. Dual Supervisor engines for concurrent processing

   Answer: B, D. Again, focus on the entire answer. E is incorrect, as the Supervisors operate in active/standby mode. The backplanes operate at 3.6Gbps for frames and 5Gbps for cells.

2. How many 24-port FastEthernet modules may be placed in the 5500 chassis? (Assume a single Supervisor module.)

   A. 0

   B. 1

   C. 4

   D. 11

   E. 12

   Answer: D. The 13th slot is reserved for the ASP (LS1010), and the first slot is used by the Supervisor engine.

3. An administrator wants to place a second Supervisor engine into the 5500 chassis. In which slot must the module be placed?

   A. Any slot

   B. Slots 2 through 5—those with access to all three backplanes

   C. Slot 2

   D. Slot 13

   E. None of the above

   Answer: C. Supervisors will operate only in slots 1 and 2.

CHAPTER

6

Catalyst 5000 Series Switch
Product Architecture

Cisco Exam Objectives Covered in This Chapter

▸**Describe the architecture and function of major components of the Catalyst 5000 series switch:** *(pages 147 – 154)*
- Processors: NMP, MCP, and LCP
- Logic Units: LTL, CBL, Arbiter, and EARL
- ASICs: SAINT, SAGE, SAMBA, and Phoenix

▸**Trace a frame's progress through a Catalyst 5000 series switch.** *(pages 154 – 158)*

Just as computers are the sum of a wide array of components, including disk drives, microprocessors, memory, and motherboard, the Catalyst system is made up of numerous systems that govern the movement of frames within the chassis.

Cisco created the Catalyst 5000 series of switches to provide a fault-tolerant backbone and workgroup switch. This will provide an internetwork with low downtime and near-wire speeds of data transfer.

This section will focus on the various processors, Logic Units, and ASICs that process and forward the frame, and the path of an Ethernet frame through the switch will also be reviewed. A thorough understanding of the frame flow through the switch and the function of each component in the system is critical to success on the exam. In addition, this material will greatly assist troubleshooting efforts.

Describe the architecture and function of major components of the Catalyst 5000 series switch:

- Processors: NMP, MCP, and LCP
- Logic Units: LTL, CBL, Arbiter, and EARL
- ASICs: SAINT, SAGE, SAMBA, and Phoenix

This first objective will give you the background you need when designing your internetwork with Catalyst switches. The different components that make up the Catalyst 5000 series of switches will be discussed.

When preparing for the CLSC exam, or any test that includes the Catalyst system, review the following material. Especially focus on how the various components are involved in the forwarding of frames and their roles and responsibilities. Understanding the various components will also assist in real-world troubleshooting and application.

Critical Information

The easiest way to may sure you understand the major components of the 5000 series switch is to present them here for review. Pay particular attention to relationships and similarities between components.

Catalyst Processors

The Catalyst processors, in concert with the ASICs, provide the intelligence behind the frame-switching process. The processors, along with their supporting systems, are presented in this section.

Network Management Processor (NMP)

The network management processor, or NMP, controls the system hardware as well as the configuration and diagnostic functions. In addition, the NMP is responsible for network management and the Spanning-Tree Protocol. In the Catalyst system, each VLAN has a separate spanning-tree construct.

Master Communication Processor (MCP)

The MCP uses the serial management bus to communicate between the NMP on the Supervisor module and the line module communication processors (LCPs) on the individual line cards in the chassis. The serial management bus operates outside of the data backplane at 761Kbps.

The MCP includes an 8051 processor, 32KB of EPROM, 64KB of SRAM for code, and 32KB of SRAM for data. In addition, 32KB are allocated for I/O space. The 8051 processor contains a built-in universal asynchronous receiver and transmitter (UART).

The MCP also handles the testing and configuration of local ports, the control of local ports, the download of runtime code, and the diagnostics of onboard chips including memory, ASICs, and the local target logic (LTL) and color blocking logic (CBL).

NOTE Cisco documentation uses both the terms master communication processor and management control processor to define MCP.

Line Module Communication Processor (LCP)

The LCP is located on each line module and is responsible for communication with the MCP on the Supervisor engine. The LCP is an 8051 processor, and communication over the management bus uses the Serial Communication Protocol (SCP). During module initialization, the LCP boots from local ROM and prepares an information package called *resetack*, which includes the boot-up diagnostics and module information. This package is sent to the MCP, which forwards the parameters to the NMP.

Logic Units

Logic Units provide forwarding logic based on VLAN, MAC address, and ingress port. The specifics of these units are described for review below.

Arbiter

The Catalyst system uses a two-tier method of arbitration to control the switching process. The local bus arbiter, located on each module, assigns priorities for queuing and handles all traffic on all ports of the module. This process then uses the central bus arbiter, located on the Supervisor module, to obtain permission to transmit frames to the switching engine. The central bus arbiter uses a round-robin process, with special handling for high-priority frames, to service all modules and all ports. The priority levels are configured by the administrator, and provide flexibility for the switching of time-sensitive traffic, including voice and video, in addition to server ports.

Collectively, the arbiter system is referred to as the ARB.

Local Target Logic (LTL)

The LTL works with the EARL (discussed later in this chapter) to determine the destination port or ports for each frame. This function accommodates differences in unicast, multicast, and broadcast forwarding. The LTL uses index values provided by the EARL to select one, many, or all ports on the line module for receipt of the frame.

Color Blocking Logic (CBL)

Cisco uses the concept of colors to help administrators visualize different VLANs. The color blocking logic works by blocking traffic from entering or leaving a port that is not part of the VLAN. In addition, the CBL participates in the spanning-tree process to block ports and prevent bridging loops. Recall that each port is associated with a single VLAN (assuming a nontrunk port). As will be presented in the frame flow diagram (Figure 6.1, later in this chapter), each incoming frame is tagged with an identifier for the VLAN noting its color within the switch. A frame tagged from the green VLAN would thus be blocked from exiting a red VLAN port.

EARL

No kingdom would be complete without an EARL, and building on this pun, the Catalyst 5000 is no different. In switching, however, EARL refers to the Encoded Address Recognition Logic. This chip works with the bus arbitration system to control access to the data-switching bus. EARL also controls the destination ports of packet transfers.

More specifically, the EARL monitors frame flow and compiles the list of MAC addresses as related to port numbers and the VLAN ID. In addition, the ASIC determines the destination port of frames and maintains the timer for aging entries out of the forwarding table. By default, entries are discarded after 300 seconds, although the administrator can change this value. Valid parameters are limited between 1 and 20 minutes. The EARL can maintain a table of up to 128,000 addresses—actually stored in the CAM, or MAC address table. Simply put, the EARL handles forwarding and filtering decisions within the switch.

Administrators do not troubleshoot the EARL per se. Rather, issues with MAC address and port mappings controlled by EARL are more a part of the diagnostic process. Understanding the significant function of the EARL in the Catalyst line, and its role in all switching, can assist in hardware-related debugging.

ASICs

ASICs operate in hardware at wire speed, performing a single, pre-defined function. The critical ASICs of the 5000/5500 system are described below. For both the exam and real life, understand the similarities and differences between each ASIC.

SAMBA

The Synergy Advanced Multipurpose Bus Arbiter, or SAMBA, ASIC is located on the line modules and the Supervisor modules. On the line cards, this chip is responsible for broadcast suppression based on thresholds established by the administrator. This ASIC also maintains statistics on packets.

The SAMBA operates in either master or slave mode. Master mode is used on the Supervisor engine, and slave mode is used on the line cards. The master is capable of addressing up to 13 line modules, while the slave is capable of serving up to 48 individual ports.

In the master/slave model, the slave SAMBA must wait for permission from the master before granting access to the port. This process is described in greater detail in the next section of this chapter; however, it is most important to note that SAMBA is involved in granting access to the switching bus, and that in master mode, this election is granted on a per-module basis. In slave mode, this election is per port.

WARNING Cisco's SAMBA should not be confused with the SAMBA utility for providing SMB (Windows NT) services on Unix platforms.

SAINT

The SAINT (Synergy Advanced Interface and Network Termination) handles Ethernet switching on the Catalyst 5000 platform, and it also handles ISL encapsulation. Each Ethernet port has an independent 192KB buffer for inbound and outbound packets, which is divided to provide 168KB to outbound traffic and 24KB for inbound frames.

The buffer arrangement controlled by the SAINT has proven itself in hundreds of networks and rarely presents a troubleshooting issue—however, administrators must always consider buffer overflows and underruns as a factor. Again, capturing the appropriate counters with the show commands will provide the administrator with troubleshooting tools.

SAGE

The SAGE (Synergy Advanced Gate-Array Engine) is similar to the SAINT, except that it is used for non-Ethernet applications, including FDDI, ATM LANE, Token Ring, and the network management processor on the Supervisor engine. The SAGE is also used on the RSM module (there are two—one for each channel).

Phoenix

The Phoenix ASIC provides both a technical and an economical expansion of the Catalyst line. First, the gate array is responsible for interconnecting the three 1.2Gb backplanes in the Catalyst 5500 chassis to create a crossbar fabric that bridges traffic between backplanes at gigabit speeds. Second, the architecture permits the use of legacy modules, providing administrators with investment protection when upgrading from the Catalyst 5000. While the chassis needs replacement in such circumstances, some companies choose to defer trade-in or replacement of specific modules because of cost concerns.

The Phoenix ASIC includes a 384KB buffer to address congestion and is treated as a port by the bus arbiter and EARL modules.

Exam Essentials

Understand the roles of the different ASICs. Remember that the Phoenix ASIC is only on the 5500 platform, not the 5000. Also, understand the similarities between the SAGE and SAINT ASICs— the SAINT is responsible for Ethernet, and the SAGE is used for Token Ring, FDDI, and ATM.

Remember the different roles of the Logic Units and processors. Be familiar with the roles of the MCP, NCP, CBL, and LTL systems. Understand that Cisco refers to VLANs with colors— they're really number based, but visually, it's helpful to use blue for VLAN 1, red for 2, and so on.

Key Terms and Concepts

ASIC: Application Specific Integrated Circuit. ASICs are specifically programmed chips that perform a function at wire speed.

Buffer: A storage area dedicated to handling data while in transit. Buffers are used to receive/store sporadic deliveries of data bursts, usually received from faster devices, compensating for the variations in processing speed. Incoming information is stored until everything is received prior to sending data on. Also known as an information buffer.

CAM: Content Addressable Memory. This is the storage area for the MAC (hardware) layer 2 address table.

EARL: Encoded Address Recognition Logic. While a number of other Logic Units and ASICs are involved, the EARL is responsible for the majority of forwarding decisions.

Management bus: A separate communications bus for communication between the line modules and the Supervisor engine. It operates at 761Kbps.

Switching bus: A 1.2Gbps backplane in the Catalyst chassis used for user-data forwarding.

Sample Questions

1. Which ASIC provides a bridge between the backplanes in the Catalyst 5500?

   A. SAGE.

   B. SAINT.

   C. Phoenix.

   D. EARL.

   E. There is only one backplane in the Catalyst 5500.

   Answer: C. The Phoenix interconnects the three 1.2Gbps backplanes in the 5500.

2. The MCP is responsible for which of the following functions?

   A. Communication between the LCPs and NMP

   B. Route forwarding

   C. CAM table updates

   D. ISL trunking and SPAN ports

   Answer: A. The MCP communicates with the NMP and the LCPs on the line cards.

3. The SAGE ASIC is similar to which of the following?

A. The EARL ASIC

B. The Phoenix ASIC

C. The LCP and NMP

D. The SAINT ASIC

E. None of the above

Answer: D. The SAGE ASIC is a SAINT ASIC without Ethernet support.

Trace a frame's progress through a Catalyst 5000 series switch.

In this section, the process by which the Catalyst 5000 processes frames will be reviewed. This will give you the basic understanding of the interaction among the hardware components.

For the exam, it is important to understand the roles and responsibilities of the various components described previously, and how they interoperate to direct a frame from one port to another. In a production environment, understanding of the information provided here can help you troubleshoot internetwork switch problems.

Critical Information

It is highly recommended that readers learn the method by which the Catalyst 5000 forwards frames, as an entire exam objective is based on this process. This example is based on an Ethernet frame.

The Catalyst system processes frames by store-and-forward switching. This differs from the theoretical alternative of cut-through switching, and provides additional control and management of the forwarding process. Recall that cut-through switching is not an option in the Catalyst 5000/5500. The Catalyst avoids the traditional latency of store-and-forward switches by sending all frames to every port and then purging those destinations that are inappropriate. While still subject to variable latency, this provides a good compromise between speed and accurate frame propagation.

When a frame enters a port, it is placed into the receive buffer by the port's DMA controller. The checksum of the frame is verified by the ASIC, and a 12-byte header denoting the source port, VLAN number, and FCS is added. The Ethernet MIB and RMON counters are also incremented to provide proper accounting of the data flow. Once the frame is stored in the frame buffer, a request is made to access the switching bus for frame forwarding. Note that this request is made via the management bus.

The bus arbiter receives the request on the management bus from the SAINT ASIC for permission to transmit the frame over the switching bus. The Supervisor is responsible for granting access to each line module, and the individual line module is responsible for granting access to an individual port. Permission is granted for a single frame only.

Once the bus arbiter grants access to the switching bus, the SAINT ASIC transmits the contents of the buffer. The frame is transmitted to all ports in the switch and stored in each individual port's input buffer. This is an important concept in the Catalyst system—as each port receives every frame, there are no rebroadcast issues for broadcast or multicast frames. In addition, there is no delay in receiving the frame at the destination port.

At this point, the switch has acted more like a hub than a switch. The frame has been forwarded to all ports, regardless of VLAN considerations and MAC-layer addresses. Clearly, the transmitted frame cannot be forwarded to all ports on the switch.

It is at this point in the switching process that the EARL instructs each port to forward or drop the frame. This is coordinated with the LTL and CBL functions, and depends on the VLAN, source port, MAC table, and nature of the frame—broadcast, unicast, or multicast. The

EARL does not command the forwarding of frames on individual ports. Rather, the EARL commands all ports to drop the frame except those that should forward the frame.

Figure 6.1 provides a visual representation of the frame flow within the Catalyst. Note again that this example is for an Ethernet-to-Ethernet flow—a flow to FDDI or another medium might require additional processing and frame conversion.

FIGURE 6.1: Frame flow within the Catalyst 5000

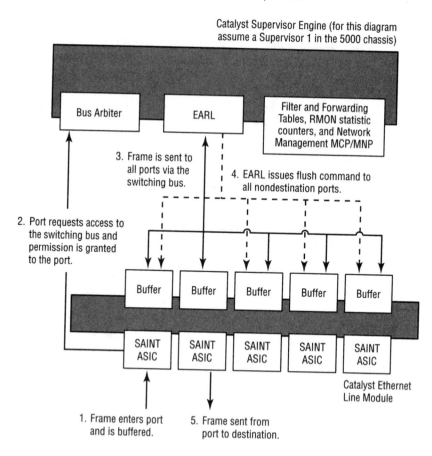

Exam Essentials

Remember that every frame is forwarded to every port on the Catalyst.   Understand that regardless of the VLAN or other destination criteria, all frames are sent to every port on the Catalyst system via the ASIC switching bus. The EARL commands nondestination ports to discard the frame.

Remember that a separate management bus is used to control frame flow.   Remember that the Catalyst modules communicate with each other using a management bus. This avoids contention with the switching bus for bandwidth and increases performance.

Understand how the EARL, CBL, and LTL are used to make forwarding decisions on a frame.   Understand the process by which frame forwarding occurs. Upon ingress, the switch tags the frame with the ingress port and VLAN information. This information, in addition to the CAM (MAC address table), works to forward frames to only the appropriate ports.

Key Terms and Concepts

CAM: Content Addressable Memory. This is the storage area for the MAC (hardware) layer 2 address table.

EARL: Encoded Address Recognition Logic. While a number of other Logic Units and ASICs are involved, the EARL is responsible for the majority of forwarding decisions.

Sample Questions

1. Order the following steps documenting the process by which an Ethernet frame is processed within the Catalyst switch.

   A. EARL commands the dropping of the frame on nondestination ports.

   B. The frame enters the switch, and the port's DMA buffer stores it in the port's receive buffer.

   C. The frame is transmitted to all ports via the high-speed switching bus.

   D. The frame is received by all ports in the switch.

   E. The port is granted bus access by the central bus arbiter.

   F. Permission to transmit the frame on the high-speed switching backplane is requested by the SAINT ASIC.

   G. The EARL, along with the LTL and CBL functions, selects the destination ports.

   Answer: B, F, E, C, D, G, A. Review this material and be very comfortable with this process.

2. Where is MAC address information stored?

   A. CAM

   B. CBL

   C. LTL

   D. EARL

   E. SAINT

   Answer: A. Content Addressable Memory contains the MAC table.

3. The EARL commands ports to forward frames.

   A. True

   B. False

   Answer: B. The EARL commands ports to discard frames in their buffer, rather than forward them.

CHAPTER 7

Catalyst 5000 Series Switch Hardware

Cisco Exam Objectives Covered in This Chapter

▶ **Describe the hardware features, functions, and benefits of Catalyst 5000 series switches.** *(pages 160 – 165)*

▶ **Describe the hardware features and functions of the Supervisor engine.** *(pages 165 – 168)*

▶ **Describe the hardware features and functions of the modules in the Catalyst 5000 series switches.** *(pages 168 – 171)*

In previous chapters, the differences between the various chassis in the Catalyst 5000 product line were covered, and the role of the Supervisor was presented. This section will augment that foundation with three new exam objectives. You will see that these objectives are targeted toward troubleshooting and physical systems, in addition to considerations regarding cabling.

For the CLSC exam, review this chapter as you would prepare for a troubleshooting session without access to the console (CLI). Almost all of the material presented here is exclusive of commands and software processing.

This is important information to understand for the exam as well as when designing and working in an internetworking environment with Catalyst switches.

Describe the hardware features, functions, and benefits of Catalyst 5000 series switches.

While seemingly broad, this objective is focused on both how the Catalyst 5000/5500 platform would be used and why they should be used in certain situations. In the following section, some of the considerations, including the chassis itself and redundancy—an option in the 5500—will be broken down.

This is an important objective, and a precursor to understanding the other two objectives in this chapter. This will help you when designing and installing the Catalyst switches in a production environment as well as when gathering information for the CLSC exam.

Critical Information

Between the Catalyst 5000 and 5500 platforms, Cisco has offered a wide array of networking options for both large and small networks. This platform diversity includes offerings that scale in terms of both topologies and port densities.

General Information

The *CLSC Study Guide* provides greater information regarding the basic 5000/5500 systems; however, readers should be comfortable with the three bus systems of the Catalyst 5000. These buses are described in Table 7.1.

T A B L E 7.1: The Catalyst 5000 Bus Architecture

Bus	Function
Management Bus	Interconnects NMPs and carries statistical information.
Index Bus	Also referred to as the Control Bus, the Index Bus is used to signal port selections from the EARL.
Frame Switching Bus	A 1.2Gbps bus for the transmission of user data. In the 5500, this bus is interconnected as a 3.6Gbps backplane fabric when using the Supervisor III.

The most significant item to remember is that the management of frame forwarding is handled via a different bus than that of the data. Of lesser import for this objective, recall the different chassis configurations, including slots and power-supply capabilities. As presented in the next section, be comfortable with the differences and configurations of the 5500 chassis. These differences include the expanded backplane capacity and the inclusion of the LS1010 cell backplane.

The 5500 Chassis

The 5500 chassis provides a 3.6Gbps backplane for frame switching. This backplane consists of three separate 1.2Gbps backplanes accessible from the various module slots. These backplanes are interconnected via the Phoenix ASIC, which was described in greater detail in Chapter 6. Table 7.2 documents the backplane interface options. Each letter (A, B, C) represents one of the three separate 1.2Gbps backplanes.

T A B L E 7.2: The 5500 Backplane

Slot	Backplane and Use
1	Supervisor Engine II or III (primary); A, B, C backplanes
2	Redundant Supervisor module or A, B, C backplanes
3	A, B, C backplane
4	A, B, C backplane
5	A, B, C backplane
6	B backplane
7	B backplane
8	B backplane
9	LS1010 module or B backplane
10	LS1010 module or C backplane
11	LS1010 module or C backplane
12	LS1010 module or C backplane
13	ATM Switching Engine (ASP module only)

NOTE Slot 13 is not available for frame-based services and is reserved for the ASP module exclusively.

Redundancy

The Catalyst 5000/5500 platforms are designed to provide limited redundancy by way of their redundant power supplies; however, this option fails to address the most significant single point of failure in the Catalyst system. As the Supervisor engine is responsible for forwarding decisions on all frames in the switching fabric, its failure will effectively stop the flow of frames through the switch.

To address this issue, Cisco provides for the Supervisor II or Supervisor III to be configured for redundancy in the 5500 chassis. While not without limitations, this configuration can greatly reduce the impact of Supervisor engine failure. These limitations include the placement of the Supervisor engines in the chassis—they must occupy slots 1 and 2—and that the ports on the standby Supervisor are disabled, which effectively reduces the total port count of the switch to the ports on the line modules.

In addition, failure scenarios may require up to 3 minutes for the standby to become active, although typical fail-over times are much faster. This delay usually results in the loss of some frames.

Exam Essentials

The Supervisor engines are limited to specific slots in the Catalyst chassis. Remember that the Supervisor engine must go into the first slot of the chassis, with the exception of the redundant Supervisor, which may be placed in the second slot. By default, the Supervisor in slot 1 will be loaded as primary, and the Supervisor in slot 2 will be in standby.

The 5500 chassis incorporates two separate backplane structures. Recall that the 5500 contains a cell-based backplane for ATM cells, based on the LS1010 platform. In addition, a crossbar-connected 3.6Gbps backplane is provided for frame-based traffic.

The Catalyst 5000 series offers different redundancy options.
Remember that dual power supplies provide one form of redundancy in the Catalyst product, while dual Supervisor engines are an option for some installations.

Key Terms and Concepts

Backplane: Typically passive, the backplane interconnects the various modules within a chassis. Similar to the motherboard in a computer.

Gbps: Gigabits per second. A gigabit is equal to 1024 million bits.

Redundancy: An automatic, occasionally concurrent, process by which network failures are addressed. Redundancy in the Catalyst addresses power-supply failure and Supervisor failure. While these are both intraswitch fault-tolerance options, administrators may use duplicate systems for redundancy—dual routers with HSRP, for example.

Sample Questions

1. Which of the following is true regarding the Catalyst 5500?

  A. Supports dual Supervisors

  B. Provides 3.6Gbps for frame traffic

  C. Provides 5Gpbs for cell traffic

  D. Provides 3.6Gbps for cell traffic

  E. Supports Token Ring, FDDI, ATM, and Ethernet in the same chassis

Answer: A, B, C, E. All of the answers are true except the 3.6Gbps cell backplane. It operates at 5Gbps.

2. Which of the following slots may be used for the Supervisor engine?

   A. Slot 13

   B. Slot 5

   C. Any slot that accesses all three backplanes

   D. Slot 1

   E. Any slot

   Answer: D. In redundant configurations, a second Supervisor is placed in slot 2.

Describe the hardware features and functions of the Supervisor engine.

W hile there is a wide array of Supervisor engine options available for the Catalyst 5000/5500 series, this objective primarily focuses on the differences between the Supervisor engine and its two current successors, the Supervisor II and Supervisor III.

For this objective, pay careful attention to the features of each Supervisor and the limitations of each engine in terms of the different Catalyst chassis. This will help you in a production environment as well as when gathering information for the CLSC exam.

Critical Information

The Supervisor engine is responsible for the management and forwarding processes within the switch. By upgrading the engine, administrators can improve performance and add additional features (within the limitations of the chassis). For example, the Supervisor III is required to access the three 1.2Gbps backplanes in the 5500 chassis, while a Supervisor II or III may be used for Supervisor redundancy. EtherChannel support was added with the Supervisor II as well.

The Supervisor engine also provides the interface for out-of-band management (the console port) and the diagnostic LEDs that indicate switch status and current load. This information is helpful in troubleshooting.

The Supervisor I engine is available with the following interface options.

- Two multimode SC 100Mbps Ethernet ports

- Two single-mode ST 100Mbps Ethernet ports

- Two RJ-45 100Mbps Ethernet ports

The ports available on the Supervisor engine are considered important by Cisco regarding this objective; however, as a general rule, there is an available module for any typical installation. Remember the physical-media distance limitations presented in other chapters of this book, and that these limits also impact the functionality of the ports on the Supervisor engine.

TIP   Refer to Cisco's online resource, Cisco Connection Online, for current information regarding the Supervisor module. The site is at www.cisco.com.

As noted previously, the Supervisor engine must be installed in the first slot of the chassis, except in redundant configurations, where a Supervisor engine must be installed in both slots 1 and 2. Theoretically, on the 5500 chassis, a Supervisor could be installed in slot 2 only; however, this configuration would unnecessarily consume a line-module slot.

Exam Essentials

Understand the significance of the Supervisor engine. Know that the Supervisor is responsible for managing the flow of frames within the switch and that the SC0 and SL0 interfaces, in addition to the console connection, are terminated on the Supervisor.

Know that new features may be added to the switch by upgrading the Supervisor engine. While limited to the capabilities of the chassis, new features may be added to the Catalyst by upgrading the Supervisor engine.

Key Terms and Concepts

EtherChannel: Available for Fast and Gigabit Ethernet links, EtherChannel disables Spanning Tree on up to four ports and permits those four connections to combine into one logical connection. So, bandwidth across an EtherChannel using FastEthernet is 800Mbps (full-duplex). This can greatly improve trunk performance.

Sample Questions

1. The Supervisor I is available with which of the following interfaces?

   A. There are no interfaces on the Supervisor, just the console port.

   B. FastEthernet, multimode fiber.

   C. FastEthernet, single-mode fiber.

   D. Fast Ethernet, RJ-45.

   Answer: B, C, D.

2. Which of the following is true?

A. The Supervisor engine is built into the Catalyst 5000 chassis.

B. Placing three Supervisor II engines in the 5500 will permit access to the 3.6Gbps backplane.

C. The SC0 interface is bonded to a single physical port on the Supervisor engine.

D. The Supervisor can support FastEthernet on copper media with an RJ-45 connector.

Answer: D. RJ-45 connectors are available on the Supervisor.

Describe the hardware features and functions of the modules in the Catalyst 5000 series switches.

T he modular nature of the Catalyst 5000 series significantly adds to the value afforded by the platform. This objective is primarily concerned with two facets of the Catalyst switch that have been covered in other sections—the interaction between the Supervisor module and the line modules, and the functions and limitations of the line modules themselves.

This is an important objective to understand. It will help you when troubleshooting the Catalyst switch and adding new cards in a production environment. Also, when studying for your CLSC exam, you can gain an understanding of the different modules used in the Catalyst switches.

Critical Information

The Catalyst 5000 series modules provide services for FDDI/CDDI, ATM LANE, Ethernet and FastEthernet, Token Ring, and in the newest modules, Gigabit Ethernet. The 5500 chassis supports modules from the LS1010 product, including the ASP (ATM Supervisor) and ATM cell-based modules.

Table 7.3 documents some of the significant items to keep in mind for the different modules.

T A B L E 7.3: Catalyst Modules

Module Type	Features and Information
Ethernet	192KB buffer per port with support for full- or half-duplex operation. Modules may be inserted online. One SAINT ASIC per port. Various modules support fiber or copper connections. The Catalyst supports 10/100/1000Mbps Ethernet.
Token Ring	Uses the SAGE ASIC and supports fiber or copper connections. Various switching/bridging options are available, including source-route switching (SRS), source-route bridging (SRB), and source-route transparent bridging (SRT).
FDDI/CDDI	Supports single- or dual-attachment station connections on copper RJ-45 (CDDI) or fiber (MM or SM).
ATM	Supports ATM LANE with full support for LECS, LES, BUS, and LEC. The LANE modules may be used in any Catalyst 5000 series switch. In addition to ATM LANE, true ATM cell switching is available in the 5500 chassis with the LS1010 line cards. Slot 13 on the 5500 chassis is reserved for the ASP module—a Supervisor engine for ATM cell switching.

It is also important to note that the line modules on the Catalyst 5000/5500 are removable while the switch is online. This feature permits recovery from failures without affecting the remainder of the switch.

Exam Essentials

Remember that the line modules may be removed online.
Understand that each line module operates independently from the
other modules, and that replacement of a line card is permitted while
the switch is in operation.

**Understand the limitations of the modules in the different
chassis.** Recall that only the 5500 chassis (of the 5000/5500 series)
may accept the ASP module and other ATM cell-switching line cards
from the LS1010 product line.

**Know the different types of line modules available for the 5000
series.** Recall that Ethernet, ATM LANE, Token Ring, and FDDI/
CDDI modules are available.

Key Terms and Concepts

LED: Light-emitting diode. A light source used in multimode
fiber installations.

Multimode: Abbreviated MM, multimode fiber uses LEDs for
transmission. Multimode fibers typically operate over shorter distances than single mode.

Single-mode: Abbreviated SM, single-mode fiber connections
use a laser for transmission. As single-mode connections travel far-
ther than multimode connections, they are useful in large campus
and metropolitan installations.

SRB: Source-route bridging. Created by IBM, it's the bridging
method used in Token Ring networks. The source determines the
entire route to a destination before sending the data and includes
that information in fields within each packet. Contrast with transparent bridging.

SRT: Source-route transparent bridging. A bridging scheme
developed by IBM, merging SRB and transparent bridging. SRT

takes advantage of technologies in one device, fulfilling the needs of all end nodes. Translation between bridging protocols is not necessary.

Sample Questions

1. The 10/100 Ethernet module on the Catalyst 5000 is responsible for making frame-forwarding decisions.

   A. True

   B. False

   Answer: B. The EARL on the Supervisor engine is responsible for forwarding decisions.

2. Which of the following is false regarding the Catalyst 5000 series modules?

   A. Modules may be removed from the chassis without disrupting frame flow on other modules.

   B. Ethernet ports use the SAINT ASIC.

   C. Token Ring ports use the SAINT ASIC.

   D. Single-mode fiber ports typically provide the greatest distance functionality.

   Answer: C. Token Ring, FDDI, and ATM LANE use the SAGE ASIC.

CHAPTER

8

Configuring Catalyst 5000
Series Switches

Cisco Exam Objectives Covered in This Chapter

▶ **Prepare network connections.** *(pages 175 – 178)*

▶ **Establish a serial connection.** *(pages 179 – 181)*

▶ **Use the Catalyst 5000 switch CLI to:** *(pages 181 – 187)*
- Enter privileged mode
- Set system information
- Configure interface types

In this chapter, the Cisco exam objectives that address Catalyst 5000/5500 switch configuration will be examined. These issues include the two methods for accessing the management system of the Catalyst—in-band and out-of-band. In addition, this chapter will focus on the use of the Catalyst command line interface (CLI).

The Catalyst 5000 series is capable of processing numerous physical interface types, including Ethernet, Token Ring, FDDI/CDDI, and ATM LANE. These connections can, depending on type, use copper (Category 3 or Category 5) or fiber (multimode or single-mode) connections. Administrators need to evaluate the needs of the network and the functional abilities of each medium.

This chapter is important because it will teach you how to configure the Catalyst 5000 series switches. This is important to understand because finding a Cisco Catalyst switch in a production environment is typical these days. By using the commands taught in this chapter, you'll be prepared for a production environment as well as the CLSC exam.

Prepare network connections.

There are a great many things to consider when installing Catalyst switches, including power, cooling, rack space, and budgets. However, network connections are what make the switch useful, so Cisco has included specific details of network connections as an exam objective.

In this objective, the physical distance limitations of the different media types, as well the power margins when running the Catalyst 5000 series switches, will be discussed.

This is an important objective to understand when planning your installation and troubleshooting an existing environment.

Critical Information

It is important to know the specified maximum distances that are permitted for the various media available on the Catalyst 5000 series switches. In addition, because of the complexities involved in fiber interconnections, the preparation of network connections includes the calculation of power budgets in these installations.

The specifications incorporated into each physical media standard for each protocol virtually guarantee successful connectivity. While such values are more than rules of thumb, they are easy to incorporate into network designs, and insulate the administrator from having to understand the detailed electrical criteria involved in twisted-pair wiring and fiber optics (see Table 8.1).

T A B L E 8.1: Physical Media Distance Limitations

Media/Protocol	Distance
CDDI (CAT 5)	100 meters
FDDI (MM)	2000 meters
FDDI (SM)	30,000 meters
ATM LANE (OC-3 MM)	2000 meters
ATM LANE (OC-3 SM)	10,000 meters
Token Ring (UTP, 16Mb)	200 meters
Ethernet (CAT 3 or 5)	100 meters
Ethernet (MM)	2000 meters
FastEthernet (CAT 5)	100 meters
FastEthernet (MM Full)	2000 meters
FastEthernet (MM Half)	400 meters
FastEthernet (SM Full)	10,000 meters

Table 8.2 presents Cisco's suggested LED link loss values for multi-mode fiber connections. These values are used with the following formulas to determine the power margin:

- The letters PB represent the power budget, which is the maximum amount of power transmitted. The formula is PB = PT − PR. PT stands for power transmitter, and reflects the minimum transmitter power. The PR variable represents the minimum receiver sensitivity.

- This formula provides the PB value for the formula that provides the power margin, or PM. The other value is the maximum link loss value (LL). The power-margin formula is expressed as PM = PB − LL.

T A B L E 8.2: Approximate LED Link Loss Values

Element	Link Loss Value (Estimated)
Fiber attenuation	1 dB per kilometer
Splice	0.5 dB per splice
Connectors	0.5 dB per connector
Clock recovery module	1 dB
High-order mode losses	0.5 dB

The most significant factor to note with regard to these formulas is that the power margin (PM) must be positive for the link to work, under most circumstances. If the value is negative, the link may not function properly.

Exam Essentials

Maximum media distances are specified for fiber and copper connections. Know the limitations for both the media and the protocol in use. Note from Table 8.1 that single-mode fiber permits the longest distances, but ATM and FDDI have different maximum distances.

If the power margin is positive, the multimode fiber connection should function correctly. Review and understand the concepts behind the formulas presented in this section. Beyond the basic guidelines for fiber connections, the power loss and margin considerations presented here account for the signal degradation introduced by splices, connectors, and fiber distance.

Key Terms and Concepts

Decibel: Decibels (dB) measure the power output of an acoustical or electrical device.

Link loss value: An estimate of the loss experienced at an interconnect point in a fiber connection.

Power budget: The power budget defines the maximum amount of power received on a fiber connection.

Sample Questions

1. After calculating the power margin, the result is negative. What does this probably mean?

   A. The link will work.

   B. The link will not work.

   C. The calculation is incorrect.

   D. Not enough information is provided.

   Answer: B. Positive power margins typically indicate that a link will function correctly.

2. To obtain the greatest distance from a FastEthernet link, an administrator should use which of the following?

   A. Half-duplex, multimode

   B. Full-duplex, multimode

   C. Half-duplex, single-mode

   D. Full-duplex, single-mode

   Answer: D. Single-mode connections typically provide the greatest distance options between stations. Full-duplex connections eliminate the collision detection criteria from Ethernet.

Establish a serial connection.

Typically, administrators initially configure the switch with a cable connected to the console port. This connection is important enough that Cisco has included an exam objective concerning the fundamentals of this connection. In this section, the default parameters for this connection will also be defined.

This is not a large objective, but it is important. You need to be able to connect to a switch and bring up the command line interface (CLI). This is important when using Catalyst 5000 switches in a production environment and when studying for your CLSC exam.

Critical Information

The serial connection is established via the console port on the Supervisor engine of the Catalyst 5000/5500 switch. This port is a DB-25 connector on the original Supervisor engines; however, the Supervisor III engine has changed to the RJ-45 serial connector. By default, this connection is configured as follows:

- 9600 baud

- Eight data bits

- One stop bit

- No parity

From this connection, the administrator can access the command line interface, or CLI. Initially, no password is configured on the switch— pressing Enter a few times will provide a prompt.

The serial connection also provides service for the SL0 interface, which is used for SLIP connections. This type of connection is useful for out-of-band connectivity.

Exam Essentials

Understand how the serial connection is used to access the CLI. The command line interface (CLI) is reachable via the serial console port. This port is typically used for the initial configuration of the switch.

Key Terms and Concepts

In-band management: In-band management is the management of a network device through the network using Simple Network Management Protocol (SNMP) or Telnet.

Out-of-band management: Out-of-band management is management outside of the network using a console connection.

SLIP: Serial Line Internet Protocol. A variation of TCP/IP used as an industry standard for point-to-point connections.

Sample Questions

1. What is the console port on the Catalyst 5000 used for?

   A. Initial configuration of the Supervisor

   B. Access to the CLI

   C. Connections via the SLIP protocol

   D. All of the above

   E. None of the above

   Answer: D. The console (serial) port is used for initial configuration, access to the CLI, and SLIP connections.

2. How is the SLIP interface identified on the switch?

A. SC0

B. SL0

C. SLIP0

D. SC1

E. SL0/0

Answer: B. The SLIP interface is SL0.

Use the Catalyst 5000 switch CLI to:

- Enter privileged mode
- Set system information
- Configure interface types

In this series of books, it has been noted numerous times that it is highly beneficial to get some time on an actual switch so that you can enter the various commands and directly view the results.

This section will provide sufficient examples to prepare you for the exam; however, even a half-hour on the switch would be time well spent.

This objective is important when using Catalyst 5000 switches in a production environment and when gathering information for your CLSC exam.

Critical Information

Cisco's exam objectives include tasks related to the use of the command line interface (CLI) for the initial configuration of the Catalyst 5000 series switches. These tasks are straightforward and typically part of every installation.

First and foremost, you will need to enter privileged mode. As with the Cisco router platforms, the switch's privileged mode is accessed with the enable command. In the default configuration, there is no password associated with enable mode.

NOTE   Privileged mode provides a level of authority that permits changes to the switch configuration. Because of this, access to the enable password should be limited.

Second, most administrators will choose to configure the switch with system information. The Catalyst 5000/5500 provides for the documentation of administrative information within the switch. This information includes:

- System contact
- System location
- System name
- System prompt

This information is most helpful in identifying the switch that is being accessed remotely and the administrator responsible for maintenance of that switch. The commands to configure these settings are listed in the following sections.

System Contact

The commands to configure system contact are as follows:

- `set system contact` *contact_string*
- `set system contact Joe Administrator x.60842`

System Location

The commands to configure system location are as follows:

- `set system location` *location_string*
- `set system location Bldg. 7, Sydney Campus`

System Name

The commands to configure system name are as follows:

- `set system name` *name_string*
- `set system name Switch_A`

System Prompt

The commands to configure the system prompt are as follows:

- `set prompt` *prompt_string*
- `set prompt Switch_A`

The system clock and passwords for both console and enable modes may be configured as well.

System Clock

The commands to configure the system clock are as follows:

- `set time` *day_of_week mm/dd/yy hh:mm:ss*
- `set time Monday 05/05/99 12:00:00`

TIP Consult the Cisco Web site at www.cisco.com for the latest information regarding year 2000 (Y2K) and other date compliance issues.

Console Password

The command to configure the password for console mode is as follows:

- `set password`

The system will prompt for the old password and verification of the new password. A password of zero characters is permitted; however, this is not recommended from a security perspective.

Enable Password

The command to configure the enable password is as follows:

- `set enablepass`

The system will prompt for the old enable password and verification of the new enable password.

Configuring the Catalyst 5000/5500 System Interfaces

Once the switch is configured with basic information, including an IP address, it is possible to Telnet to the system to make configuration changes. This occurs via the SC0 interface, which is initially placed in VLAN 1. An IP address, subnet mask, default gateway, and broadcast value must all be set from their default values of 0.0.0.0 as well.

To configure the SC0 interface, use the `set interface sc0 [vlan_number] ip_address [netmask[broadcast]]` command. For example, to set the SC0 interface to VLAN 1 using IP address 10.1.1.10 on a subnet, type **set interface sc0 1 10.1.1.10 255.255.255.0 10.1.1.255**. This command could be shortened to omit the VLAN number and broadcast address.

It may be necessary to issue the equivalent of the `no shutdown` command on the interface. On the Catalyst, this command to enable the interface is `set interface sc0 up`. It may also be necessary to establish a default route, which is configured with the `set ip route default gateway [metric]` command. This would be needed to reach a switch on a different subnet from the management or Telnet console. The `show ip route` command should be used to verify routes, and additional routes may be established with the `set ip route destination gateway [metric]` command. The switch does not learn routes via a routing protocol such as EIGRP or RIP.

Necessary Procedures

Configure Switch_A for use in a test network. Use the values in Table 8.3 for your configuration.

T A B L E 8.3: Values for Lab Configuration Example

Parameter	Value
IP address	10.20.30.10
Network mask	255.255.255.0
Default gateway	10.20.30.1
System name	Switch_A
System contact	Administrator
System location	Maui, Hawaii
Password	sybex
Enable password	cisco

Commands for Table 8.3 Configuration

The commands for the configuration of the values in Table 8.3 are as follows:

```
set interface sc0 10.20.30.10 255.255.255.0
set ip route default 10.20.30.1
set system name Switch_A
set system contact Administrator
set system location Maui, Hawaii
set password (Note: Follow the prompts for the old and new passwords.)
set enablepass (Note: Follow the prompts for the old and new passwords.)
```

Exam Essentials

Be able to enter privileged mode on the Catalyst Supervisor.
While this is a fairly straightforward objective, understand the use of the enable command and that limits should be placed on the number of administrators with privileged access.

Understand the commands needed to configure the Catalyst with system information. While the commands are optional in deployments, administrators should be familiar with the commands needed to configure a system name and other information that can facilitate management.

Be able to identify the SC0 and SL0 interfaces. Be able to configure both interfaces and understand how each is used. The SC0 interface is used for in-band connections, and the SL0 is used for out-of-band SLIP connections.

Practice the commands listed in this chapter. Understand the purpose of each command and when it would be used. The commands presented in this chapter address the basic functions of the Catalyst 5000/5500 platform.

Key Terms and Concepts

In-band management: In-band management is the management of a network device through the network using Simple Network Management Protocol (SNMP) or Telnet.

Out-of-band management: Out-of-band management is management outside of the network using a console connection.

Sample Questions

1. The SC0 interface provides Telnet access to the Catalyst Supervisor engine.

   A. True

   B. False

   Answer: A.

2. Which of the following items is incorrect?

   A. The Catalyst 5500 Supervisor III learns routes via EIGRP.

   B. The SL0 interface is used for SLIP connections.

   C. The switch uses `set` commands to configure the system as opposed to using a configuration mode.

   D. Privileged mode is accessed with the `enable` command.

   Answer: A. Specific routes and the default route must be configured statically.

3. The privileged-mode password is set with which of the following commands?

   A. `set enable password`

   B. `set password enable`

   C. `enablepass`

   D. `set enablepass`

   Answer: D.

CHAPTER

9

Managing the Catalyst 5000
Series Switch Family

Cisco Exam Objectives Covered in This Chapter

► **Upon completion of this module, you will be able to describe the different ways of managing the Catalyst 5000 series switch, including:** *(pages 191 – 196)*

- Out-of-band management (console port)
- In-band management (network connection using SNMP)
- RMON
- SPAN
- CWSI

Management of any switch, including the Catalyst 5000 series switches, is the single most significant element presented in this book. Without management, all of the configuration and troubleshooting skills garnered in other chapters would be irrelevant. In addition, because resource management consumes the greatest amount of administration time, this chapter will touch upon some of the tools that greatly reduce the time required to manage the switch—although the configuration of these tools frequently is time consuming in and of itself.

This chapter is important when connecting your switch with a console cable and when monitoring your switched internetwork with management devices. For this chapter and its single objective, keep in mind that Cisco is concerned only with the high-level understanding of the various management options with a slight degree of detail regarding the interfaces used. Other objectives add detail to this component.

Upon completion of this module, you will be able to describe the different ways of managing the Catalyst 5000 series switch, including:

- Out-of-band management (console port)
- In-band management (network connection using SNMP)
- RMON
- SPAN
- CWSI

As defined in the objective, there are two different access methods for managing the Catalyst system. These will be reviewed as out-of-band and in-band, and then the different in-band resources, including RMON, Telnet, and CWSI, will be added. SPAN is an interesting in-band option, in that it augments protocol analysis and extended RMON functionality.

This is an important objective because it shows you configurations that you will use in a day-to-day production environment. This objective will also provide useful information you will need when studying for your exam.

Critical Information

The Catalyst 5000 series is managed with either in-band or out-of-band connections. These two connections as they relate to this objective will be reviewed in this section.

Out-of-Band Connections

Most out-of-band connections make use of the Supervisor-engine console port. This port is used to set up the preliminary switch configuration for in-band connections under most circumstances.

Depending on the Supervisor engine in use, the console connection uses a DB-25 connector or an RJ-45 (the Supervisor III). All connections are configured for 9600 baud by default, with eight data bits, one stop bit, and no parity. The console port may also be used with a modem connection, which can use SLIP (Serial Line IP) as an interface. This requires configuration of the SL0 interface prior to use.

The advantage to the out-of-band connection is that it is independent of the standard network traffic. Because of this, discounting CPU burdens, the out-of-band connection should be available even if the data network is down or under heavy load. This advantage is particularly important when the switch is in a remote location without on-site technical resources.

In-Band Connections

Catalyst 5000 series switches are almost always configured with in-band management. This requires the use of the IP protocol and configuration of the SC0 interface. Once this interface is configured, administrators may connect to the switch via Telnet, or with an SNMP/RMON tool, including CWSI.

Telnet

Telnet is a simple method for accessing the command line interface (CLI) of the switch. From the Telnet session, an administrator may change the switch configuration as though they were physically connected to the switch.

In addition to accepting inbound Telnet sessions, the Catalyst 5000 series switches are capable of providing up to eight outbound Telnet sessions. This feature is very helpful in troubleshooting situations.

SNMP/RMON

Within the Catalyst 5000 series, there are four supported RMON groups—Alarms, Events, Statistics, and History. Additional RMON groups are available via the network analysis module (NAM) or an external probe. External probes would be connected via the SPAN port, discussed later in this chapter. Cisco markets the Cisco SwitchProbe product for this purpose.

CiscoWorks for Switched Internetworks   CiscoWorks for Switched Internetworks (CWSI) is one of the more popular SNMP management tools. Given its Cisco-centric design, it is helpful in all Cisco networks. Depending on the version and installation, administrators may use the application with or without a management platform, such as HP OpenView or Sun Net Manager (Sun Domain Manager). CWSI includes different applications targeted toward specific tasks, as outlined in Table 9.1.

T A B L E 9.1:   The CWSI Major Applications

Application	Description
CiscoView	This is a graphical application that provides virtual chassis viewing, configuration tools, performance monitoring, and minor troubleshooting functions.
VLANDirector	This is a graphical administration tool for adding users, assigning ports, and changing associations.
TrafficDirector	This application provides a united view of the switched network, including trunk links and switch ports.
ATMDirector	In ATM networks, this tool facilitates installation and administration.
User Tracking	Cisco switches permit VLAN assignments based on dynamic parameters, including the MAC layer address. User Tracking defines these dynamic VLANs and tracks stations within the network.

SPAN

While Cisco includes SPAN (Switched Port Analyzer) as an in-band management function, in reality it is not. The SPAN port may be used with an external RMON probe or a protocol analyzer. Typically, protocol analysis is used in troubleshooting scenarios, although analyzer features may be helpful in baselining. Via a port configured with SPAN, the administrator may copy the frame flow from another port or the entire VLAN. Recall that switches typically copy frames to a port with the destination MAC address only. SPAN, or port mirroring, copies the data from one port to another—modifying this typical behavior.

Exam Essentials

Understand that there are two connectivity options for managing the Catalyst. Know that in-band and out-of-band connections may be used to configure and administer the Catalyst 5000 series switch, and understand the differences between these two connection options.

Be familiar with the in-band management options. Understand that Telnet, RMON, and SNMP are all in-band management systems. SPAN is not a management option, per se, but is a useful tool for the administrator.

Understand SPAN and its uses. Know that SPAN is Cisco's port-mirroring technology and that both individual ports or an entire VLAN may be mirrored for protocol analysis or RMON probes.

Be familiar with CiscoWorks for Switched Internetworks. Review and understand the various applications included in this SNMP/RMON tool.

Key Terms and Concepts

Baselining: Establishing a reference point for the network in terms of typical traffic load and type. This information is then used in capacity planning and troubleshooting.

In-band management: In-band management uses the same connections as user data to access the managed resource. While this adds to the overall traffic on the LAN/WAN, in-band connections also provide a great deal more bandwidth than out-of-band connections. In-band is used with RMON and SNMP systems.

Out-of-band management: Management using out-of-band connections eliminates the management traffic from the normal data flow. This eliminates the impact of the traffic on user applications and can provide access to the resource in the event of network failure.

RMON: Remote monitoring. Used with SNMP, RMON provides enhanced management functions of network devices. These services are defined to include historical data and real-time packet captures.

SNMP: Simple Network Management Protocol. A method for obtaining information and configuring network devices.

SPAN: Switched Port Analyzer. Cisco's method for mirroring a port within the switch for RMON or protocol analysis. An individual port or the entire VLAN may be copied to the SPAN port.

Sample Questions

1. The Catalyst 5000 switch support for Telnet includes which of the following?

   A. Secure, encrypted Telnet.

   B. A Telnet client.

   C. A Telnet server.

   D. Support for up to eight outbound Telnet sessions.

   E. Telnet is not supported; only SNMP is permitted.

   Answer: B, C, D. The switch operates as both a Telnet client and a server, and up to eight outbound connections are permitted. In the current versions of Catalyst 5000 series software, secured versions of Telnet are not supported. Support for this feature may be added in the future.

2. The Catalyst 5000 switch may be managed from which of the following?

   A. A directly connected console using the CLI

   B. A directly connected console using the CDP

   C. A modem connection configured for PPP protocol and CHAP

   D. An X Window application served by the Supervisor engine

   Answer: A. All of this material wasn't presented in this chapter, but at this point, you should be aware that CDP is Cisco Discovery Protocol and that PPP is unavailable on the switch—it uses SLIP. The switch does not include an X Window feature. Review the other chapters if this question was a problem.

3. Which of the following would be used to add ports to a virtual LAN?

   A. TrafficDirector

   B. ATMDirector

   C. VLANDirector

   D. CLI

   E. VTP

   Answer: C, D.

CHAPTER

10

Troubleshooting the Catalyst
5000 Series Switches

Cisco Exam Objectives Covered in This Chapter

Upon completion of this module, you will be able to:
(pages 199 – 220)

- Describe the approach for troubleshooting Catalyst
- Describe the physical-layer problem areas
- Use the **show** commands to troubleshoot problems
- Describe the switch hardware status
- Describe network test equipment

T

roubleshooting is a pivotal role in the administration of any network device, including the Cisco Catalyst 5000 switches. Because of this, Cisco includes test objectives targeted toward the tools and commands used to research problems involving the Catalyst, in addition to providing some identification of common problem areas.

Also, the objectives include describing the process by which problem diagnostics should proceed. For all of these areas, test preparation should include basic troubleshooting processes and methodologies, in addition to the specifics that will be outlined in this chapter.

Although a single objective, troubleshooting of the Catalyst 5000 series switches is one of the most important topics. In the academic arena, troubleshooting requires a level of understanding that incorporates many of the other exam objectives. In production networks, troubleshooting transcends installation, administration, and design considerations. Administrators should consider troubleshooting concerns in the design phase of the network.

Upon completion of this module, you will be able to:

- Describe the approach for troubleshooting Catalyst
- Describe the physical-layer problem areas
- Use the show commands to troubleshoot problems
- Describe the switch hardware status
- Describe network test equipment

Often, troubleshooting is involved following one of three specific events: Either the installation is new, the installation was changed (intentionally or unintentionally), or a system or component in the installation failed. Given these case scenarios, troubleshooting typically follows a flow that begins with a series of questions. The answers typically provide an indication of what steps to follow in the actual research and diagnostic phases.

Troubleshooting begins with asking simple questions to isolate the scope of the problem. The answers to these questions frequently yield clues as to the areas that may be causing the problem. These questions should include the root cause of the problem, including the details of the problem. For example, knowing if the installation ever worked is as important as knowing if something changed. Changes can be caused by intentional modifications or failure of a device. Knowing the cause at the beginning of the troubleshooting process can save significant amounts of time.

Further, be familiar with the resources available to assist you in the troubleshooting process. For example, the LEDs on the chassis modules can report utilization, line-card status, and failures. Knowing what these lights mean and how to use the information effectively are two important skills to have for the exam. Know that red LEDs typically indicate failure, while orange indicates a problem, and green usually means proper operation.

Finally, be familiar with the power-on sequences of the switch and the POST test. The "Necessary Procedures" section later in this chapter provides details regarding these processes and the output, but know that review of the POST process can be a powerful tool in the troubleshooting arsenal.

Critical Information

The answers to preliminary troubleshooting questions will frequently lead to the cause of the problem. Some of these questions should include:

- Is this installation new or incorporating a system/service that has never been used before?

- Was the configuration (physical or logical) changed recently? This should include changes to other systems in the same site or interconnected logically. For example, a routing-table change could impact devices elsewhere in the network.

- Did a device in the network fail, or is it overloaded?

Once one of these questions has yielded a course of action, proceed along that path. For example, lack of a power light on the switch would direct a different response than a new installation with untested copper wiring.

A useful troubleshooting tool available on the Catalyst 5000/5500 is the LED indicator lights. The LEDs on the Catalyst switch flash and eventually turn green to indicate operational status on power-up. Red LEDs indicate a failure or problem, while orange lights indicate a problem on the module. Troubleshooting should include a quick check of the LEDs to make sure that all are indicating proper operation, and on power-up, the output from the POST should be reviewed for any error indications. During normal operation, the active LED is lit on the active Supervisor, for example.

Describing the Physical-Layer Problem Areas

Switch installations inevitability find wiring problems. Because of this, the CLSC exam objectives include typical problem areas in the physical layer. The majority of the cabling problems discovered involve either poor installation quality or cable lengths beyond the specifications.

Physical-layer problems fall into three categories:

- Determining if the media is within the specifications and length limitations of the protocol used is one of the most important considerations in determining the cause of physical-layer problems. As noted later in this section, each medium (fiber and copper) is rated for a maximum distance. In addition, punch-downs and other interconnection points may impact the performance of the cable. Older installations of Category 3 cable are common, yet will not support FastEthernet.

- Assuming that the physical medium is of the correct type and installation, the troubleshooting process naturally leads to defects in the wiring. Breaks in the wire, in addition to crimps and loose connections, can easily cause connectivity problems. These breaks can occur at punch-down blocks or within the connectors (RJ-45 cubes, for example).

- Lastly, the interface connection to the equipment, including the switch and workstation, needs to be understood. LEDs are frequently available to assist in the troubleshooting process. These LEDs may light even when a crossover cable is used in place of a straight-through connection.

Table 10.1 reflects the distance limitations of CDDI/FDDI, ATM LANE, Ethernet, and Token Ring. These limitations are important to consider in network design and cable plant implementations, in addition to being an area to understand for the Cisco exam objectives.

T A B L E 10.1: Physical Media Distance Limitations

Media/Protocol	Distance
CDDI (CAT 5)	100 meters
FDDI (MM)	2000 meters
FDDI (SM)	30,000 meters
ATM LANE (OC-3 MM)	2000 meters
ATM LANE (OC-3 SM)	10,000 meters
Token Ring (UTP, 16Mbps)	200 meters
Ethernet (CAT 3 or 5)	100 meters
Ethernet (MM)	2000 meters
FastEthernet (CAT 5)	100 meters
FastEthernet (MM Full)	2000 meters
FastEthernet (MM Half)	400 meters
FastEthernet (SM Full)	10,000 meters

NOTE The distance limitations for Gigabit interfaces are being updated as new standards and equipment are developed. Please review the latest information on Cisco's Web site for more details.

The "Describe network test equipment" objective expands upon the various tools that can be used to troubleshoot wiring problems; however, exam takers should be familiar with the following common problems and the tools that could be used to examine these issues. This list provides more detail than the bulleted list at the beginning of this section.

Cross-connect and punch-down points: Are the wires loose, disconnected, broken, or mis-wired? Visual inspection and cable testers should be used to address these issues. In addition, some installations require crossover cables, as opposed to straight-through cables. Is the cable of the correct type? Cables may be damaged in conduits as well. Testers are helpful in locating these problems.

Cable distance: Is the cable beyond the distance limitations? Recall that Category 5 is limited to 100 meters. A TDR (Time Domain Reflectometer) can provide distance information regarding the media.

Link lights: Is there a link light? Does a known good connection work in the port? While the objective focuses on wiring, keep in mind that problems may be caused by interface or hardware issues.

Using the show Commands to Troubleshoot Problems

One of the more helpful commands on the Catalyst 5000 is the show command. This command provides information regarding the status of VLANs, trunks, interfaces, environmental systems, and individual modules. In addition, the MAC addresses in the CAM table are viewable for diagnostics on the bridging process.

To apply this information in the real world, think of how these commands would work in a troubleshooting scenario. Such an event would likely include two workstations not communicating, possibly on the same switch and VLAN. For the exam, continue to think of where the show commands would apply in different situations, and what the output would tell you under those circumstances.

For the exam, also bear in mind that the show commands are tools that can assist in the troubleshooting process. In addition, understand the output of the various show commands and know which commands provide key pieces of information. For example, understand this material at a level where you know that the show interface command reports the SL0 and SC0 virtual interfaces, while the status of each physical port is viewed with the show port command.

While the "Necessary Procedures" section provides examples of the more common show commands, direct experience with the switch greatly assists in the exam preparation process.

Describing the Switch Hardware Status

While software is an important component of the Catalyst 5000 system, the hardware portion of the system is typically part of the troubleshooting process. So, it is included as an objective for the CLSC exam.

Be aware of the hardware dependencies and independencies within the Catalyst 5000 system. For example, recall that the Supervisor engine is critical to the forwarding of packets within the system and that line cards may be removed/replaced hot. This is a great benefit when an individual interface card fails.

In addition, the diagnostic process may include researching failures of individual Logic Units or ASICs. While such failures may cause the entire switch to halt, it is possible to have an individual ASIC fail. This scenario might include forwarding errors or isolation of individual backplanes in the 5500, for example.

Describing Network Test Equipment

While the show, debug, and ping commands are quite powerful, a number of network testing products are available to augment these systems and add to the feature set of the router. These devices include physical media testers and protocol analyzers, which can capture each frame for further analysis.

Be familiar with the devices that can assist you with the troubleshooting process. Such devices include the following:

Time Domain Reflectometer: A Time Domain Reflectometer, or TDR, is used to measure the length of a cable and the electrical resistance, or impedance. Recall that as switches are installed, copper media is frequently asked to support FastEthernet connections. While exceeding the 100-meter distance limitation may work for 10Mbps Ethernet, errors may prevent such installations from supporting 100Mbps. A TDR can quickly validate the distance of the cable. Fiber-optic TDRs are called OTDRs (Optical Time Domain Reflectometers).

Cable tester: Many cable testers include a TDR function; however, these devices expand upon the TDR role and can be used to diagnose layer 2 and layer 3 issues. A good cable tester can also be used by workstation support staff to verify that the port is mapped to the correct VLAN.

Network monitor: Network monitors can provide a great deal of historical information regarding the network, including traffic by station and protocol. While the actual packet is not stored for further review, the monitor can provide baseline information and trend data as it continuously monitors network traffic.

Protocol analyzer: Protocol analyzers are capable of capturing and displaying entire frames/packets for review. This function provides the administrator with the opportunity to diagnose different layers separately, and to identify specific points in the file transfer where errors occur. Also called Sniffers (a trade name of Network Associates/Network General), these devices are well suited to layer 3 and higher problems.

Necessary Procedures

The commands in this section are provided to augment an understanding of the troubleshooting process on the Catalyst 5000 system. Please review them with attention to how the commands are used and information provided by each command. Think about how the commands might be used in real-world troubleshooting processes. These commands should afford the reader with a broad overview of the tools available and how they would be used.

The reset Command

The Catalyst switch may be reloaded with the reset command. This command causes the operating software to reload and is comparable to a power-on. When troubleshooting, it may be helpful to reload the switch to see if the problem clears up—even if the problem is unrelated to the switch, the blockage of packets will sometimes cause the problem station to reset. Please note the output of the POST test included in the following:

```
Switch_A> (enable) reset

This command will reset the system.
Do you want to continue (y/n) [n]? y

Switch_A> (enable)
System Bootstrap, Version 3.1(2)
Copyright (c) 1994-1997 by cisco Systems, Inc.
Presto processor with 32768 Kbytes of main memory

Autoboot executing command: "boot bootflash:cat5000-sup3.4-5-1.bin"

System Power On Diagnostics
NVRAM Size ..................512KB
ID Prom Test ................Passed
DPRAM Size ..................16KB
DPRAM Data 0x55 Test ........Passed
DPRAM Data 0xaa Test ........Passed
DPRAM Address Test ..........Passed
Clearing DPRAM ..............Done
System DRAM Memory Size ......32MB
DRAM Data 0x55 Test .........Passed
DRAM Data 0xaa Test .........Passed
DRAM Address Test ...........Passed
Clearing DRAM ...............Done
EARLII ......................Present
EARLII RAM Test .............Passed
EARL Serial Prom Test .......Passed
Level2 Cache ................Present
Level2 Cache test...........Passed

Boot image: bootflash:cat5000-sup3.4-5-1.bin
Downloading epld sram device please wait ...
Programming successful for Altera 10K50 SRAM EPLD

Running System Diagnostics from this Supervisor (Module 1)
This may take up to 2 minutes....please wait

1999 Feb 08 14:21:52 Pacific -08:00 %SYS-5-MOD_OK:Module 1 is online
```

TIP   In addition to using the **reset** command, which reloads the entire switch, it is also possible to reload an individual module. This can augment troubleshooting efforts.

NOTE   While the switch includes a wide array of **show** commands, some are more common than others. As stated previously, firsthand experience with the switch is desirable.

The show config **Command**

The show config command displays the current configuration of the switch. This output has been abbreviated for space.

```
Switch_A> (enable) show config

begin
!
#version 4.5(1)
!
set password $1$FMFQ$HfZR5DUszVHIRhrz4h6V70
set enablepass $1$FMFQ$HfZR5DUszVHIRhrz4h6V70
set prompt Console>
set length 24 default
set logout 20
set banner motd ^C^C
!
#system
set system baud  9600
set system modem disable
set system name  Switch_A
set system location Maui, Hawaii
set system contact
!
```

```
#snmp
set snmp community read-only       public
set snmp community read-write      private
set snmp community read-write-all secret
set snmp rmon disable
set snmp trap disable module
set snmp trap disable chassis
set snmp trap disable bridge
set snmp trap disable repeater
set snmp trap disable vtp
set snmp trap disable auth
set snmp trap disable ippermit
set snmp trap disable vmps
set snmp trap disable entity
set snmp trap disable config
set snmp trap disable stpx
set snmp trap disable syslog
set snmp extendedrmon netflow disable
set snmp extendedrmon vlanmode disable
set snmp extendedrmon vlanagent disable
set snmp extendedrmon enable
!
#ip
set interface sc0 1 10.1.1.10 255.255.255.0 10.1.1.255

set interface sc0 up
set interface sl0 10.1.1.254 255.255.255.0
set interface sl0 down
set arp agingtime 1200
set ip redirect    enable
set ip unreachable    enable
set ip fragmentation enable
set ip route 0.0.0.0          10.1.1.1      1
set ip alias default         0.0.0.0
!
```

```
#Command alias
!
#vmps
set vmps server retry 3
set vmps server reconfirminterval 60
set vmps tftpserver 0.0.0.0 vmps-config-database.1
set vmps state disable
!
#dns
set ip dns disable
!
#tacacs+
set tacacs attempts 3
set tacacs directedrequest disable
set tacacs timeout 5
!
#authentication
set authentication login tacacs disable console
set authentication login tacacs disable telnet
set authentication enable tacacs disable console
set authentication enable tacacs disable telnet
set authentication login local enable console
set authentication login local enable telnet
set authentication enable local enable console
set authentication enable local enable telnet
!
#bridge
set bridge ipx snaptoether    8023raw
set bridge ipx 8022toether    8023
set bridge ipx 8023rawtofddi snap
!
#vtp
set vtp domain Domain
set vtp mode client
set vtp pruneeligible 2-1000
clear vtp pruneeligible 1001-1005
!
```

```
#spantree
#uplinkfast groups
set spantree uplinkfast disable
#backbonefast
set spantree backbonefast disable
set spantree enable  all
#vlan 1
set spantree fwddelay 15    1
set spantree hello    2     1
set spantree maxage   20    1
set spantree priority 32768 1
```

The show interface Command

Unlike the router, a Catalyst switch does not include physical ports as interfaces. The show interface command provides information regarding the in-band SC0 interface and the SLIP SL0 interface.

```
Switch_A> (enable) show interface

sl0: flags=51<UP,POINTOPOINT,RUNNING>
        slip 10.1.2.254 dest 255.255.255.0
sc0: flags=63<UP,BROADCAST,RUNNING>
vlan 1 inet 10.1.1.10 netmask 255.255.255.0
broadcast 10.1.1.255
```

The show module Command

While the output here is abbreviated, the show module command provides information regarding the individual modules in the chassis including serial number, model, number of ports, and position within the chassis.

```
Switch_A> (enable) show module
```

Mod	Ports	Module-Type	Model	Serial-Num	Status
1	2	100BaseFX MMF Supervi	WS-X5530	013481217	ok
2	12	100BaseFX MM Ethernet	WS-X5201R	013387240	ok
3	1	Network Analysis/RMON	WS-X5380	012771226	ok
4	24	10/100BaseTX Ethernet	WS-X5225R	013420561	ok

The show spantree **Command**

The show spantree command provides information regarding the Spanning-Tree Protocol and the status of the process. This output shows that the switch is the root bridge, and that the ports are in a forwarding state.

```
Switch_A> (enable) show spantree


VLAN 1
Spanning tree enabled
Spanning tree type          ieee


Designated Root             00-50-f0-1b-31-00
Designated Root Priority    0
Designated Root Cost        0
Designated Root Port        1/0
Root Max Age 20 sec    Hello Time 2 sec Forward Delay 15 sec


Bridge ID MAC ADDR          00-50-f0-1b-31-00
Bridge ID Priority          0
Bridge Max Age 20 sec Hello Time 2 sec Forward Delay 15 sec


Port Vlan  Port-State Cost Priority
1/1    1  forwarding  19      32
1/2    1  forwarding  19      32
```

The show trunk **Command**

The show trunk command reports the status of all ports running a trunking protocol. Note that ISL is configured on both ports.

```
Switch_A> (enable) show trunk

Port    Mode    Encapsulation  Status    Native vlan
1/1     on      isl            trunking  1
1/2     on      isl            trunking  1
```

```
Port       Vlans allowed on trunk
1/1        1-1005
1/2        1-1005


Port       Vlans allowed and active in management domain
1/1        1-1005
1/2        1-1005
```

The show vlan Command

To view the status of the various VLANs on the switch and the ports bound to the VLAN, use the show vlan command. This command also reports the name and number of the VLAN. Note that no ports are bound to the Marketing VLAN.

Switch_A> (enable) **show vlan**

VLAN	Name	Status	IfIndex	Mod/Ports, Vlans
1	default	active	5	2/1-12
2	Marketing	active	23	

The show port Command

The show port command provides information regarding the speed, duplex, VLAN membership, trunk status, and connection for each physical port on the switch. Note that port 2/1 is a member of VLAN1, while the other ports are configured for trunking. This output is truncated from the original.

Switch_A> (enable) **show port**

Port	Status	Vlan	Level	Duplex	Speed	Type
1/1	connected	trunk	normal	full	100	100BaseFX MM
1/2	connected	trunk	normal	full	100	100BaseFX MM
2/1	connected	1	high	full	100	100BaseFX MM

The show cam dynamic Command

To view the MAC layer addresses on each port, use the show cam dynamic command. This command is useful in locating errors in the

forwarding database and duplicate MAC addresses, in addition to
bridging loops.

```
Switch_A> (enable) show cam dynamic

VLAN  Dest MAC/Route Des  Dest Ports or VCs/[Protocol Type]

2     00-d0-06-c4-10-00   1/2 [ALL]
1     00-50-f0-d5-b3-ff   1/1 [ALL]
3     00-00-0c-17-ad-83   1/1 [ALL]
```

The show ip route Command

The SC0 and SL0 interface routing table may be viewed with the show
ip route command.

```
Switch_A> (enable) show ip route

Fragmentation   Redirect   Unreachable
enabled         enabled    enabled

The primary gateway: 10.129.1.1

Destination     Gateway          Flags   Use     Interface
default         10.129.1.1       UG      3837    sc0
10.129.1.0      10.129.1.10      U       4388    sc0
255.255.255.0   10.129.1.254     UH      0       sl0
```

The show system Command

The show system command provides information regarding the
status of CPU utilization, power-supply availability, and system
location.

```
Switch_A> (enable) show system

PS1-Status PS2-Status Fan-Status Temp-Alarm Sys-Status
ok         ok         ok         off        ok
```

```
PS1-Type   PS2-Type   Modem   Baud  Traffic Peak
WS-C5508   WS-C5508   disable 9600  0%      0%


System Name    System Location        System Contact
Switch_A       Maui, Hawaii
```

The show log Command

The show log command provides information regarding failures and errors in the system. In addition, the number of resets and their times are included.

```
Switch_A> (enable) show log

Network Management Processor (ACTIVE NMP) Log:
  Reset count:   3
  Re-boot History:
  May 25 1999 11:34:15 0
  May 25 1999 10:30:36 0
  Jan 17 2000 18:13:55 0

  Bootrom Checksum Failures:      0
  UART Failures:                  0
  Flash Checksum Failures:        0
  Flash Program Failures:         0
  Power Supply 1 Failures:        3
  Power Supply 2 Failures:        4
  Swapped to CLKA:                0
  Swapped to CLKB:                0
  Swapped to Processor 1:         0
  Swapped to Processor 2:         0
  DRAM Failures:                  0
  Exceptions:                     0
  MCP Exceptions/Hang:            0

Heap Memory Log:
Corrupted Block = none
```

The show test Command

The show test command is well suited to displaying the hardware status of the Catalyst 5000/5500 system.

TIP Use this command and the other **show** commands outlined in this chapter on a real switch before taking the exam.

```
Switch_A> (enable) show test

Environmental Status (. = Pass, F = Fail,
   U = Unknown, N = Not Present)
   PS (3.3V):   N   PS (12V): .   PS (24V):   .
   PS1: .     PS2: F
   PS1 Fan:      .   PS2 Fan : F   Clock(A/B): A
   Chassis-Ser-EEPROM: .
   Temperature: .   Fan:      .

Module 1 : 2-port 100BaseFX MMF Supervisor
Network Management Processor (NMP) Status:
   ( . = Pass, F = Fail, U = Unknown)
   ROM:  .   Flash-EEPROM: .   Ser-EEPROM: .   NVRAM: .   MCP Comm: .

   EARL III Status :
DisableIndexLearnTest:   .
DontLearnTest:           .
DisableNewLearnTest:     .
ConditionalLearnTest:    .
MonitorColorFloodTest:   .
EarlTrapTest:            .
StaticMacAndTypeTest:    .
BadDvlanTest:            .
BadBpduTest:             .
IndexMatchTest:          .
ProtocolTypeTest:        .
IgmpTest:                .
SourceMissTest:          .
```

Exam Essentials

Know the right questions to ask when starting the trouble-shooting process. Understand the problem-determination process and the process of elimination used by administrators in trouble-shooting. This process should include methods for eliminating potential problem causes.

Understand the LEDs on the switch and how to use them in the troubleshooting process. Review the significance of the LED colors and the steps by which lights illuminate. Understanding how to use these tools, along with the show commands and other diagnostic systems, is essential to the administration of the Catalyst system.

Understand the distance limitations for different protocols over various media. You should be familiar with the distances permitted with different protocols and media in network design and trouble-shooting. For example, most Category 5 specifications call for a maximum distance of 100 meters.

Be able to state the various ways to troubleshoot wiring problems and to describe the common wiring issues. Be able to list the common problems noted previously and the steps and tools to locate these problems. Common problems and issues include improperly terminated cables and cables beyond the specified distance.

Know which show commands to use in different situations. The specific output of some show commands is provided in the "Necessary Procedures" section. When reviewing these items, consider when it would be necessary to use such a command. For example, bridging loops would be best researched with the show spantree command. A high number of collisions and CRC errors would likely be solved with the show port command.

Understand the output of the show commands. Be able to read the speed and duplex output of the show port command, for example. Understanding how to read the output of the show commands will greatly assist in real-world applications of this material;

however, it can also assist in knowing which command to use for each troubleshooting step.

Realize that the Catalyst is designed to prevent complete failure. Understand that the failure of an individual line module is designed to impact only that module and not the entire switch. In addition, failed components can be swapped online.

Know that a number of commands and visual indicators are provided to assist troubleshooting. Understand the show commands outlined previously, including the function of each command—for example, the show test command will report the status of various diagnostics on the switch. Also, LEDs are provided to visually indicate the status of the switch.

Understand that in addition to the router functions, a number of tools are available to test the network. Know that cable testers, TDRs, protocol analyzers, and network monitors are all tools that can diagnose the health of the network and resolve problems. Solid network documentation can further augment these tools.

Key Terms and Concepts

ASIC: Application Specific Integrated Circuit. An ASIC provides wire-speed processing of packets through the switch. The SAINT, SAGE, and Phoenix are all ASICs in the Catalyst system.

Duplex: The capacity to transmit information between a sending station and a receiving unit at the same time is called full-duplex. Half-duplex permits only transmission or reception at one time.

Failure scenario: In network design, the projected results of a partial or complete system failure. In troubleshooting, the isolation of the problem scope should incorporate the failure scenario. This is accomplished via understanding cause and effect within the problem. For example, a group of 24 workstations failing would likely be related to the failure of a single module in the switch.

LED: Light-emitting diode. A light source that, on the Catalyst hardware, illuminates to provide diagnostic information.

POST: Power On Self Test. A diagnostic process that computing devices execute on startup to verify correct operation.

Punch-down: A point where individual wires are terminated onto a wiring block. Typically, such blocks are called 66 or 110 blocks, from their telco origins.

TDR: Time Domain Reflectometer. A device to measure cable length and impedance.

Telco: Shorthand for telecommunications. Frequently used to refer to the local telephone company.

Sample Questions

1. A steady green active light is displayed on the Supervisor module. What does this mean?

   A. The Supervisor is active and functioning.

   B. The Supervisor has failed.

   C. All modules on the switch are functioning.

   D. The switch is operating at 100%. The light should flicker under normal operation to represent load.

   Answer: A. The active light indicates an active Supervisor.

2. The Supervisor fails to load in a new installation. To find the cause, what should the administrator do?

   A. Replace the Supervisor engine.

   B. Unplug all connections from the switch and reload.

   C. Observe the POST output.

   D. Use the debug utility on the switch.

   Answer: C. The POST reports failures with the system.

3. For FastEthernet, what is the longest approved copper media length and type?

   A. CAT 3, 100 meters

   B. CAT 3, 10 meters

   C. CAT 4, 100 meters

   D. CAT 5, 100 meters

   Answer: D. FastEthernet specifies the use of Category 5 cable with a maximum distance of 100 meters.

4. Which of the following are common cable problems?

   A. Substitution of Category 3 cable for FastEthernet

   B. Broken wires in patch panels or other interconnect points

   C. Crossover cables confused for straight-through ones

   D. Crimped cables in conduit

   E. All of the above

   Answer: E. Each of these items is a common cause of cable problems.

5. Which command would report the port speed and duplex?

   A. show spantree

   B. show port

   C. show system

   D. show speed duplex

   Answer: B. The show port command is used to display the port speed, duplex, trunk status, and VLAN membership.

6. The show log command displays which of the following?

   A. All RMON error statistics

   B. Power-supply errors

   C. The spanning-tree configuration

   D. The time of the last reset

   Answer: D. The command provides information regarding the last reset and system failures.

7. The show test command displays which of the following?

   A. Power-supply status

   B. NVRAM test information

   C. Fan-system status

   D. EARL status

   E. All of the above

   Answer: E.

CHAPTER

11

Catalyst 5000 Series Switch
FDDI Module

Cisco Exam Objectives Covered in This Chapter

▶ **Describe the major features and functions of the Catalyst 5000 FDDI/CDDI Module.** *(pages 223 – 231)*

▶ **Describe IEEE 802.10 VLANs.** *(pages 231 – 235)*

▶ **Configure the Catalyst 5000 FDDI/CDDI Module.** *(pages 236 – 241)*

T his chapter will cover the features, functions, and configuration of the Catalyst 5000 FDDI/CDDI modules. It will also describe IEEE 802.10 VLANs and how they can be used to internetwork FDDI/CDDI VLANs with Ethernet ISL VLANs and ATM ELANs.

The chapter will begin with a quick review of FDDI technology, go through the features of the FDDI/CDDI modules including in-depth coverage of APaRT and fddicheck, then move on to overviews of the three different available modules and cursory examinations of two major categories of use for the modules.

After that, the IEEE 802.10 protocol to the level of detail necessary to understand how it can be utilized to provide VLAN capability over FDDI and CDDI rings; the general concept of associating 802.10 VLANs with Ethernet VLANs; the recommended use of a VLAN numbering scheme; the overall principle of mapping Ethernet and FDDI VLANs together; and the management support built-in to the modules will all be examined.

Finally, the default configuration for the modules, how to customize the configuration, and the considerations of whether to disable APaRT and/or enable fddicheck will be covered.

It is important to understand the characteristics of these modules and protocols not just for the exam, but also because FDDI and, to a lesser degree, CDDI were once very popular core technologies in many data centers and campus networks.

This chapter is important because although FDDI and CDDI are not commonly implemented anymore, it is highly likely that you will encounter them in legacy environments and be asked to come up with a way to migrate from the legacy environment to, or least interoperate with, newer internetworking technologies—e.g., switched FastEthernet and ATM.

Describe the major features and functions of the Catalyst 5000 FDDI/CDDI Module.

This objective will very briefly review FDDI technology and list the features of the modules, then explore both APaRT and fddicheck in more detail, proceeding to descriptions of the three different types of available modules focusing on media supported, transmission distances, and how to interpret the LEDs. In closing, a brief overview of the two major categories of use for the modules and the features important to the two scenarios will be discussed.

On the exam and in production, being knowledgeable about the features and functions of the FDDI/CDDI modules is important because knowing both the capabilities and limitations of any device you propose to deploy into an internetwork is an extremely important part of knowing whether the device will provide the solution you have in mind.

Critical Information

The American National Standards Institute (ANSI) X3T9.5 specifies FDDI as a 100Mbps, token-passing LAN standard using multimode fiber-optic cabling, with transmission distances of up to 2 kilometers, arranged in a dual-ring architecture for redundancy. Copper Distributed Data Interface (CDDI) is the implementation of Fiber Distributed Data Interface (FDDI) protocols over Shielded

Twisted Pair (STP) and Unshielded Twisted Pair (UTP) based on the ANSI Twisted Pair-Physical Medium Dependent (TP-PMD) standard. CDDI also uses a dual-ring architecture for redundancy and operates at 100Mbps, but is limited to transmission distances of approximately 100 meters.

The major features and functions of the FDDI/CDDI modules include:

- 85,000 packets per second (pps) translational bridging between FDDI and Ethernet
- Ability to participate in up to 1000 IEEE 802.10 VLANs
- IEEE 802.1d Spanning-Tree Algorithm
- Cisco Discovery Protocol (CDP)
- VLAN Trunking Protocol (VTP)
- Up to 4000 active MAC addresses
- A variety of connectors and media types
- The ability to have multiple modules in the same chassis
- MTU discovery
- APaRT
- fddicheck

The FDDI module is an FDDI-Ethernet translational switch, as opposed to an FDDI concentrator or true FDDI switch. In an FDDI concentrator, the major goal is increased FDDI port density, and in a true FDDI switch, frames are switched in FDDI format between FDDI ports. The FDDI module translates packets on the attached FDDI ring into Ethernet packets within the Catalyst 5000, even between two FDDI ports.

The Catalyst 5000 series switch supports up to 1000 VLANs, IEEE 802.1d Spanning-Tree Protocol, Cisco Discovery Protocol, and VLAN Trunking Protocol as features of the overall platform, so these are not features of the FDDI module per se. The three different available modules and the connector and the media options they support will be covered later in this objective. The module uses the MTU discovery protocol to determine the maximum size of packets allowed by each interface. The Catalyst 5000 will enable any end hosts running MTU discovery to discover the maximum allowable MTU size of the various links along the path.

APaRT

The Automated Packet Recognition and Translation (APaRT) uses Content Addressable Memory (CAM) entries on the FDDI or CDDI module to associate a specific layer 2 frame type with each MAC address. This enables it to automatically translate frames being transferred between FDDI/CDDI and Ethernet to the native format of the destination device—e.g., Ethernet 802.3, FDDI_802.2, Ethernet II, Raw, FDDI_SNAP, or Ethernet_SNAP. This allows nodes to be attached to CDDI or FDDI without having to reconfigure applications or network protocols.

Fddicheck

Fddicheck was created to solve a very specific, potentially critical problem. FDDI/CDDI specifications require that, to transmit, a station must possess the token and transmit two void frames after every data frame it transmits.

The specifications further require that in the interim between transmission of the data frame and receipt of a void frame, which should be the frame immediately following the return of the originally transmitted data frame, the station should strip all data frames from the ring as they are considered spurious. However, older, noncompliant FDDI/CDDI stations sometimes transmit spurious void frames even though they are not in possession of the token. This can lead a compliant station, such as the Catalyst 5000 FDDI/CDDI module, to receive a void frame prior to its originally transmitted data frame circumnavigating the ring. This causes the compliant station to stop stripping frames from the ring, which results in two things:

- The originally transmitted data frame is *not* stripped and can theoretically circle the ring forever, consuming valuable bandwidth.

- If the originally transmitted data frame were placed on the ring via translational bridging from a non-FDDI/CDDI source station, the source address in the frame would now incorrectly be interpreted as being part of the FDDI/CDDI ring. Frames destined for that address will no longer be forwarded, but rather repeated back on to the ring, effectively severing communications between the node at that address and the FDDI/CDDI ring.

To prevent this loss of connectivity, fddicheck examines the module's CAM and discards frames incoming from the FDDI ring if the source address in the FDDI frame was learned on the non-FDDI side. However, if APaRT is disabled, fddicheck is automatically disabled.

The FDDI and CDDI backbone modules are available in a variety of connector/media options:

- RJ-45 connector, Category 5 UTP (CDDI)

- MIC connector(s), multimode fiber

- ST connectors, single-mode fiber

CDDI Module

The CDDI module provides a single- or dual-attachment station (SAS or DAS) connection via two female RJ-45 connectors used for connecting to the 100Mbps CDDI ring with Category 5 UTP over a maximum distance of approximately 100 meters. The LEDs on the module provide status indications for the module and each port as follows:

Status LED: Green if all self and diagnostic tests pass. Red if any test, other than an individual port test, fails. Orange if the module is disabled, and during system boot and self-test diagnostics.

RingOp LED: Green if the ring is operational. Off if the ring is not operational.

Thru LED: Green if the FDDI/CDDI A and B ports are connected to the primary and secondary rings. Off otherwise.

Wrap A LED: Green if the FDDI/CDDI A port is connected to the ring and the B port is isolated. Off otherwise.

Wrap B LED: Green if the FDDI/CDDI B port is connected to the ring and the A port is isolated. Off otherwise.

A Port Status LED: Green if the A port is connected to the ring. Orange if the A port receives a signal but fails to connect or a dual homing condition exists. Off if no receive signal is detected on the A port.

B Port Status LED: Green if the B port is connected to the ring. Orange if the B port receives a signal but fails to connect or a dual homing condition exists. Off if no receive signal is detected on the B port.

The FDDI MMF module provides an SAS or DAS to the FDDI ring via two MIC connectors used with 62.5/125-micron multimode fiber-optic cables over a maximum transmission distance of 2 kilometers. It also has a six-pin min-DIN connector for connecting an external optical bypass switch to the module. An optical bypass switch can prevent the ring segmentation that occurs when there are multiple ring failures by bypassing, instead of wrapping, failed stations from the ring.

For example, when two ring failures occur, the ring would normally be wrapped in both cases, effectively segmenting the ring into two separate rings incapable of communicating with each other. Additional failures cause further ring segmentation. By bypassing the failed node instead of having the switch or concentrator wrap it, an optical bypass switch prevents ring segmentation.

NOTE   If you install or remove an optical bypass switch, you must reset the FDDI module.

The LEDs on the front provide status information for the module and the individual FDDI ports. They are identical to the LEDs detailed under the CDDI module above, with the addition of the following LED:

Optical Bypass in LED: On when the external optical bypass switch is activated and is in Thru mode. Off otherwise.

The single-mode fiber FDDI module provides an SAS or DAS connection to the FDDI backbone via two pairs of straight-tip (ST) connectors used with 8/125-micron single-mode fiber-optic cabling over a transmission distance of up to 32 kilometers. Similar to the FDDI MMF module, the FDDI SMF module comes with a six-pin min-DIN external optical bypass switch connector.

The most basic use of the FDDI/CDDI line modules is connecting Ethernet stations to an FDDI backbone. In this role, the key features are IP fragmentation, where frames from the FDDI backbone larger than the maximum frame size for Ethernet are divided into legal-sized frames, and APaRT. The other common use for the FDDI/CDDI modules is integration of multiple legacy rings into heterogeneous environments utilizing VLAN technology. The key features for this role are the ability to support multiple FDDI/CDDI modules in the same chassis and the VLAN capability provided by the IEEE 802.10 protocol.

Exam Essentials

Know that the FDDI/CDDI module is not an FDDI concentrator or true FDDI switch. The FDDI module is an FDDI-Ethernet translational switch and translates packets on the attached FDDI ring into Ethernet packets within the Catalyst 5000, even between two FDDI ports, at a rate of up to 85,000 packets per second (pps).

Remember what the APaRT does. The Automated Packet Recognition and Translation (APaRT) associates a frame type with each MAC address.

Understand how fddicheck compensates for the "spurious void frame" problem. It discards frames seen on the FDDI ring if the frame's source address was learned on the non-FDDI side.

Know the types of media and connectors supported and the transmission distances supported by each media. They are as follows:

- The CDDI module supports Category 5 Unshielded Twisted Pair (UTP) via RJ-45 connectors and is capable of transmitting up to 100 meters over this media.

- The FDDI MMF module supports multimode fiber (MMF) via Media Interface Connectors (MICs) and is capable of transmitting up to 2000 meters (2 kilometers) over this media.

- The FDDI SMF module supports single-mode fiber (SMF) via straight-tip (ST) connectors and is capable of transmitting up to 32,000 meters (32 kilometers) over this media.

Remember that more than one FDDI/CDDI module can be supported in the same chassis. This feature is considered the key to integrating multiple legacy rings into a heterogeneous environment.

Key Terms and Concepts

APaRT: Automated Packet Recognition and Translation. Associates a frame type with each MAC address in FDDI networks.

fddicheck: Specially developed feature designed to overcome the "spurious void frame" problem by discarding frames seen on the FDDI ring if the frame's source address was learned on the non-FDDI side.

Raw: A reference to a frame type that preceded the finalization of the IEEE 802.3 specification—the primary difference being the lack of any 802.2 LLC functionality.

Sample Questions

1. What protocol makes it possible to provide VLAN functionality on the FDDI/CDDI modules?

   A. 802.3

   B. 802.1d

   C. 802.10

   D. 802.2

   Answer: C. The Security Association Identifier (SAID) field in the Clear Header portion of 802.10 can be used to carry VLAN numbers.

2. What is the function of the APaRT?

   A. To separate FDDI rings that are on different VLANs

   B. To associate a specific layer 2 frame type with each MAC address in the module's CAM

   C. To translate frames transferred between FDDI/CDDI and Ethernet to the destination device's native frame format

   D. Both B and C

   Answer: D. By associating a specific layer 2 frame type with each MAC address in the FDDI/CDDI module's CAM, the APaRT can translate frames being transferred between FDDI/CDDI and Ethernet to the destination device's native frame format.

3. What problem was fddicheck designed to overcome?

A. Incompatible frame check sequences between older and newer FDDI devices

B. Failure of older FDDI devices to remove their frames from the ring

C. Fragmentation of FDDI frames translationally bridged to Ethernet that are larger than the Ethernet MTU

D. Transmission of spurious void frames by older FDDI/CDDI devices causing the module not to strip frames it transmitted off the ring and incorrectly adding non-FDDI/CDDI source addresses to its CAM for the FDDI/CDDI port

Answer: D. fddicheck overcomes the "spurious void frame" problem by discarding frames seen on the FDDI ring if the frame's source address was learned on the non-FDDI side.

Describe IEEE 802.10 VLANs.

This objective explores the IEEE 802.10 protocol in some detail and covers how the Security Association Identifier field of the Clear Header portion of the frame can be used to create VLANs on FDDI/CDDI rings. The general concept of how 802.10 VLANs are associated with Ethernet VLANs, numbering schema for VLANs, an overview of mapping FDDI and Ethernet VLANs together, and the management support built-in to the modules will also be examined.

Understanding the concepts presented in this objective is crucial to understanding later coverage of how to actually configure the modules, which, in turn, is critical both on the exam and in the real world.

Critical Information

FDDI networks can be integrated into enterprisewide VLAN architectures by using the 802.10 protocol on Cisco routers and switches. By using Cisco's VLAN network management software and the VLAN Trunking Protocol, it is possible to map ISL, ATM emulated LANs, and 802.10 VLANs together to provide a way for VLANs to propagate over a variety of media types.

Originally conceived to address the growing need for security within shared LAN/metropolitan-area network (MAN) environments, the IEEE 802.10 Interoperable LAN/MAN Security (SLS) standard incorporates authentication and encryption techniques to ensure data integrity and confidentiality throughout the network. Ratified in late 1992, the SLS standard functions at the Data Link layer of the OSI reference model, so it is well-suited to low-latency, high-throughput switching environments.

An inner header, known as the Protected Header, and an outer header, known as the Clear Header, comprise the 802.10 header. The Protected Header through the ICV may be encrypted. The Protected Header contains a duplicate of the source address contained in the MAC header to allow for address validation, which prevents another node from attempting to identify itself as the real source of the frame (i.e., spoofing). Support for each portion of the 802.10 header, including encryption, is optional.

The protocol can be used with a Security Management Information Base (SMIB) when used to fully secure data transfer across shared media. The SMIB provides the Security Association Identifier (SAID) and encryption keys used by LAN devices to exchange data within the same secured virtual community.

The 802.10 frame's Clear Header is preceded by a 3-byte IEEE 802.2 LSAP indicating an 802.10 VLAN frame, and contains a 4-byte Security Association Identifier (SAID) and an optional Management-Defined Field (MDF), which can carry information to facilitate PDU processing. VLAN ID is the essential piece of required header information when any protocol is used to effect a VLAN topology.

The 802.10 SAID field is used as the VLAN ID and identifies traffic as belonging to a particular 802.10 VLAN. Forwarding decisions based on which interfaces are configured for which VLANs can then be made by internetworking devices with VLAN intelligence—e.g., the Catalyst 5000. Therefore, when incurring the performance penalties brought about by applying security algorithms to encrypt the data is undesirable and only the establishment of logical VLAN topologies across a physical network is the goal, high-throughput devices must minimally support only the Clear Header portion of the 802.10 frame format. In this case, only the SDE Designator (3-byte 802.2 LSAP indicating 802.10 VLAN frame) and the actual VLAN ID (4-byte SAID field) must be carried, which adds the advantage of low processing overhead.

The 4-byte SAID allows for 2^{32}, or 4,294,967,296 (4.29 billion), distinct VLANs, making it possible to configure ports for multiple VLANs and, in the future, potentially extend the criteria for VLAN membership to interface and protocol, for example.

FDDI 802.10 SAIDs are associated by the Catalyst 5000 with non-FDDI VLANs to form a single broadcast domain. Native frames that originate from stations assigned non-FDDI VLANs and whose destination address is on an 802.10 FDDI ring acquire an 802.10 header that contains the appropriate VLAN ID (SAID) as the frames are forwarded on to the FDDI ring.

When a new non-FDDI VLAN is created, the Catalyst 5000 software anticipates that it will be mapped to FDDI 802.10 VLAN and assigns it a SAID. The default SAID value that it selects is the non-FDDI VLAN number plus 100,000. However, with the exception of needing to configure a router interface with SDE encapsulation, it is not necessary to note this value. Only the FDDI VLAN that is created and subsequently mapped to it will join its broadcast domain.

When two or more Catalyst 5000s are connected by an FDDI ring, the 802.10 protocol's ability to carry VLAN identifiers (the SAID) in each frame enables the FDDI/CDDI interfaces to act as interswitch trunks. This makes it possible to extend logical broadcast domains (VLANs) across an FDDI network.

Exam Essentials

Know what software release 802.10 functionality first became available in. The 802.10 functionality requires Catalyst 5000 NMP Release 2.1 and FDDI module Software Release 2.1.

Remember which part of the 802.10 frame contains the SAID. The Clear Header includes the 4-byte Security Association Identifier (SAID) field as well as the optional Management-Defined Field (MDF).

Remember how many VLANs the 4-byte SAID allows for. Four bytes is 32 bits. 2^{32} equals 4,294,967,296, or roughly 4.29 billion possible VLANs.

Key Terms and Concepts

APaRT: Automated Packet Recognition and Translation. Associates a frame type with each MAC address in FDDI networks.

fddicheck: Specially developed feature designed to overcome the "spurious void frame" problem by discarding frames seen on the FDDI ring if the frame's source address was learned on the non-FDDI side.

SAID: Security Association Identifier that can identify up to 4.29 billion possible VLANs.

Sample Questions

1. What release of Catalyst 5000 NMP and FDDI module software is required for 802.10 functionality?

   A. 4.2

   B. 2.1

   C. 2.4

   D. 3.1

   Answer: B. 802.10 functionality requires Catalyst 5000 NMP Release 2.1 and FDDI module Software Release 2.1.

2. In what portion of the 802.10 frame is the SAID contained?

   A. Clear Header

   B. Protected Header

   C. ICV

   D. LSAP

   Answer: A. The Clear Header includes the Security Association Identifier (SAID) and an optional Management-Defined Field (MDF).

3. What is the maximum number of VLANs that may be defined using the SAID?

   A. 1000

   B. 32

   C. 2

   D. 4.29 billion

   Answer: D. The 4-byte SAID field allows for 2^{32}, or approximately 4.29 billion, Security Association Identifiers.

Configure the Catalyst 5000 FDDI/CDDI Module.

The default configuration, which is adequate for most applications, of the FDDI/CDDI module and how to customize various facets of it will be covered in this objective. The configurable settings are numerous, but the focus will be on setting the port name, creating FDDI VLANs, assigning VLANs to ports, displaying VLAN information, mapping Ethernet VLANs to FDDI VLANs and vice versa, establishing and verifying trunking operation on ports, disabling APaRT with verification, and enabling fddicheck with verification. Prior to covering the disabling of APaRT and the enabling of fddicheck, the considerations for taking either of these actions will be reviewed.

As you well know, being familiar with concepts without actually knowing how to apply them is of little value. Consequently, learning the configuration commands and decision processes presented in this objective are important to success in production environments as well as on the exam.

Critical Information

The configurable features of the FDDI/CDDI modules have default values that were selected to work in the most common environments. The default values are as follows:

- All FDDI/CDDI ports are enabled.

- Default IPX protocol translations are as follows: Ethernet 802.3 Raw to FDDI SNAP, FDDI 802.2 to Ethernet 802.3, and FDDI SNAP to Ethernet 802.3 Raw.

- The TL_MIN parameter sets the minimum time to transmit a FDDI physical sublayer (PHY) line state before advancing to the next physical connection management (PCM) state. Forty micro-seconds is the default value for TL_MIN.

■ The TNotify parameter sets the interval, in seconds, between neighbor notification frames. The default value is 30 seconds.

■ The TRequest parameter is set, by default, to 165,000 microseconds. This parameter specifies the FDDI switch's desired value for the Token Ring Timer (TRT) when negotiating the TRT with other stations.

■ The user data string, used to identify the FDDI module in the SMT MIB, is set to *Catalyst 5000*.

■ IP fragmentation is enabled.

■ ICMP unreachable messages are enabled.

■ The Link Error Rate (LER) alarm value defines the threshold at which the LER is considered excessive. LER-Alarm is set to 8 (10^{-8}).

■ LER-Cutoff is set to 7 (10^{-7}). The LER-Cutoff value defines the LER at which the link will be flagged as faulty.

If necessary, any of the above defaults can be modified to suit the environment. Some of the more common customizations are the focus of the following section, including setting the port name, setting up an FDDI 802.10 configuration, creating VLANs, and then assigning switch ports to a VLAN.

Necessary Procedures

In this section, you will learn about the commands you can use to set a port name, set up an FDDI 802.10 configuration, create a VLAN, and then assign a port to an FDDI card.

Setting a Port Name

Setting a port name is accomplished by performing the following steps in privileged mode:

Task	Command
Configure a name for a port.	**set port name** mod_num/port_num [name string]
Verify that the port name is correct.	**show port** mod_num/port_num

Examples of each command follow.

Command Example

```
Console> (enable) set port name 4/1 FDDI A
Port 4/1 name set.
Console> (enable) set port name 4/2 FDDI B
Port 4/2 name set.
```

Command Example

```
Console> show port 4
Port  Name             Status    Vlan        Level  Duplex Speed Type
----  ---------------- --------- ----------  ------ ------ ----- -----
4/1   FDDI A           standby   1                  half   100   FDDI
4/2   FDDI B           connect   1                  half   100   FDDI

Port CE-State Conn-State Type Neig Con Est Alm Cut Lem-Ct Lem-Rej-Ct Tl-Min
---- -------- ---------- ---- ---- --------------- ------ ---------- ------
4/1  isolated standby    A    U    yes 9  11  10  0   0          40
4/2  isolated active     B    U    yes 9  11  10  0   0          1340000

Last-Time-Cleared
--------------------------
Fri Nov 29, 1996, 18:28:51

Console>
```

Setting Up an FDDI 802.10 Configuration

In this section, you will learn how to create an FDDI VLAN and assign a VLAN to a port.

Creating an FDDI VLAN

To create an FDDI VLAN number in the management domain, specifying the MTU and SAID (if desired), use the following command:

set vlan *vlan_num* **type fddi mtu** *mtu* **said** *said*

An example of this command follows.

Command Example

```
Console> (enable) set vlan 610 type fddi said 610
VTP: vlan addition successful
```

Assigning a VLAN to a Port

To assign a VLAN to a port, use the following command:

set vlan *vlan_num* *mod_num/port_num*

Command Example

```
System1> (enable) show vlan 10
```

VLAN	Name	Type	Status	Mod/Ports
10	VLAN0010	enet	active	4/1-2

VLAN	SAID	MTU	RingNo	BridgeNo	StpNo	Parent	Trans1	Trans2
10	100010	1500	0	0	0	0	0	0

Command Example

```
System1> (enable) show vlan
```

VLAN	Name	Type	Status	Mod/Ports
1	default	enet	active	1/1-2
10	VLAN0010	enet	active	4/1-2
20	VLAN0020	enet	active	2/1-24
1002	fddi-default	fddi	active	
1003	token-ring-default	tring	active	
1004	fddinet-default	fdnet	active	
1005	trnet-default	trnet	active	

```
VLAN SAID       MTU   RingNo BridgeNo StpNo Parent Trans1 Trans2
---- ---------- ----- ------ -------- ----- ------ ------ ------
1    100001     1500  0      0        0     0      0      0
10   100010     1500  0      0        0     0      0      0
20   100020     1500  0      0        0     0      0      0
1002 101002     1500  0      0        0     0      0      0
1003 101003     1500  0      0        0     0      0      0
1004 101004     1500  0      0        0     0      0      0
1005 101005     1500  0      0        0     0      0      0
System1> (enable)
```

Command Example

```
Console> (enable) set vlan 10 translation 610
VTP: vlan modification successful
```

Command Example

```
Console> (enable) set trunk 2/3 on 1 10
VTP: vlan modification successful
```

Exam Essentials

Remember how to set a VLAN. This is done with the following command:

```
Console> (enable) set vlan 10 translation 610
```

Remember how to set a trunk port. This is done with the following command:

```
Console> (enable) set trunk 2/3 on 1 10
```

Key Terms and Concepts

APaRT: Automated Packet Recognition and Translation. Associates a frame type with each MAC address in FDDI networks.

SAID: Security Association Identifier that can identify up to 4.29 billion possible VLANs.

Sample Questions

1. What is the correct command to set port 3 on card 2 to VLANs 1 through 10?

A. trunk 2 3 in 1/10

B. set trunk 3/2 1 10 on

C. set trunk 2/3 on 1 10

D. set trunk 1-10 vlan 2.3

Answer: C.

2. What is the correct command to set VLAN 10 with translation of 610?

A. vlan 10 translation 610

B. set vlan 10 translation 610

C. set 10 vlan translation 610

D. set 610 vlan 10

Answer: B.

CHAPTER

12

Introduction to
ATM LAN Emulation

Cisco Exam Objectives Covered in This Chapter

▶ **Define LAN Emulation.** *(pages 245 – 250)*

▶ **Describe the LAN Emulation components.** *(pages 251 – 257)*

▶ **Describe the start-up procedure of a LAN Emulation Client.** *(pages 257 – 261)*

▶ **Describe how one LEC establishes communication with another LEC.** *(pages 262 – 270)*

▶ **Discuss how internetworking is achieved in a LANE environment.** *(pages 271 – 274)*

In this chapter, LAN Emulation (LANE) and the Asynchronous Transfer Mode (ATM) protocol stack will be discussed. You will also read about the different components that make up a LAN Emulation Client (LEC) and the procedures of a client when a client starts up in an ATM LANE network. This is an important chapter if you are working on ATM, or are interested in achieving any type of Cisco certification, since ATM is becoming more important in the Cisco world.

ATM is a very robust transport with many features that make it advantageous as a point-to-point or backbone protocol. However, utilizing the benefits of ATM in a LAN (local area network) environment presents some challenges. The challenge is to cohabitate the point-to-point characteristics of ATM and the connectionless/broadcast characteristics of a LAN, thus accomplishing a synergistic network solution. This solution is known as LANE (LAN Emulation).

The general idea behind LANE is to define a standard means of forwarding layer 2 data-link traffic over ATM. With LANE, it is possible to make an ATM interface "look" like one or more separate Ethernet or Token Ring interfaces, allowing existing LAN-based applications to run without modification over an ATM network. It is even possible, where necessary, to run multiple LANE networks over a single physical ATM network.

Define LAN Emulation.

LAN Emulation can be defined as the configuration of all local area network services such as ARP (Address Resolution Protocol) on ATM: a nonbroadcast, multiaccess network. LANE allows legacy LAN users to take advantage of the benefits of ATM without modifying end-station hardware or software.

This first objective will give you the understanding of the basics of ATM and the ATM protocol stack. This will help you throughout this chapter as you learn about the different components that make up ATM LANE clients.

Critical Information

To be able to understand ATM and LANE, you must first understand the ATM protocol stack and the different protocols that make up ATM. The ATM protocol dictates how two end devices communicate with each other across an ATM network through switches. The ATM protocol model contains three functional layers:

The ATM physical layer: Bit timing and the physical medium

The ATM layer: Generic flow control, generation of call header, and multiplexing and demultiplexing

The ATM adaptation layer: Support for higher-layer services such as signaling, circuit emulation, voice, and video

These layers are very similar to layer 1 and layer 2 of the OSI reference model, as you can see in Figure 12.1.

FIGURE 12.1: The ATM model compared to the OSI reference model

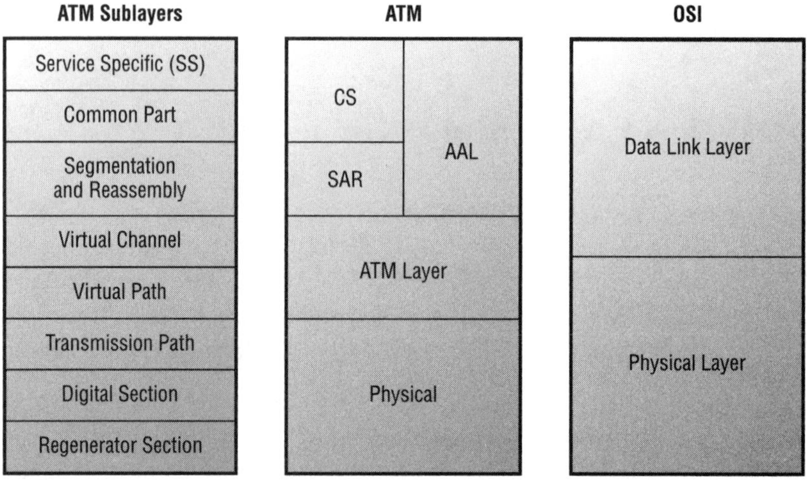

The ATM Physical Layer

The ATM physical layer is responsible for sending and receiving bits on the physical level. This layer also manages ATM cell boundaries and controls the cell packaging in the correct frame type for the ATM media you use.

The ATM Layer

The ATM layer connects the virtual connections and carries ATM cells through the network. It accomplishes this by using information contained within the header of each ATM cell. The ATM layer is responsible for:

- Multiplexing and demultiplexing ATM cells from different virtual connections. You can identify these different connections by their VCI and VPI values.

NOTE   A VCI (Virtual Circuit Identifier) can also be called a virtual channel. This is simply the identifier for the logical connection between the two ends of a connection. A VPI (Virtual Path Identifier) is the identifier for a group of VCIs that allows an ATM switch to perform operations on a group of VCIs.

- Translation of VCI and VPI values at the ATM switch or cross-connect.

- Extraction and insertion of the header before or after the cell is delivered from or to the ATM adaptation layer.

- Governing the implementation of a flow-control mechanism at the User Network Interface (UNI). The UNI is basically two ports connected by a pair of wires, typically fiber.

- Passing and accepting cells from the ATM adaptation layer (AAL).

The ATM Adaptation Layer (AAL)

The ATM adaptation layer (AAL) provides the translation between the larger service data units of the upper layers of the OSI reference model and ATM cells. This function works by receiving packets from the upper-level protocols and breaking them into 48-byte segments to be dumped into the payload of an ATM cell. The AAL has two different sublayers: Segmentation and Reassembly (SAR) and the Convergence Sublayer (CS). The CS can further be subdivided into additional layers: the Common Part (CP) and the Service Specific (SS). Like with protocols specified in the OSI reference model, Protocol Data Units (PDUs) are used to pass information between these layers.

Specifications exist for a few different ATM adaptation layers:

AAL1 (Class A):   Used for transporting telephone traffic and uncompressed video traffic. Known as Constant Bit Rate (CBR) service. Uses end-to-end timing and is connection oriented. Examples are DS1, E1, and nx64 Kbps emulation.

AAL2 (Class B): Does not use the CS and SAR sublayers. Multiplexes short packets from multiple sources into a single cell. Uses a Variable Bit Rate (VBR) and end-to-end timing, and is connection oriented. Examples are packets, video, and audio.

AAL3/4 (Class C): Designed for network service providers and uses VBR with no timing required, but is still connection oriented. Examples are Frame Relay and X.25.

AAL5 (Class D): Used to transfer most non-SMDS data and LAN Emulation. Also uses VBR with no timing required, but is a connectionless service. Examples are IP and SMDS.

ATM networks can provide the transport for several different independent emulated LANs. When a device is attached to one of these emulated LANs, its physical location no longer matters to the administrator or implementation. This process allows you to connect several geographically dispersed LANs with switches to create one large emulated LAN. This can simplify moves, adds, and changes as attached devices can now be administered easily using emulated LANs. For example, a marketing group can belong to one LANE, and a design group can belong to another LANE. Individual members can be located anywhere in the building and still maintain their group membership without regard to physical location.

LANE also provides translation between disparate media environments, allowing data sharing. For instance, Token Ring or FDDI networks can share data with Ethernet networks as if they were part of the same network.

Exam Essentials

Understand what the ATM physical layer provides to a LANE Client. The ATM physical layer provides bit timing and the physical medium.

Remember what the ATM layer provides. The ATM layer provides generic flow control, generation of call header, and multiplexing and demultiplexing.

Understand the ATM adaptation layer and what it supports.
The ATM adaptation layer provides support for higher-layer services such as signaling, circuit emulation, voice, and video.

Understand the big picture of LANE. LANE also provides translation between multiple media environments, allowing data sharing.

Key Terms and Concepts

AAL: ATM adaptation layer. A service-dependent sublayer of the Data Link layer that accepts data from other applications and brings it to the ATM layer in 48-byte ATM payload segments.

ATM: Asynchronous Transfer Mode. The international standard, identified by fixed-length, 53-byte cells, for transmitting cells in multiple-service systems such as voice, video, or data.

LANE: LAN Emulation. The technology that allows an ATM network to operate as a LAN backbone. To do so, the ATM network is required to provide multicast and broadcast support, address mapping (MAC to ATM), SVC management, and an operable packet format.

LEC: LAN Emulation Client. Software providing the emulation of the Data Link layer interface that allows the operation and communication of all higher-level protocols and applications to continue. The LEC Client runs in all ATM devices, which include hosts, servers, bridges, and routers.

LECS: LAN Emulation Configuration Server. An important part of emulated LAN services, providing the configuration data that is furnished upon request from the LES. These services include address registration for Integrated Local Management Interface (ILMI) support, configuration support for the LES addresses and their corresponding emulated LAN identifiers, and an interface to the emulated LAN.

LES: LAN Emulation Server. The central LANE component that provides the initial configuration data for each connecting LEC. The LES typically is located on either an ATM-integrated router or a switch.

Sample Questions

1. What media types can utilize ATM LANE?

   A. Token Ring

   B. Ethernet

   C. ATM

   D. All of the above

   E. None of the above

Answer: D. ATM LANE supports ATM, Ethernet, Token Ring, and FDDI.

2. How many bytes long is an ATM cell?

   A. 45

   B. 48

   C. 52

   D. 53

   E. 64

Answer: D. An ATM frame contains 48-byte payload and a 5-byte header totaling 53 bytes.

3. At what layer of the OSI model is ATM defined?

   A. Layers 2 and 3

   B. Layers 3 and 4

   C. Layers 4 and 5

   D. The Data Link layer

   E. Layers 1 and 2

Answer: E. ATM operates at the Physical and Data Link layers of the OSI model.

Describe the LAN Emulation components.

To be able to successfully configure a functional ATM LANE network, it is first necessary to have a complete working knowledge of the interworkings of the LANE protocols and subsequently to have a full understanding of each of the components and the respective roll they play.

This chapter will briefly explain each component and its function. It is important to understand the different components described in this objective because there are many similar terms, and they can get confusing if not studied closely.

Critical Information

LANE consists of several components that interact and relate in different ways to provide network connectivity based upon the client-server model. The interaction of these components allows for many functions that are foreign to ATM, such as broadcast searching, address registration, and address caching. The LANE model is made up of the following components:

- The LAN Emulation Client (LEC)

- The LAN Emulation Server (LES)

- The LAN Emulation Configuration Server (LECS)

- The Broadcast-and-Unknown Server (BUS)

WARNING LEC and LECS are completely different terms and components.

Figure 12.2 illustrates the components of LANE and their relation-ships, which will be discussed in the following sections. All the com-ponents will be defined before you read about how they work together within LANE.

F I G U R E 12.2: Components of LANE

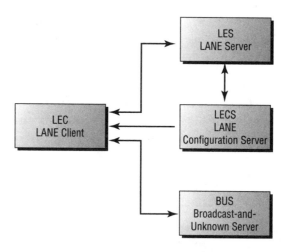

The LAN Emulation Client (LEC)

The LEC is the client portion of the LANE components that allows par-ticipation in all of the other services. The LEC will reside in all devices on the LANE network. Each LEC will register its MAC (Media Access Control) address with the LES. The LEC will perform data forwarding and address resolution very much the same way that ARP (Address Resolution Protocol) would in a broadcast-based network environ-ment. Subsequently, LEC will provide an emulated interface at the MAC level to the higher layers such as Ethernet and Token Ring.

The core responsibilities of the LEC are as follows:

Address resolution: Provides MAC-to-ATM address resolution through an LE_ARP request. Each LEC can be a member of only one emulated LAN (ELAN). Cisco routers will provide data among multiple ELANs.

Data transfer: Allows the transport of frames among other LECs and the BUS. If there is no destination LEC address, frames are forwarded to the BUS server for distribution to other LECs.

Address caching: Will "remember" the addresses of other LECs to reduce the amount of address resolution required.

Interfacing to the ELAN and driver support for higher-level services: Allows the receipt of the initial configuration services. This may include receiving the LES ATM address based upon the LANE identifier.

Driver support for higher-level services: Allows existing applications and protocols to continue operation on the ELAN without change.

The LAN Emulation Server (LES)

The LAN Emulation Server (LES) provides initial configuration data for each LEC and typically lives in an ATM switch or router. The LES acts as the command center, or the helm if you will, for the LANE services. It is responsible for allowing the clients to join the LANE, address resolution, and registration of addresses for all of the clients. The LES serves as a central repository for all of the clients to register their unicast and multicast MAC addresses as well as their ATM address. Additionally, it holds a database containing all of the information for MAC-to-ATM addresses as well as BUS server information.

Responsibilities of the LES include:

Configuration support for the LEC: Each time an LEC boots, it will request the ATM address, a LAN identifier, optional MAC address, and possible joining permission.

Address registration for the LEC: The LES will maintain the database for address resolution. Each LEC is allowed one address entry.

Database storage and response concerning ATM addresses: The LES contains the ATM address database and responds in kind with the ATM addresses for the destination ELANs.

Interfacing to the ELAN: The LES arranges control connections with the LEC. This handles address resolution as well as providing the LEC verification for joining LECs. However, the LES does not maintain a constant connection with the BUS; rather, it provides each LEC with the ATM of the BUS for forwarding.

The LAN Emulation Configuration Server (LECS)

The LAN Emulation Configuration Server (LECS) assigns the individual LECs to their respective ELANs by first assigning them to the LES server for their corresponding ELAN. This assignment is accomplished by the LECS, maintaining a copy of the database containing the LES ATM addresses and ELAN information. The LECS makes these assignments based on policies, configuration database, or information provided by the LEC. It is necessary to have only one LECS per ATM switched network.

The LECS supplies:

Registration of the LECS ATM address: The LECS uses ILMI functions connecting to the ATM network, usually based on a switch. Once registered, the network can supply the LEC with the address using ILMI on the return trip.

Configuration support for the LES: Ensures the correct LES address is supplied to the LEC.

Interface to the ELAN: LECS supplies configuration data directly to the LECs. An LEC queries for configuration data and then receives the LES address. The LECS, based upon the attributes received, assigns the correct LES address for each LEC. The LES can also establish a connection with the LECS, verifying each LEC's request to join the LES.

The Broadcast-and-Unknown Server (BUS)

The Broadcast-and-Unknown Server (BUS) is solely responsible for handling broadcast and multicast traffic. All traffic sent by clients to a destination address of 0xFFFFFFFF will be picked up by the BUS server and distributed as a multicast forward. There can be only one active BUS per ELAN. This single BUS will sequence and distribute multicast and broadcasts as well as unicast flooding, such as unicast frames that are sent out by an LEC prior to its resolving an address or before the VCC-to-target-ATM address has been resolved. The BUS knows of all LECs and will forward to them, even itself. BUSes should be configured carefully so as to not waste traffic and resources on processing unnecessary broadcast traffic.

The BUS must provide the following services:

Distributing multicast data to all LECs: ATM is a point-to-point protocol and will not support any type of broadcast required by LANs.

Distributing unicast data: Again, unicasts are not supported by ATM and require a BUS for assistance.

Interface to the ELAN: Establishes a bidirectional connection, allowing forwarding of multicast and unknown-destination unicast frames.

Exam Essentials

Understand what the LAN Emulation Client (LEC) does. The LANE Client software allows participation in the LANE.

Remember what the LAN Emulation Server (LES) is responsible for. The LAN Emulation Server is responsible for the control center, address registration for the LEC, and address database storage.

Remember what the LAN Emulation Configuration Server (LECS) is responsible for. The LAN Emulation Configuration Server (LECS) provides the configuration data that is furnished upon request from the LES.

Understand what the Broadcast-and-Unknown Server (BUS) is used for. The Broadcast-and-Unknown Server is used to distribute multicast and unicast traffic to LAN Emulation Clients.

Understand the difference between LECs and LECS. LEC is the LAN Emulation Client and is the software responsible for attaching all devices to the ATM network. LECS is the LAN Emulation Configuration Server and is responsible for handing configuration data, including address registration, to the LES.

Key Terms and Concepts

ARP: Address Resolution Protocol. Defined in RFC 826, the protocol that traces IP addresses to MAC addresses.

LANE: LAN Emulation. The technology that allows an ATM network to operate as a LAN backbone. To do so, the ATM network is required to provide multicast and broadcast support, address mapping (MAC to ATM), SVC management, and an operable packet format.

Sample Questions

1. What does the address 0xFFFFFFFF do?

   A. It is a request for the location of the BUS from the LEC.

   B. It is a broadcast address.

   C. Both A and B.

   D. None of the above.

   Answer: C. The BUS is responsible for all broadcast traffic.

2. What performs MAC-to-ATM address resolution?

   A. LECS

   B. LES

   C. BUS

   D. LEC

   Answer: B. The LES performs a similar function to ARP.

3. How many LANEs can a single LEC belong to?

　　A. Any amount configured

　　B. 5

　　C. 1

　　D. None

　　E. 10

Answer: C. An LEC can be connected to only a single LANE.

4. Which two of the following are not functions of the LEC?

　　A. Control

　　B. Data forwarding

　　C. Address resolution

　　D. ELAN assignment

Answer: A, D. An additional LEC function would be address caching.

Describe the start-up procedure of a LAN Emulation Client.

This section will help to explain the procedure a LAN Emulation Client (LEC) uses to attach to the LANE network. It is important to understand this procedure because all devices that attach to the LANE will use these same LEC start-up procedures.

Critical Information

In a LANE environment, all devices on the network are LECs. Even the devices that have server components such as the LAN Emulation Configuration Server (LECS) and the LAN Emulation Server (LES) have LEC components to attach themselves to the LANE network. Whereas, for the balance of this chapter, it will be assumed that the LEC that is worked with is *not* a serving device, even though most of the same procedures apply.

When a client boots up and attempts to join the ELAN, the first thing it must do is obtain its own ATM address. It can accomplish this in one of two ways: The address can be either preconfigured by the network administrator or dynamically discovered through the Integrated Local Management Interface (ILMI) protocol.

ILMI is a protocol that is used for the exchange of any auto-configuration information among ATM devices. The ILMI protocol utilizes a Data Link level of the SNMP protocol and its MIB (Management Information Base) database structures, and it can provide clients with the location of the LECS or provide their own address by looking at the prefix of the ATM NSAP (Network Service Access Point) address from the local ATM switch. This implementation of ILMI includes management as well as agent functions and utilizes the ATM VPI=0 and VCI=16.

Once the local ATM address has been discovered, the LEC must then determine the address of the LECS. This can be done in one of three possible ways:

- By using the ILMI procedure

- By using the well-known LECS address

- By using a well-known permanent connection to the LECS through VPI=0 and VCI=17

When the knowledge of the LECS address has been received, it is then necessary to establish a direct connection to the LECS by way of a configuration-direct VCC (Virtual Control Connection). Upon establishment of the connection, the LECS will inform the LEC of any information required for joining its ELAN, such as the LES's ATM address, the ELAN type, the ELAN name, and the maximum frame size.

There needs to be only one LECS for all of the clients within an administrative domain, and each LECS must be configured by the network administrator with all of the correct information. The LECS will then assign the individual client to their respective ELANs by directing them to the controlling LES. After the configuration information has been learned, the configuration-direct VCC can be discontinued because all configuration information has been exchanged, thus the circuit is no longer necessary.

The LEC now sets up another control-direct VCC—this time, the connection will be bidirectional to the LES. The LES will then have the option to check with the LECS to verify permissions to join the ELAN. If the permissions are granted, the LES will respond by assigning the LEC a unique LEC Identifier (LECID). The LEC will then register its MAC address and ATM address with the LES, at which point the LEC will be added to the point-to-multipoint control-distribute VCC. This VCC is established to handle the LE_ARP (LAN Emulation Address Resolution Protocol) request, as well as to send information to all of the LECSes in the ELAN.

Once the LEC has officially joined the ELAN, it must still learn the address of the BUS (Broadcast-and-Unknown Server). The LEC will send out a broadcast LE_ARP request. The LES, not the BUS, will then respond to the request with the address of the BUS. After the LEC has learned the address, it will set up a multicast-send VCC with the BUS. The BUS will add the address of the LEC into its multicast-forward VCC. This VCC is how the BUS works around the point-to-point characteristics of ATM. The BUS will use the multicast-forward VCC that is set up with each client in the ELAN to "broadcast" data to all of the LECs in the domain. In a true LAN environment, a broadcast packet is put out on the network and is read by all clients. In the case of ATM, the BUS will pick up any broadcast packets and resend them via multicast-forward VCC to each of the LECs.

Exam Essentials

Know the LEC start-up order. The order is as follows:

1. Client resolves address.

2. Client contacts LECS for configuration.

3. Client contacts LES for attachment to ELAN.

4. Client finds the BUS.

Remember what ILMI is and its use. Integrated Local Management Interface is used for auto-configuration information exchange (VPI=0 and VCI=16).

Understand that an LEC can contact the LECS in three ways. The three ways are as follows:

- By using the ILMI procedure

- By using the well-known LECS address

- By using a well-known permanent connection to the LECS through VPI=0 and VCI=17

Key Terms and Concepts

ARP: Address Resolution Protocol. Defined in RFC 826, the protocol that traces IP addresses to MAC addresses.

Control-direct VCC: One of three control connections defined by Phase I LAN Emulation—a bidirectional Virtual Control Connection (VCC) established in ATM by an LEC to an LES.

Control-distribute VCC: One of three control connections defined by Phase 1 LAN Emulation—a unidirectional Virtual Control Connection (VCC) set up in ATM from an LES to an LEC. Usually, the VCC is a point-to-multipoint connection.

Sample Questions

1. What type of connection is set up between the LEC and the LES?

   A. Bidirectional connection

   B. Point-to-point connection

   C. Bidirectional multipoint-to-point connection

   D. Broadcast connectionless

   Answer: A. The LEC establishes a bidirectional connection to allow two-way communication.

2. Which of the following is the well-known permanent connection that the LEC will use to determine the LECS address?

   A. VPI=0 and VCI=16

   B. VPI=0 and VCI=17

   C. VPI=16 and VCI=0

   D. VPI=17 and VCI=0

   Answer: B. The ATM values VPI=0 and VCI=17 are reserved for configuration data.

3. What ATM values are used for Integrated Local Management Interface to gather auto-configuration information?

   A. VPI=0 and VCI=16

   B. VPI=0 and VCI=17

   C. VPI=5 and VCI=19

   D. VPI=16 and VCI=0

   Answer: A. These values are reserved for configuration information.

Describe how one LEC establishes communication with another LEC.

To this point, you have read about what LAN Emulation is, looked closely at all of the key components, and learned how the LEC attaches to the LANE and retrieves its configuration data. This seems like a lot of information, but you must keep in mind that you have not passed actual usable data traffic from one device to the other. This objective will continue down the winding road of ATM LANE communication by completing the journey from one end station to another.

It would be advantageous to have the entire end-to-end picture if you were ever to install an ATM network, or needed to troubleshoot why a client was not communicating.

Critical Information

Since the LEC attachment process has already been reviewed, this section will now trudge a little deeper into the communication process. LANE components communicate by Switched Virtual Circuits (SVCs). There are several type of SVCs: unidirectional, bidirectional, point-to-point, and point-to-multipoint. LANE configurations use Virtual Channel Connections (VCCs), also known as Virtual Circuit Connections.

Building an ATM-Address-to-Ethernet-MAC-Address Table

When a client first attempts to join the ELAN, it must build an ATM-address-to-Ethernet-MAC-address table. Here is how:

- The LEC sends an LE_ARP to the LES (a point-to-point VCC).

- The LES forwards the LE_ARP to all clients on the ELAN (a point-to-multipoint control-distribute VCC).

- Any client that recognizes the MAC address responds.

- The LES forwards the response (a point-to-multipoint control-distribute VCC) to the LEC.

Figure 12.3 shows the path each LEC takes as it establishes a connection with the emulated LAN and another LEC. After a quick look at each step, this section will go into more detail about the internetworking and the mechanics behind what's happening.

F I G U R E 12.3: How an LEC establishes communication

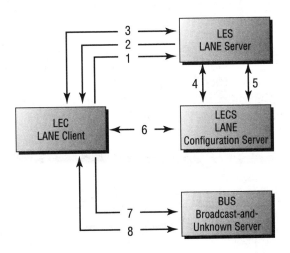

1. A query is made to the ATM switch containing the LECS, using ILMI. The query requests the ATM address of the LES for its emulated LAN. The switch contains an MIB variable containing the requested ATM address. This connection is a bidirectional, point-to-point, configure-direct VCC. The LEC will attempt to locate the LES using these steps:

   A. Use ILMI to connect to LECS.

   B. Look for a locally configured ATM address.

   C. Receive a fixed address defined by the MIB variable using UNI.

   D. Access PVC 0/17, a well-known permanent virtual circuit.

NOTE What is inside the query? The LEC fires off a cell with the ATM address of the LECS (locally configured). This wakes the configure-direct VCC, sending an LE_CONFIGURE_REQUEST down the pipe. The query is compared to the LECS database, and if a match is found, an LE_CONFIGURE_RESPONSE is returned, providing the ATM address for the local LES server for that emulated LAN.

2. The LECS responds across the established connection, providing the ATM address and name of the LES for the LEC's emulated LAN.

3. The LEC then establishes a connection with the LES based upon the configuration data received in the previous connection. Again, the connection is a bidirectional, point-to-point, control-direct VCC and remains up for the duration of the process. Figure 12.4 illustrates steps 1 through 3.

F I G U R E 12.4: LES-to-LEC communication (steps 1–3)

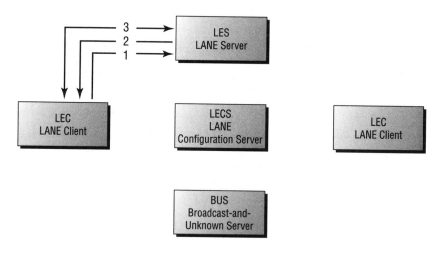

4. While the connection is established with the LEC requesting entry (a configure-direct VCC) to the emulated LAN, the LES makes a bidirectional connection to the LECS asking for verification so that

the requesting LEC may enter the emulated LAN. The server configuration that was received in the first connection is now verified against the LECS database, determining authenticity and allowing membership. Figure 12.5 shows the difference from step 3 to step 4.

FIGURE 12.5: LES-to-LEC communication (step 4)

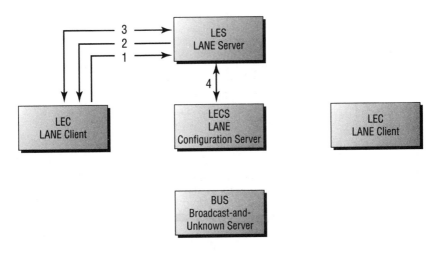

NOTE What's going on? The LEC creates another packet—now with the correct ATM address for the LES, again causing the control-direct VCC to establish a connection. The LEC fires out an LE_JOIN_ REQUEST to the LES containing the LEC ATM address and the MAC address to register with the emulated LAN. The LES makes a quick check with the LECS verifying the LEC. The LES receives the data and creates a new branch for the LEC as well as issuing an LE_JOIN_ RESPONSE back to the LEC. This response contains the LANE Client Identifier (LECID)—a unique identifier for each client. This ID is used to filter return broadcasts from the BUS.

---

5. The LES replies to the LEC's request (through the existing configure-direct VCC) by either allowing or denying membership in the emulated LAN.

6. If the LES allows the connection, the LEC is added to the point-to-multipoint control-distribute VCC. Then the LEC is granted a connection using the point-to-point control VCC to the corresponding LEC or service it was searching for originally, and the higher-level protocols take over. If the LES rejects the LEC's request, the session is terminated. Figure 12.6 provides a view of what has occurred in steps 5 and 6.

F I G U R E 12.6: LES-to-LEC communication (steps 5 and 6)

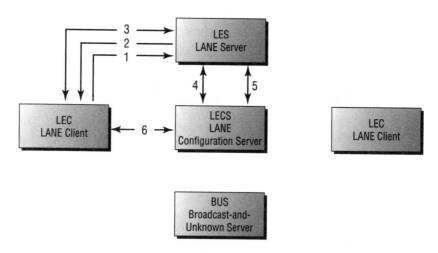

7. After being given permission by the LES, the LEC must now find the ATM address for the BUS and become a member of the broadcast group.

NOTE What is going on? The LEC must locate the BUS, so an LE_ARP_REQUEST packet containing the MAC address 0xFFFFFFFF is sent. This packet is sent down the control-direct VCC to the LES, which understands the request for the BUS. The LES then responds with the ATM address for the BUS.

---

8. Eventually the BUS is located, and the LEC becomes a member of the emulated LAN. Figure 12.7 shows the final outcome as the emulated LAN is joined.

F I G U R E 12.7: LES-to-LEC communication (final outcome)

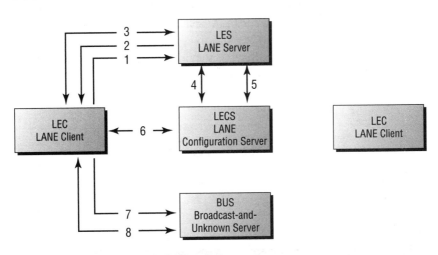

Upon completion of this entire process, you will be able to successfully pass user data from one place to the other, which is the whole point of a LANE network. LANE will provide an ATM forwarding path to allow communication with an unknown destination.

Accomplishing this means the LEC issues an LE_ARP_REQUEST to the LES using the control-direct VCC. The LES takes the request and forwards it out the control-distribute VCC to all the LECs listening. At the same moment, the unicast packets are fired away to the BUS, where they are forwarded out to all endpoints. Remember that this sudden influx of unicast traffic isn't great for the network and will continue passing through until the LE_ARP_REQUEST is answered.

As the ARP request is translated and forwarded along by interfaces belonging to the emulated LAN, hopefully another LEC down the line resolves everything by replying with an LE_ARP_RESPONSE. The response is forwarded back to the LES, and the address is added to the database, relating a new MAC address to an ATM address.

Once it receives the resolution, the LEC immediately does two things: First, it requests a data-direct VCC that will carry the unicast traffic among the LECs. (Remember that at this moment, the BUS is still forwarding unicast traffic at 10 packets per second.) As soon as the data-direct VCC becomes available, the LEC performs its second duty and generates a flush packet on the multicast-forward VCC. After passing through the network, the flush packet will return to the sending LEC, signaling that the LEC can begin communication with the located LEC. Figure 12.8 summarizes the process, showing how each connection is accomplished and where it is going.

FIGURE 12.8: Complete LES-to-LEC communication

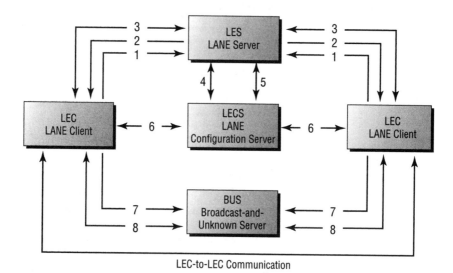

LEC-to-LEC Communication

Exam Essentials

Remember the key steps in LEC-to-LEC communication. The key steps are as follows:

1. A query is made to the ATM switch containing the LECS, using ILMI. The query requests the ATM address of the LES for its emulated LAN.

2. The LECS responds across the established connection, providing the ATM address and name of the LES for the LEC's emulated LAN.

3. The LEC then establishes a connection with the LES based upon the configuration data received in the previous connection.

4. The LES makes a bidirectional connection to the LECS asking for verification so that the requesting LEC may enter the emulated LAN.

5. The LES replies to the LEC's request.

6. If the LES allows the connection, the LEC is added to the point-to-multipoint control-distribute VCC.

7. After being given permission by the LES, the LEC must now find the ATM address for the BUS and become a member of the broadcast group.

8. Eventually the BUS is located, and the LEC becomes a member of the emulated LAN.

Key Terms and Concepts

SVC: Switched Virtual Circuit. A virtual circuit that is dynamically established on demand and is torn down when transmission is complete. SVCs are used in situations where data transmission is sporadic. Sometimes called a Switched Virtual Connection in ATM terminology.

VCC: Virtual Channel Connection. Logical circuit, made up of VCLs, that carries data between two endpoints in an ATM network. Sometimes called a Virtual Circuit Connection.

VCI: Virtual Channel Identifier. A 16-bit field in the header of an ATM cell. The VCI, together with the VPI, is used to identify the next destination of a cell as it passes through a series of ATM switches on its way to its destination. ATM switches use the VPI/VCI fields to identify the next network VCL that a cell needs to transit on its way to its final destination. The function of the VCI is similar to that of the DLCI in Frame Relay.

Sample Questions

1. What type of request is sent by the LEC to the BUS?

   A. Uses ILMI

   B. LE_CONFIGURE_REQUEST

   C. LE_ARP_REQUEST

   D. LE_JOIN_REQUEST

   Answer: C. A LAN Emulation ARP request is used to determine the address of the BUS.

2. Once an LEC has established the ATM address of another LEC (via the LES) using an LE_ARP, what type of VCC is used to contact the LEC?

   A. Point-to-multipoint control-distribute VCC

   B. Point-to-point control-direct VCC

   C. Point-to-point data-direct VCC

   D. Multicast-forward VCC

   Answer: C. Point-to-point data-direct VCC is used for the LES server. Point-to-multipoint is used for the BUS.

3. What is a VCI?

   A. Virtual Circuit Identifier

   B. Virtual Channel Identifier

   C. Virtual Connection Integration

   D. Both A and B

   E. Both A and C

   Answer: B. VCI is a 16-bit field in the header of an ATM cell used to identify the next destination of a cell.

Discuss how internetworking is achieved in a LANE environment.

Now that you have a good understanding of how the ATM LAN Emulation works, it is time to bring that knowledge into the real world. As important as it to understand *how* it works, it is perhaps even more important to understand *when* and *where* to utilize the technologies that have been discussed, as well as *what* products to use.

Critical Information

Cisco Systems offers many products that provide LANE. All of the Cisco switches from the smallest 1900 series to the largest 6000 series will support LANE services.

Many Cisco routers will also support LANE services, including the 4000, 4500, 7000, and 7500. Although each of these products will provide basic ATM cell forwarding, they may still vary in interface offerings, redundancy, and traffic-management capabilities.

Aside from these functional differences, the Cisco products offer a wide range of performance levels as well. If you are looking to install a network of any type, not just ATM, it is very important to thoroughly examine the Total Cost of Ownership, including price, level of performance, and dependability. Cisco offers an entire line of ATM devices providing an appropriate solution for any environment, from the small office to the corporate enterprise.

Workgroup ATM Switches

Workgroup switches are generally the smallest. This series can include the 2820 and the 1900 series. However, the Catalyst 5000 and 6000 can be implemented as a workgroup switch. Workgroup switches tend to be Ethernet oriented and provide an ATM uplink to a campus switch. These are usually located in the closet, close to the desktop user.

Campus ATM Switches

Campus switches include those in the LightStream 1010 family of ATM switches. Campus ATM switches are typically implemented to relieve the network congestion across the existing backbone by providing new services such as VLANs. Campus switches support a wide variety of interfaces, often having connections to the current backbone and WAN, yet they provide a price-to-performance break that makes them suitable for local backbone installations. This type of switch also needs a higher level of management and congestion control, allowing several switches to be tied together.

Enterprise ATM Switches

Enterprise switches are the next step up from the campus ATM switch, allowing multilevel campus ATM switches to be tied together in enterprise installations. They provide the internetworking necessary for the multiprotocol traffic of an enterprise network to travel. These are not used as core backbone switches, but instead they act as single point of integration for the varying technologies found within the enterprise. Cisco's BPX/AXIS is designed to meet the needs of high-traffic enterprises, or even public service providers.

Multiservice Access Switches

Multiservice access switches are there to provide a multitude of services for the growing needs of blossoming networks. They can provide the services to support the MAN, the WAN, and the campus.

Exam Essentials

Know the different series of switches. They are as follows:

Workgroup ATM switches: Located close to the user, in wiring closets 1900–6000.

Campus ATM switches: Used in backbone or switch-consolidation points. Require faster hardware and more management.

Enterprise ATM switches: Allow integration of large systems, often including Broadband and/or public service providers.

Multiservice access switches: More versatile switches for the MAN, WAN, or campus.

Key Terms and Concepts

Broadband: Any channel having a bandwidth greater than a voice-grade channel (4KHz). Also called *wideband*.

MAN: Metropolitan area network. Network that spans a metropolitan area. Generally, a MAN spans a larger geographic area than a LAN, but a smaller geographic area than a WAN.

VLAN: Virtual LAN. Group of devices on one or more LANs that are configured (using management software) so that they can communicate as if they were attached to the same wire, when in fact they are located on a number of different LAN segments. Because VLANs are based on logical instead of physical connections, they are extremely flexible.

WAN: Wide area network. Data-communications network that serves users across a broad geographic area and often uses transmission devices provided by common carriers such as Frame Relay, SMDS, and X.25.

Sample Questions

1. What routers in the Cisco series can implement LANE?

    A. Cisco 2500, 2510, and 2511

    B. Cisco 5000 and 5500

    C. Cisco 4000 and 4500

    D. Cisco 8000 and 8001

    Answer: C. Cisco 5000 series are switches. The 2500 series do not support ATM, and there is currently no 8000.

2. Which models of Cisco switches are considered for workgroups?

    A. 1900–2820

    B. Catalyst 5000–6000

    C. BPX/AXIS

    D. 2500–2600

    Answer: A. There are several switches in the 1900–2820 family that support all types of interface configurations.

3. What is the best price and performance solution for a campus switch?

    A. Catalyst 5000–6000

    B. LightStream 1010

    C. 1900–2820

    D. BPX/AXIS

    Answer: B. The LightStream campus ATM switches are typically implemented to relieve the network of congestion across the existing backbone by providing new services such as VLANs.

CHAPTER

13

Catalyst 5000 Series Switch ATM
LANE Module

Cisco Exam Objectives Covered in This Chapter

▶ **List the features of the Catalyst 5000 LANE module.**
(pages 276 – 281)

▶ **Outline the performance ratings for the ATM bus and the switching bus.** *(pages 281 – 284)*

▶ **Describe how to access the CLI for the LANE module.**
(pages 284 – 287)

▶ **Describe the Simple Server Redundancy Protocol (SSRP).**
(pages 287 – 289)

In this chapter, the Catalyst 5000 series switch ATM LANE module will be discussed. The installation and configuration of both ATM and switches in an internetwork and how they perform in an internetwork environment will be examined.

You will also learn how to configure ATM through the command line interface (CLI). How to configure the ATM LANE will be shown to you in Chapter 14. The chapter will finish by describing the Simple Server Redundancy Protocol (SSRP).

This is an important chapter to read and understand if configuring ATM LANE and when gathering information for your CLSC exam.

▶ List the features of the Catalyst 5000 LANE module.

In this first objective, the features of the Catalyst 5000 LANE module will be listed. This is an important objective to understand, as it will give you the background needed on the ATM LANE module.

By understanding the Catalyst 5000 series LANE module, you will be able to configure and troubleshoot the Catalyst ATM modules.

Critical Information

The physical LANE module for the Catalyst 5000 is available in three versions of 155Mbps SONET/SDH OC-3. These include multimode, single-mode, and Unshielded Twisted Pair interfaces. While two interfaces of each type are available, only one may be active at any time. This provides for link failure or the loss of ILMI (Integrated Local Management Interface) signaling. The Catalyst 5000 supports a maximum of three LANE modules and up to 256 LANE clients. In addition, the module supports permanent and switched virtual circuits (PVCs and SVCs). SVC support is provided with the Q.2931 signaling protocol.

TIP   The ATM configuration is contained within the LANE module, not the Supervisor.

Integrated Local Management Interface cells provide for automatic configuration between ATM systems. This is accomplished using SNMP and MIB command structures, and uses a Virtual Path Identifier (VPI) of 0 and a Virtual Circuit Identifier (VCI) of 16, or VP/VC 0,16. Many telecommunications providers and administrators will use the VP/VC shorthand to document VPI/VCI pairs—as with other acronyms, any shortcut is appreciated.

NOTE   The ILMI SNMP functions include both manager and agent functions. This is different from the unidirectional relationship normally associated with SNMP.

ILMI can provide sufficient information for the ATM end station to find an LECS. In addition, ILMI provides the ATM NSAP (network service access point) prefix information to the end station. This prefix is configured on the local ATM switch and is 13 bytes long. It's combined with the MAC address (6 bytes) of the end node, called an end system identifier, and a 1-byte selector to create the 20-byte ATM address.

The LANE module includes functionality for the LEC, LES/BUS, and LECS functions, while supporting up to 256 LANE clients. The multimode fiber module uses an SC connector and is documented in Table 13.1.

T A B L E 13.1: The Multimode LANE Module

Function	Parameter
SAR (Segmentation and Reassembly)	Capable of reassembling 512 packets simultaneously
Virtual circuits	Support for up to 4096 virtual circuits
ATM Adaptation Layer	AAL5
Optical source	LED
Maximum distance between devices	2 kilometers
Wavelength	1270 to 1380 nm
Receiver sensitivity	–32.5 dBm to –14 dBm
Transmitter output	–19 dBm to –14 dBm

The single-mode module is similar to the multimode module; however, single-mode is recommended in larger campus installations where distance is a significant factor. The single-mode module is outlined in Table 13.2.

The UTP version of the LANE module is similar to the fiber modules; however, it is limited to very short distances and uses Category 5 cabling with an RJ-45 connector.

T A B L E 13.2: The Single-Mode LANE Module

Function	Parameter
Optical source	Laser
Maximum distance between devices	10 kilometers
Wavelength	1261 to 1360 nm
Receiver sensitivity	–32.5 dBm to –8 dBm
Transmitter output	–14 dBm to –8 dBm

NOTE The ATM configuration is stored within the LANE module, not the NVRAM on the Supervisor module, and is not displayed by the show config command.

The LANE module includes LEDs to indicate the status and functionality of the unit. The LEDs are interpreted as shown in Table 13.3.

T A B L E 13.3: The LANE Module LEDs

Function	Red	Orange	Green
Status	One or more diagnostic tests failed.	The module is disabled in software, or the system is booting.	All diagnostic tests passed.
TX—Transmit			Port is transmitting a cell.
RX—Receive			Port is receiving a cell.
Link			The link is active.

Exam Essentials

Remember what type of cabling the LANE module supports.
The cabling types supported include multimode, single-mode, and Unshielded Twisted Pair interfaces.

Key Terms and Concepts

ATM: Asynchronous Transfer Mode. The international standard, identified by fixed-length, 53-byte cells, for transmitting cells in multiple-service systems such as voice, video, or data.

LANE: LAN Emulation. The technology that allows an ATM network to operate as a LAN backbone. To do so, the ATM network is required to provide multicast and broadcast support, address mapping (MAC to ATM), SVC management, and an operable packet format.

Sample Questions

1. How many clients does the LANE module support?

   A. 25

   B. 26

   C. 250

   D. 256

   Answer: D. The LANE module includes functionality for the LEC, LES/BUS, and LECS functions, while supporting up to 256 LANE clients.

2. What type of cabling does the ATM LANE module support? (Choose all that apply.)

A. Single-mode

B. Multimode

C. UTP

D. STP

Answer: A, B, D. These include multimode, single-mode, and Unshielded Twisted Pair interfaces.

Outline the performance ratings for the ATM bus and the switching bus.

In this objective, the different ATM implementations in the Catalyst series internetwork will be discussed. Both the ATM and switching networks as used in an internetwork will be examined.

This is an important objective to understand when working in a mixed network environment as well as when gathering information for the CLSC exam.

Critical Information

Planning the design of an ATM network involves many of the same criteria as in designing frame-based networks. Issues of cost, corporate or business units, security, bandwidth, and technical limitations must all be considered.

A single ELAN network design is the simplest to understand and implement, and is recommended for lab installations to assist in comprehension of ATM LANE and potential issues in larger networks. Such a network may incorporate multiple LECs, with a single LECS and LES/BUS.

More advanced ATM LANE implementations may contain a single LECS serving multiple ELANs. Different switches in the network may be configured as LES/BUS pairs for an individual ELAN—recommended for removing a single point of failure—or with all ELANs served by LES/BUS pairs on a single switch in the data center. Note that ELANs cannot communicate with each other without a layer 3 device, either a router or the RSM module in the Catalyst. All multiple ELAN designs must include a router. It is also possible for the router to serve as the LECS and LES/BUS.

Most modern networks relate well to the client-server model. This model reflects the relationship between clients, workstations and other user interfaces, and servers, or those resources that supply clients with services. Servers should include printers and other shared devices.

In networking, the client is sometimes referred to as a demand node. This reflects the fact that these devices frequently request the information—a demand for networking purposes. Resource nodes are synonymous with servers, as they respond to demands. In the network, routers, servers, and mainframes all serve as resource nodes.

Recall that switches can provide a number of services; however, one of their most basic functions is the control of the collision domain. VLANs, including those connected via ATM and FDDI, still benefit from Ethernet stations sitting on single switch ports. Performance within the network increases because the desktop is no longer burdened with collisions (full-duplex), and integration into other media augments this increased performance.

It would be wrong to assume that buffers are incapable of overflowing—surpassing their ability to handle incoming traffic. Buffer overflows can be resolved by identifying the packet flow within the network. Usually resources, or resource nodes, are more prone to congestion and buffer problems.

To address these problems, administrators should increase the size of the switch buffers and the size of the links to resource nodes, including servers. In addition, aggregating links can greatly address this issue. The Catalyst 5000/5500 products support Fast Ether-Channel, a bonding process that can link up to four FastEthernet connections. This results in a full-duplex 800Mbps connection between switches and trunked servers, which may also suffer from congestion and buffer overflows.

The Catalyst switch also supports a higher priority setting on a per-port basis. When you increase this setting, servers can be given more access to the Catalyst backplane. The commands for this configuration are included in the following chapter. Lastly, a packet retry process can address buffer overflow.

While the Catalyst 5000/5500 can service Token Ring, Ethernet, FDDI, and ATM connections, the overriding goal of the switch is to improve network performance. In addition, the switch can improve performance and scalability by clustering servers, providing 10/100Mbps service to workgroups and FastEthernet to the desktop. The Catalyst can also serve in the backbone, providing an aggregation point for the various workgroups. As a result, poor network response problems, high collision rates, and broadcasts can all be addressed within a design that includes switches.

Exam Essentials

Remember that by creating ELANs, you can break up the LANE broadcast domains.   Emulated LANs are created in ATM LANE networks to break up users and groups into broadcast domains.

Key Terms and Concepts

ATM: Asynchronous Transfer Mode. The international standard, identified by fixed-length, 53-byte cells, for transmitting cells in multiple-service systems such as voice, video, or data.

LANE: LAN Emulation. The technology that allows an ATM network to operate as a LAN backbone. To do so, the ATM network is required to provide multicast and broadcast support, address mapping (MAC to ATM), SVC management, and an operable packet format.

Sample Questions

1. Advanced ATM LANE implementations may include what?

   A. More than two routers

   B. More than three routers

   C. A double LECS serving one ELAN

   D. A single LECS serving multiple ELANs

   Answer: D.

2. What is a possible solution for buffer overflows?

   A. Identifying router locations

   B. Identifying the packet flow within the network

   C. Buying more Cisco switches

   D. ISDN backup links

   Answer: B.

Describe how to access the CLI for the LANE module.

When configuring the LANE module, it is important to remember that the ATM LANE configuration is not stored or modified in the Supervisor engine. As a result, the administrator must connect to the ATM LANE module to continue.

This objective is important when studying for your CLSC exam and when gathering information to configure your internetwork.

Critical Information

In the "Necessary Procedures" section of this objective, you will read about the procedures to connect and configure an ATM LANE module. Chapter 14 will give you an example of how to use the following commands to configure the ATM LANE module.

Necessary Procedures

In this section, you will see the procedures used to configure an ATM LANE module.

1. Connect to the ATM LANE module and enter configuration mode.

2. The administrator must enter enable mode and configure the ATM interface on the LANE module.

3. The ATM addresses of the LEC, LES, BUS, and LECS should be obtained and recorded. Note that this assumes that the LANE module is connected to the LS-1010 ASP via an LS-1010 line card or an external ATM switch. While it may be necessary to configure the LS-1010 during this process, this example will focus on the LANE module.

4. Start the LES and BUS.

5. Each connection will require an LEC.

6. If an LECS is desired, configure the LECS database and start the LECS.

Exam Essentials

Remember where the LANE configuration is stored. When configuring the LANE module, it is important to remember that the ATM LANE configuration is not stored or modified in the Supervisor engine.

Remember the step to perform after connecting to the ATM LANE module. Configure the ATM interface on the LANE module.

Key Terms and Concepts

ATM: Asynchronous Transfer Mode. The international standard, identified by fixed-length, 53-byte cells, for transmitting cells in multiple-service systems such as voice, video, or data.

CLI: The command line interface is used on Cisco routers and switches for configurations of routers and switches. Other management tools are also available to configure the devices.

LANE: LAN Emulation. The technology that allows an ATM network to operate as a LAN backbone. To do so, the ATM network is required to provide multicast and broadcast support, address mapping (MAC to ATM), SVC management, and an operable packet format.

Sample Questions

1. Which is true regarding ATM LANE configuration?

    A. The ATM LANE configuration is done on the Supervisor module.

    B. The ATM LANE configuration is done on the ATM LANE module.

    C. The ATM LANE configuration is done on the redundant Supervisor module.

    D. The ATM LANE configuration is done on T/r modules.

    Answer: B.

2. What is the third step in the LANE configuration process?

A. The ATM addresses of the LEC, LES, BUS, and LECS should be obtained and recorded.

B. The ATM addresses of the LANE module should be obtained and recorded.

C. Start the LES and BUS.

D. Each connection requires an LEC.

Answer: A.

Describe the Simple Server Redundancy Protocol (SSRP).

In this objective, the Simple Server Redundancy Protocol (SSRP), which is used with ATM LANE configurations and Catalyst 5000 switches, will be discussed.

This is an important objective to understand when configuring LANE and you need redundancy, as well as when gathering information for the CLSC exam.

Critical Information

Given the initial limitations of the LANE specification, administrators quickly identified that a single LES/BUS pair would represent a single point of failure in the network. To address this limitation, Cisco introduced SSRP, or Simple Server Redundancy Protocol, in the 11.2 release of the IOS. This feature adds a slight measure of fault tolerance in all Cisco LANE implementations.

When configured with the Catalyst 5000 ATM Release 3.1 or higher, SSRP provides redundancy by allowing backup LECS and LES/BUS servers for an ELAN. The feature is always enabled with Cisco LANE.

For simple LANE service replication or fault tolerance to work, the ATM switch must support multiple LANE server addresses. These addresses must be identical on all LANE configuration servers on your internetwork, and must be in the same priority order.

LANE Simple Server Redundancy Protocol is supported on Cisco IOS Release 11.2 and later software. Older LANE configuration files continue to work with this new software.

Exam Essentials

Remember when you would use SSRP. This feature adds a slight measure of fault tolerance in all Cisco LANE implementations.

Remember to make sure all addresses are the same. SSRP addresses must be identical on all LANE configuration servers on your internetwork, and must be in the same priority order.

Key Terms and Concepts

ATM: Asynchronous Transfer Mode. The international standard, identified by fixed-length, 53-byte cells, for transmitting cells in multiple-service systems such as voice, video, or data.

LANE: LAN Emulation. The technology that allows an ATM network to operate as a LAN backbone. To do so, the ATM network is required to provide multicast and broadcast support, address mapping (MAC to ATM), SVC management, and an operable packet format.

SSRP: Simple Server Redundancy Protocol adds a slight measure of fault tolerance in all Cisco LANE implementations.

Sample Questions

1. For server redundancy to work correctly, which is true?

    A. All LANE configurations must have the same SSRP addresses, and must be in the same order.

    B. All LANE configurations must have the same SSRP addresses, but can be in any order.

    C. Each SSRP server has unique addresses, but in the order of priority.

    D. You must have all Cisco routers in your internetwork.

    Answer: A.

2. SSRP is supported on which IOS?

    A. 10.3 or newer

    B. 11.1 or newer

    C. 11.3 or newer

    D. 11.2 or newer

    Answer: D.

CHAPTER 14

Configuring the Catalyst 5000 Series Switch ATM LANE Module

Cisco Exam Objectives Covered in This Chapter

▶ **Explain ATM address structure.** *(pages 292 – 295)*

▶ **Describe how ATM addresses are automatically assigned.**
(pages 295 – 297)

▶ **Describe the rules for assigning ATM components to interfaces.**
(pages 297 – 301)

▶ **Configure LANE components on a Catalyst 5000 switch.**
(pages 301 – 304)

This chapter will continue with the discussion of ATM on the Catalyst 5000 series switches. The different ATM address structures and how ATM addresses are automatically assigned in an ATM internetwork will be examined.

The different components used and how ATM components are assigned to interfaces will also be described. The chapter will finish by showing you how to configure LANE on a Catalyst 5000 switch.

This chapter is important to understand when working in a switched internetwork and when gathering information for your CLSC exam.

▶ Explain ATM address structure.

This first objective will discuss MAC and ATM addresses and the function they serve within ATM LANE. Every component used with LANE must have a MAC address to uniquely identify it on the LAN, and it must be unique on the entire LANE network.

This is an important objective to understand, as it will give you the background you need on ATM addresses and how they are used in a LANE network.

Critical Information

The ATM LANE module automatically assigns ATM addresses for each of the LANE components. Besides each host, the LEC, LECS, LES, and BUS must have a unique ATM address. All LECs on the same interface must have the same address, which is automatically assigned and used as the End-System Identifier (ESI) of the ATM address. The LEC MAC addresses are not unique, but all other ATM addresses are unique.

ATM LANE Addresses

ATM LANE addresses consist of the following:

- A 13-byte prefix that includes the following fields defined by the ATM Forum:

    - Authority and Format Identifier (AFI) field (1 byte)

    - Data Country Code (DCC) or International Code Designator (ICD) field (2 bytes)

    - Domain-Specific Part Format Identifier (DFI) field (1 byte)

    - Administrative Authority field (3 bytes)

    - Reserved field (2 bytes)

    - Routing Domain field (2 bytes)

    - Area field (2 bytes)

- A 6-byte end system

- A 1-byte selector field

Exam Essentials

Remember how ATM addressing works with the LANE module and components. The ATM LANE module automatically assigns ATM addresses for each of the LANE components. Besides each host, the LEC, LECS, LES, and BUS must have a unique ATM address.

Key Terms and Concepts

ATM: Asynchronous Transfer Mode. The international standard, identified by fixed-length, 53-byte cells, for transmitting cells in multiple-service systems such as voice, video, or data.

CLI: The command line interface is used on Cisco routers and switches for configurations of routers and switches. Other management tools are also available to configure the devices.

LANE: LAN Emulation. The technology that allows an ATM network to operate as a LAN backbone. To do so, the ATM network is required to provide multicast and broadcast support, address mapping (MAC to ATM), SVC management, and an operable packet format.

Sample Questions

1. Which is true about ATM addressing?

   A. The redundant P/S module automatically assigns ATM addresses for each of the LANE components.

   B. The T/R module automatically assigns ATM addresses for each of the LANE components.

   C. The ATM LANE module automatically assigns ATM addresses for each of the LANE components.

   D. The Supervisor module automatically assigns ATM addresses for each of the LANE components.

   Answer: C.

2. Which of the following modules must have unique ATM addresses?

A. LEC

B. LECS

C. LES

D. BUS

Answer: A, B, C, D.

Describe how ATM addresses are automatically assigned.

This objective will continue the discussion of ATM addresses and how they are automatically assigned in a LANE network.

This is an important objective in this chapter because it will give you the information on how ATM addresses are automatically assigned in a LANE network. This can help in troubleshooting an ATM network and also when gathering CLSC exam information.

Critical Information

Cisco provides the following method of constructing and assigning ATM and MAC addresses in an LECS database. A pool of 16 MAC addresses is assigned to each ATM module. Although 16 are provided, the switches use only the first 4. For constructing LANE addresses, the following assignments are made to the LANE components:

- Every LEC on the interface uses the first MAC address in the pool.

- Every LES on the interface uses the second MAC address in the pool.

- Every BUS on the interface uses the third MAC address in the pool.

- The LECS on the interface uses the fourth MAC address in the pool.

All the LANE components of a specific ELAN are configured on the same subinterface. Since a subinterface can contain only one LEC and one LES/BUS, the ATM addresses are different because of the manner in which Cisco products assign MAC addresses.

Exam Essentials

Remember how many MAC addresses are used with each ATM module. A pool of 16 MAC addresses is assigned to each ATM module. Although 16 are provided, the switches use only the first 4.

Key Terms and Concepts

ATM: Asynchronous Transfer Mode. The international standard, identified by fixed-length, 53-byte cells, for transmitting cells in multiple-service systems such as voice, video, or data.

CLI: The command line interface is used on Cisco routers and switches for configurations of routers and switches. Other management tools are also available to configure the devices.

LANE: LAN Emulation. The technology that allows an ATM network to operate as a LAN backbone. To do so, the ATM network is required to provide multicast and broadcast support, address mapping (MAC to ATM), SVC management, and an operable packet format.

Sample Questions

1. A pool of how many MAC addresses is assigned to each ATM module?

   A. 8

   B. 16

   C. 24

   D. 32

   Answer: B.

2. Although __ MAC addresses are provided, the switches use only the first __.

   A. 8, 4

   B. 16, 4

   C. 2, 4

   D. 1, 2

   Answer: B.

Describe the rules for assigning ATM components to interfaces.

It is essential for administrators to understand the initial startup and connection sequences for ATM LANE. This not only provides a basis for troubleshooting, but also helps you to evaluate proper placement of the LES/BUS and LECS modules.

This objective is important because it will give you the background on ATM and the rules for assigning the components to interfaces.

Critical Information

Although it's not required, most LANE environments make use of the LECS to provide configuration information to the end node. This connection, using a configuration-direct VCC, queries for an LECS in the following order:

1. Use the address for the LECS that has been preconfigured on the local LEC.

2. Use ILMI to locate the LECS.

3. Use the LECS well-known address. This address is 47:00:79:00:00:00:00:00:00:00:00:00:00:00:A0:3E:00:0 1:00 and is specified by the ATM Forum.

After contacting the LECS, the client has sufficient information to contact the LES, including some operating information for the ELAN. The LEC-to-LES connection is established with a join command on a bidirectional control-direct VCC. The LES is responsible for registering the LEC and permitting it to join the ELAN.

The LEC is now responsible for locating the BUS. This is accomplished via LE-ARP, or LAN Emulation Address Resolution Protocol. The LES will respond to this request with the address of the BUS. The LEC then registers and joins the BUS.

Figure 14.1 illustrates the initial startup sequence of ATM LANE.

When a client needs to send data to an unknown resource, the LES and BUS cooperate to provide the correct information. The LEC will send an LE-ARP request to the LES for the destination station, and, prior to receiving a response, also will send the initial data cells to the BUS, which will forward the data cells to the destination and all other stations. Once the destination client receives the LE-ARP request from the LES, it responds, and the address information is forwarded to the source. The source then sends a "flush" message to the BUS, instructing it to stop sending any unsent cells and to discard them. The source will establish a direct connection with the destination, and the remaining data will be sent.

F I G U R E 14.1: The initial ATM LANE sequence

Phase 1: The LEC queries the LECS.

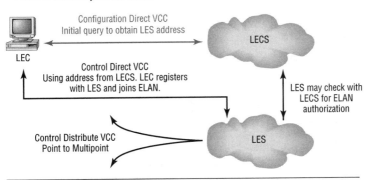

Phase 2: The LEC joins the ELAN.

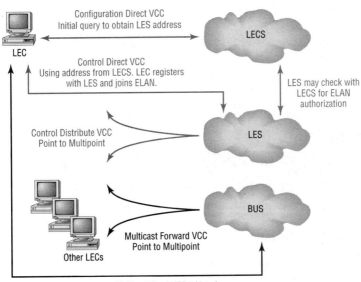

Phase 3: The LEC connects to the BUS.

Exam Essentials

Remember when LE-ARP is used. When a client needs to send data to an unknown resource, the LES and BUS cooperate to provide the correct information. The LEC will send an LE-ARP request to the LES for the destination station, and, prior to receiving a response, also will send the initial data cells to the BUS, which will forward the data cells to the destination and all other stations.

Key Terms and Concepts

ATM: Asynchronous Transfer Mode. The international standard, identified by fixed-length, 53-byte cells, for transmitting cells in multiple-service systems such as voice, video, or data.

CLI: The command line interface is used on Cisco routers and switches for configurations of routers and switches. Other management tools are also available to configure the devices.

LANE: LAN Emulation. The technology that allows an ATM network to operate as a LAN backbone. To do so, the ATM network is required to provide multicast and broadcast support, address mapping (MAC to ATM), SVC management, and an operable packet format.

Sample Questions

1. The LEC is responsible for locating the BUS. How does it do this?

   A. With LARP

   B. With LE-ARP

   C. With ARP

   D. With LEC

   Answer: B.

2. When a client needs to send data to an unknown resource, what two items cooperate to provide the correct information?

   A. LECS, BUS

   B. BUS, LECs

   C. LES, BUS

   D. LE-ARP, BUS

   Answer: C.

Configure LANE components on a Catalyst 5000 switch.

When configuring the LANE module, it is important to remember that the ATM LANE configuration is not stored or modified in the Supervisor engine. As a result, the administrator must connect to the ATM LANE module to continue.

In this objective, the commands to connect to and configure an ATM LANE module will be given. The "Necessary Procedures" section will give you an example of how to use the following commands to configure the ATM LANE module.

This objective is important when studying for your CLSC exam and when gathering information to configure your internetwork.

Critical Information

In this section, you will see the steps used to configure an ATM LANE module.

1. Connect to the ATM LANE module and enter configuration mode.

2. The administrator must enter enable mode and configure the ATM interface on the LANE module.

3. The ATM addresses of the LEC, LES, BUS, and LECS should be obtained and recorded. Note that this assumes that the LANE module is connected to the LS-1010 ASP via an LS-1010 line card or an external ATM switch. While it may be necessary to configure the LS-1010 during this process, the example will focus on the LANE module.

4. Start the LES and BUS.

5. Each connection will require an LEC.

6. If an LECS is desired, configure the LECS database and start the LECS.

Necessary Procedures

In this section, you will see an example of how to configure a LANE module.

1. Connect to the ATM LANE module and enter configuration mode. In this example, the ATM LANE module is in slot 4.

    ```
    Switch_A> session 4
    ```

2. The administrator must enter enable mode and configure the ATM interface on the LANE module:

    ```
    ATM_LANE>en
    ATM_LANE#conf t
    ATM_LANE (config)#int atm 0
    ATM_LANE (config-if)#mtu 1500
    ATM_LANE (config-if)#lane config auto-config-atm-address
    ATM_LANE (config-if)#no shutdown
    ```

3. The ATM addresses of the LEC, LES, BUS, and LECS should be obtained and recorded. Note that this assumes that the LANE module is connected to the LS-1010 ASP via an LS-1010 line card or an external ATM switch.

    ```
    ATM_LANE#show lane default-atm-address
    ```

4. While it may be necessary to configure the LS-1010 during this process, the example will focus on the LANE module. Thus, the fourth step is to start the LES and BUS:

ATM_LANE (config)#**int atm 0.1**
ATM_LANE (config-subif)#**lane server-bus ethernet elan1**

5. Each connection will require an LEC:

ATM_LANE (config-subif)#**lane client ethernet 1 elan1**

6. If an LECS is desired, the sixth step would be to configure the LECS database and start the LECS:

ATM_LANE (config)#**lane database lecs_db**
ATM_LANE (lane-config-database)#**name elan1 server-atm-address**
[server1-address]
ATM_LANE (config-if)#**lane config lecs_db**

The *server1-address* value is supplied by the show lane default-atm-address output in step 3. The LECS database may be named differently from the convention shown here. Many administrators prefer the easily understood convention shown.

NOTE   The commands to enter and leave different command modes were omitted for space considerations and clarity of the actual LANE commands.

Please use the prompts to indicate changes. Also note that this sample configured only interface ATM 0.1 and its physical interface.

Exam Essentials

Remember where the LANE configuration is stored.   When configuring the LANE module, it is important to remember that the ATM LANE configuration is not stored or modified in the Supervisor engine.

Remember the step to perform after connecting to the ATM LANE module.   Configure the ATM interface on the LANE module.

Key Terms and Concepts

ATM: Asynchronous Transfer Mode. The international standard, identified by fixed-length, 53-byte cells, for transmitting cells in multiple-service systems such as voice, video, or data.

CLI: The command line interface is used on Cisco routers and switches for configurations of routers and switches. Other management tools are also available to configure the devices.

LANE: LAN Emulation. The technology that allows an ATM network to operate as a LAN backbone. To do so, the ATM network is required to provide multicast and broadcast support, address mapping (MAC to ATM), SVC management, and an operable packet format.

Sample Questions

1. Which is true regarding ATM LANE configuration?

   A. The ATM LANE configuration is done on the Supervisor module.

   B. The ATM LANE configuration is done on the ATM LANE module.

   C. The ATM LANE configuration is done on the redundant Supervisor module.

   D. The ATM LANE configuration is done on T/r modules.

   Answer: B.

2. How do you record the ATM addressees of the LEC, LES, BUS, and LECS?

   A. `show default-atm-address lane`

   B. `show default lane-atm-address`

   C. `show lane default-atm-address`

   D. `lane show default-atm-address`

   Answer: C.

CHAPTER

15

Catalyst 1900 and
Catalyst 2820 Hardware

Cisco Exam Objectives Covered in This Chapter

▶ **Describe the major features and benefits of the Catalyst 1900 and Catalyst 2820 switches.** *(pages 307 – 311)*

▶ **Describe the hardware components and their functions of the Catalyst 1900 and Catalyst 2820 switches.** *(pages 312 – 320)*

▶ **Describe the architecture.** *(pages 320 – 325)*

In this chapter, the features, benefits, limitations, hardware, and architecture of the Catalyst 1900 and 2820 series of switches will be examined. The features and benefits unique to the Catalyst 1900 series will be discussed, followed by the features and benefits found only in the Catalyst 2820 series, closing with the features and benefits common to both series of switches.

The chapter will then move on to describe the hardware components and functions of the two series of switches. This section will deal primarily with the fixed-configuration differences in the Catalyst 1900 series models and the various expansion modules offered for the Catalyst 2820 series.

Finally, the chapter will go into some detail regarding the internal ClearChannel architecture common to both series of switches to include the forwarding engine, embedded control unit, shared buffer memory, and packet exchange bus.

The material covered in this chapter is important to know, both for the exam and in the real world, because detailed knowledge of the capabilities and potential limitations of the devices you may consider for deployment is crucial to providing solutions that are both technologically and fiscally sound. Often, the top-of-the-line technological solution is too expensive for a given scenario; however, just as often, a very low-end solution may be financially attractive at first, but end up having many hidden costs due to inability to scale or adapt. Therefore, a wise policy is to be familiar with the advantages and drawbacks of devices at all possible points in the cost spectrum.

Describe the major features and benefits of the Catalyst 1900 and Catalyst 2820 switches.

In this objective, you will receive details on the features, benefits, and some of the limitations of the Catalyst 1900 and 2820 series of switches. Again, it is important to be familiar with the advantages and drawbacks of all devices you may consider for deployment. The next two related objectives will go into further detail on the available hardware options and the internal architecture of the switches.

Critical Information

The Catalyst 1900 and 2820 switches are Cisco's low-cost switching products. As a part of the CiscoFusion scalable architecture (Cisco Systems' solution for next-generation internetworking), these switches focus on delivering cost-effectiveness primarily for desktop and workgroup applications. Although Cisco has introduced the Catalyst 2900 series of switches to their lower-end product line, the exam covers only the 1900 and 2820 series.

The Catalyst 1900 series offers the following:

- 12 or 24 switched 10BaseT ports (RJ-45)

- One or two 100Mbps switched ports, depending on model, and one 100BaseTX port, two 100BaseTX ports, or one 100BaseTX port and one 100BaseFX port for a total maximum of 27 ports

- 100Mbps ports can be set to CollisionFree full-duplex mode to support 200Mbps bandwidth and extended distances with fiber cabling

- 1024-MAC-address cache (maximum entries in forwarding table)

- No expansion slots

- One rack unit high (1.75")

The Catalyst 2820 series offers the following:

- 24 switched 10BaseT ports (RJ-45)

- Two field-pluggable expansion slots for high-speed modules (100BaseT, FDDI, and ATM modules)

- 2048- or 8192-MAC-address cache (maximum entries in forwarding table), depending on model (not field upgradable)

- Up to 100,000 pps between 10BaseT and FDDI ports

- Up to 133,000 pps between 10BaseT and ATM ports

- Two rack units high (3.5")

Both the 1900 and 2820 series offer the following:

- A 13th (12-port 1900 series model) or 25th switched 10Mbps port via AUI for attachment to thick coaxial, thin coaxial, UTP, or fiber-media transceiver

- Cut-through (FastForward and FragmentFree) or store-and-forward switching

- 320Mbps maximum forwarding bandwidth

- 450,000 pps aggregate packet-forwarding rate

- 14,880 pps between 10BaseT ports

- 133,900 pps between 10BaseT and 100BaseT ports

- 31 microsecond FIFO latency between 10BaseT ports when using cut-through switching

- 7 microsecond FIFO latency between 100BaseT ports when using cut-through switching

- IEEE 802.1d STP support

- Shared memory architecture with 3MB packet buffer

- Connection to a redundant power system

- Up to four VLANs allowing ports to be grouped into separate logical networks

- Cisco Group Membership Protocol (CGMP)

- Port security to prevent unauthorized access to the network

- Flooding and broadcast storm controls

- Management support with CiscoView device management, Cisco Discovery Protocol (CDP), four groups of embedded RMON, and Telnet and SNMP support for in-band and a menu-driven out-of-band management console

The Catalyst 1900 series replaces the Catalyst 1700 and 2100 series. The Catalyst 2820 series replaces the Catalyst 2800 series. However, the modules supported by the Catalyst 2800 series are also supported by the Catalyst 2820 series. The Catalyst 1900 and 2820 series offer a lower cost, reduced form factor, and greater functionality compared to the Catalyst switch products they are intended to replace. The lower cost was achieved by reducing the number of components, developing new and improved ASICs, and designing a smaller enclosure. The use of the shared buffer architecture allows a lower cost while providing high performance.

Exam Essentials

Remember the following about the Catalyst 1900 series switches. The 1900 series offers the following:

- 12 or 24 switched 10BaseT ports

- 13th or 25th switched 10Mbps port via AUI

- One or two fixed 100Mbps ports (three models)

- 1024-MAC-address maximum in forwarding table

- No expansion slots

- One rack unit

Remember the Catalyst 2820 series' features, benefits, and limitations. They are as follows:

- 24 switched 10BaseT ports

- 25th switched 10Mbps ports via AUI

- 2048- or 8192-MAC-address maximum in forwarding table (two models, *not* field upgradable)

- Two expansion slots for FastEthernet, FDDI, and ATM modules

- Two rack units

Remember the common features and benefits of both the Catalyst 1900 and 2820 series switches. They are as follows:

- Cut-through or store-and-forward switching

- CiscoView and Telnet management

Key Terms and Concepts

AUI: Attachment Unit Interface. A DB-15 connector used to connect an Ethernet interface to various media transceivers; e.g., thick coaxial, thin coaxial, UTP, or fiber-optic cabling.

CollisionFree: Cisco's marketing name for full-duplex operation.

Full-duplex: An Ethernet mode of operation where both the carrier-sense and collision detection circuitry are disabled because a dedicated bidirectional circuit exists between two nodes.

Rack unit: A vertical height unit of 1.75", equivalent to one space in an equipment rack.

Sample Questions

1. The Catalyst 2822 switch supports a cache of what?

   A. 1024 MAC addresses

   B. 2048 MAC addresses

   C. 4096 MAC addresses

   D. 8192 MAC addresses

Answer: B.

2. How many switched 10BaseT ports does a Catalyst 2828 switch provide?

   A. 12

   B. 24

   C. 28

   D. 56

Answer: B.

3. The Catalyst 2828 switch supports a cache of what?

   A. 1024 MAC addresses

   B. 2048 MAC addresses

   C. 4096 MAC addresses

   D. 8192 MAC addresses

Answer: D.

Describe the hardware components and their functions of the Catalyst 1900 and Catalyst 2820 switches.

The three different fixed-configuration models of the Catalyst 1900 series, the two different base platforms of the Catalyst 2820 series, and the expansion modules available for the Catalyst 2820 series will be examined in detail under this objective. It is important to know the differences between the available hardware options to avoid numerous potential real-world problems; e.g., ordering the wrong piece of equipment because you thought it was something else and now not being able to perform the upgrade for which you just flew a thousand miles and spent a week arranging!

Critical Information

There are three different models in the Catalyst 1900 series. The Catalyst 1900 offers 24 10BaseT ports, 1 AUI port, and 2 100BaseTX ports. The Catalyst 1900C has 24 10BaseT ports, 1 AUI port, 1 100BaseTX port, and 1 100BaseFX port. Lastly, the Catalyst 1912 has 12 10BaseT ports, 1 AUI port, and 1 100BaseTX port. All other features are identical in all three models.

There are two base platforms, or models, in the Catalyst 2820 series. Both models offer 24 10BaseT ports, 1 AUI port, and 2 high-speed expansion module slots. The Catalyst 2822 supports a maximum of 2048 MAC addresses in its forwarding table, whereas the Catalyst 2828 supports a maximum of 8192 MAC addresses in its forwarding table. This is the *only* difference between the two models. Unfortunately, it is not possible to field-upgrade a Catalyst 2822 to a Catalyst 2828. Both models support switched or shared FastEthernet, FDDI, and ATM expansion modules.

Also, both series of switches provide a number of LEDs as at-a-glance indicators.

System LED: Green when everything's fine with the switch, amber when the switch failed POST, and off when the switch is not powered up.

Expansion Slot Status LEDs: Found only on switches of the Catalyst 2820 series since the Catalyst 1900 series does not offer expansion slots. The LED marked A refers to the left expansion module slot, and the LED marked B refers to the right expansion module slot. They are green when the module in the expansion slot is operational, flashing green when the module is running POST, amber when the module failed POST, and off when no module is installed.

Redundant Power System LED: Green when the redundant power system is operational and the local power supply is unplugged, alternating green and off when the redundant power system is working and the local power supply is plugged in (you're not supposed to do this), amber when a redundant power supply system is connected but has a problem, and off when a redundant power supply is not installed or powered up.

Port LEDs: The LEDs located above each port are used to indicate different things depending on the setting of the Mode button. The three modes toggled by the Mode button are Port Status (STAT), Bandwidth Utilization (UTL), and Full-Duplex Status (FDUP). The default mode is STAT, and toggling to UTL or FDUP mode is accomplished by pressing the Mode button until the desired mode is illuminated. The switch will return to the default mode of STAT after 30 seconds.

> **Port Status (STAT) mode:** The individual port LED is green when *Link*, indicating a good connection to a device attached to that port, is present; flashing green/off when receiving or transmitting data; alternating green/amber when there is a problem with the link due to CRC, jabber, or alignment errors, or excessive collisions; amber when the port is not forwarding due to suspension by management, port security

violation, or Spanning-Tree Protocol; and off when there is no Link.

Bandwidth Utilization (UTL) mode: The port LEDs are used together to indicate current and peak utilization of the switch in the current bandwidth capture interval. The default interval for peak utilization is 24 hours captured every night at midnight. The interval can be modified through the management interface using the Bandwidth Usage Report option. The current bandwidth is displayed by a series of illuminated LEDs ending with one rapidly blinking LED. Peak bandwidth is indicated by the right-most solidly lit LED. The bandwidth utilization indicated for a Catalyst 1900 or 2820 series switch with 24 10BaseT ports is as follows:

Port LEDs	Mbps
1 to 8	0.1 to < 6
9 to 16	6 to < 120
17 to 24	120 to 280

The bandwidth utilization indicated for a Catalyst 1912 switch is as follows:

Port LEDs	Mbps
1 to 4	0.1 to < 1.5
5 to 8	1.5 to < 20
9 to 12	20 to 140

Full-Duplex Status (FDUP) mode: The individual port LED is green if that port is operating in full-duplex mode and is off if it is not—i.e., it's operating in half-duplex mode.

The rear panels of both series of switches are where you'll find the RS-232 serial port, the reset switch, the AUI port, the RPS connector, the AC power receptacle, and the fans. The RS-232 serial port is a DB-9 configured as DTE, so to connect a terminal, the null modem cable that ships with the switch would be required. The reset switch is a recessed, last-resort, momentary switch that would require the use of a paper clip or pen to depress. Resetting the switch has the same effect as turning the switch off and on, so resetting should be used only if the switch has stopped responding to network management or stopped forwarding frames. The AUI port is a DB-15 connector where media transceivers for thick coaxial, thin coaxial, UTP, or fiber can be connected.

The Catalyst 2820 series supports four types of FastEthernet modules, three types of FDDI modules, and two types of ATM modules. The FastEthernet modules are one switched 100BaseTX port, eight shared 100BaseTX ports, one switched 100BaseFX port, or four shared 100BaseFX ports. The FDDI modules are MMF DAS, MMF SAS, and UTP SAS (CDDI). The ATM modules are MMF OC-3 and UTP OC-3.

All of the expansion modules are hot-swappable and can be installed with power applied, without interrupting the network. Installation is directly into the expansion slots and generally will not require the use of tools, unless someone has previously tightened the thumbscrews beyond hand pressure. The Catalyst 2820 will automatically diagnose and verify the expansion module's operation.

All of the FastEthernet modules are compatible with the IEEE 802.3u standard. The 100BaseTX modules have RJ-45 connectors for connecting via Category 5 UTP cabling. The 100BaseFX modules have ST connectors and can use either 50/125- or 62.5/125-micron multimode fiber-optic cabling. Both of the single-port switched modules have four LEDs:

Link LED: Indicates good communications with a powered-up device. This LED is on when the link integrity test passes, off when it fails. To aid in troubleshooting, this LED will blink whenever an improperly formed frame is received.

Activity LED: Blinks when the port is transmitting or receiving data. If the traffic level is high, the LED is on continuously. Conversely, the LED is off if there is no activity.

Disabled LED: When the port is disabled or suspended by a network connection error, a secure address violation, or the management console, this LED is on.

Full Duplex LED: On when the port is operating in full-duplex mode and off when operating in half-duplex mode.

The two shared, multiport modules have three LEDs for each of the individual ports:

Link LED: Operates identically to the Link LED described for the single-port switched modules above.

Receive LED: Blinks when the port is receiving data. The LED will be on continuously if the traffic level is high and off if there is no activity.

Disabled LED: Operates identically to the Disabled LED described for the single-port switched modules above, with the exception of blinking if the port is automatically disabled due to a jabber or auto-partition error.

There are two LEDs for the overall group:

Group Activity LED: Blinks when any of the shared ports are transmitting or receiving data. If there is no activity, the LED is off. If the traffic level is high, the LED is on continuously.

Group Collision LED: Blinks when there is a collision within the group of shared ports. If no collisions are detected, the LED is off.

All three of the FDDI modules are compatible with the ANSI X3T12 standard. The MMF modules have MIC connectors and can use either 50/125- or 62.5/125-micron multimode fiber-optic cabling. The DAS module has two MIC connectors and a six-pin mini-DIN connector to connect to an optical bypass switch. The SAS module has only one MIC connector. The CDDI module has an RJ-45 connector for use with Category 5 UTP cabling. All three of the modules support Automatic Packet Recognition/Translation (APaRT), MTU path discovery, and IP fragmentation; automatically detect the correct Ethernet and FDDI format; and have three LEDs:

Connected: Illuminated when the module is connected to an operational FDDI ring. The LED is off when the module is not connected to the FDDI ring.

Activity: Blinks when the port is receiving or transmitting data. Continuous illumination or rapid blinking indicates the traffic level is high. When there is no activity, the LED is off.

Disabled: Lit when the port is disabled by a secure address violation or administrative intervention via the management console.

NOTE The LEDs also indicate the type of failure when the module fails the POST.

Both of the ATM modules provide a Physical-layer interface to an ATM switch and can be used to connect to a LightStream 1010, a multilayer LAN switch—e.g., Catalyst 5000 series—with an installed ATM module, or a router with an ATM interface—e.g., Cisco 7000 or 7500 series. The MM module has an SC connector, and the UTP module has an RJ-45 connector. Both modules include the following features:

- 155.52Mbps data transfer.

- Full-duplex operation.

- Store-and-forward packet relay.

- LAN Emulation Client (LEC) *only* for emulated LANs and AAL5 (ATM Adaptation Layer 5) for LANE (LAN Emulation) data transfer. The ATM module *cannot* act as the LECS, LES, or BUS.

- UNI (User-Network Interface) 3.0 and 3.1 for SVCs (Switched Virtual Circuits) and PVCs (Permanent Virtual Circuits).

Each ATM module also supports the following ATM management features:

- Integrated Link Management Interface (ILMI) for ATM UNI 3.0 and 3.1 MIBs

- Operation, administration, and maintenance (OAM)

Each model of the ATM module also complies with the following standards:

- LANE 1.0 for LANE client *only*

- Synchronous Optical Network (SONET) and Synchronous Transport Signal level 3 (STS-3c) physical layer

- SONET Digital Hierarchy (SDH)

Both modules have only a single LED, which is solid green when the module is connected to an operational ATM switch; flashing green when transmitting or receiving data; solid amber when the module is disabled due to secure address violation, POST failure, or administrative action via the management console; and off when the module is not connected to an ATM network or device.

Exam Essentials

Know the differences among the models of the Catalyst 1900 series. The features are as follows:

1900: 24 10BaseT ports, 1 AUI port, 2 100BaseTX ports

1900C: 24 10BaseT ports, 1 AUI port, 1 100BaseTX port, 1 100BaseFX port

1912: 12 10BaseT ports, 1 AUI port, 1 100BaseTX port

Remember the only difference between the Catalyst 2822 and 2828. The difference is as follows:

2822: 2048-MAC-address cache

2828: 8192-MAC-address cache

Know the meaning of the various LEDs on the Catalyst 1900 and 2820 series. Generally, solid green is good—e.g., operational or link-integrity test passed; flashing green means activity—e.g., POST running or packets moving; amber is bad—e.g., POST failed or disabled due to various reasons; and off means absence or lack of activity—e.g., not powered up, not installed, or no packets moving.

Remember the different types of modules available for the Catalyst 2820 series.   They are as follows:

FastEthernet: One switched or eight shared 100BaseTX, one switched or four shared 100BaseFX

FDDI: MMF SAS or DAS and UTP SAS

ATM: MMF or UTP OC-3

Key Terms and Concepts

Address cache: A table where a switch keeps a record of which MAC addresses are associated with which ports—e.g., given a frame with destination MAC address x, the switch should forward that frame out port y.

LED: Light-emitting diode.

Null modem: A serial "crossover" device that makes it possible for two serial devices of the same role, primarily DTE-DTE, to communicate without the need for modems.

POST: Power On Self Test.

Sample Questions

1. When the Catalyst 1900 system LED is amber, what does this mean?

   A. The switch is operating normally.

   B. The switch is running POST.

   C. The switch failed POST.

   D. The redundant power supply is not operational.

Answer: C.

2. What do the Catalyst 2820 100BaseFX modules support?

   A. One switched or four shared 100Mbps ports

   B. One shared or four switched 100Mbps ports

   C. One switched or eight shared 100Mbps ports

   D. One shared or eight switched 100Mbps ports

   Answer: A.

3. Which of the following is *not* an FDDI module supported by the Catalyst 2820 series?

   A. UTP SAS module

   B. UTP DAS module

   C. MMF DAS module

   D. MMF SAS module

   Answer: B.

Describe the architecture.

The internal ClearChannel architecture common to both the Catalyst 1900 and 2820 series will be examined in this objective. This includes the management interface(s), which are handled by the embedded control unit, the forwarding engine (the heart of the switch), the shared buffer memory, and the packet exchange bus. Knowledge of the internal architecture of any device you'll be deploying is important so that you'll be familiar with the conditions under which a limitation of the internal architecture could cause a production problem—e.g., Head-of-Line blocking in per-port buffered switch architectures.

Critical Information

The 1Gbps packet exchange bus (X-bus), forwarding engine, embedded control unit (ECU), management interface, 3MB shared buffer memory, and switched ports all comprise the ClearChannel architecture.

X-Bus

The X-bus is a 53-bit-wide bus running at 20MHz. This 1.06Gbps bandwidth enables the switch to be completely nonblocking—i.e., able to handle wire speed on all ports concurrently. The Catalyst 1900 and 2820 series switches each provide up to 27 switched ports, consuming up to 450Mbps of bandwidth, which is less than half of the 1.06Gbps available switch bandwidth. Port access to the packet exchange bus is pipelined to prevent loss of bandwidth. The X-bus is also used to transmit signals between switch components for initiating transactions associated with transmitting and receiving packets.

All traffic passing through the switch traverses the bus, so access to the bus is prioritized by a separate master scheduler, because several components might simultaneously attempt to place data on the bus. Bus access is sequenced by transaction priority and time of arrival. Transactions are scheduled by a combination of transaction priority and port priority. A transaction sending status at the end of a transmission, for example, has a lower priority than one requesting buffer memory for a packet. Port 1 has the lowest priority, and port 27 has the highest. Each port tells the forwarding engine it has a packet engine and grabs packets based on priority. Fortunately, the bus runs fast enough that no user will be able to see a difference.

Forwarding Engine

The forwarding engine is the heart of the switch. It is responsible for the defining purpose of the switch: examining packets from incoming ports, allocating packet buffers, looking up the destination address, and queuing them to the appropriate port(s) for transmission. To ensure low latency, higher throughput, reduced complexity, increased reliability, and consequently lower switch cost, the forwarding engine is implemented entirely in hardware (ASIC).

Once the forwarding engine determines that a packet is to be forwarded, it waits until it receives the number of bytes associated with the configured switching mode and then initiates forwarding to the appropriate port(s). In FastForward mode, forwarding begins as soon as the destination address is received. In FragmentFree mode, forwarding begins only after receiving 64 bytes, which eliminates forwarding of collision fragments. Finally, in Store-and-Forward mode, forwarding does not begin until after the entire frame is received, introducing a variable latency dependent on frame length.

By monitoring the packet exchange bus, the engine is able to collect and maintain switch statistics in addition to processing packets. It is able to count packet lengths, throughput, errors, and exceptions. This data can be collected by network management stations to monitor traffic patterns and construct switch statistics tables, which can, in turn, be used to help design more efficient network architectures.

Embedded Control Unit

The embedded control unit (ECU) handles configuration and supervision; the interface for both in-band and out-of-band management; statistics reporting, diagnostics, and error handling; control of the front panel display; control of the Spanning-Tree Protocol; and the embedded RMON agent that provides enhanced manageability, monitoring, and traffic analysis to a network management station. Basically, the ECU handles everything not taken care of by the forwarding engine.

The forwarding engine is an Application Specific Integrated Circuit (ASIC) and so is very fast at what it does, but this also makes it incapable of any task that is not always handled exactly the same way. The ECU is the general-purpose processor that takes care of everything else. In the case of the Catalyst 1900 and 2820 series switches, the general-purpose processor is the Intel 486 CPU. This division of labor allows for frame-forwarding functions to be handled at wire speed with minimal latency in hardware, leaving the ECU to handle more complicated processing.

The ECU subsystem is made of the following components:

- Embedded CPU

- 512KB DRAM (for CPU)

- 1MB flash memory for firmware, configuration data, and statistics

The flash memory, in turn, is partitioned into three areas:

- Switch software image (768KB)

- Switch configuration data (192KB)

- Boot sector (32KB)

The switch software image area is what changes during software upgrades. The switch configuration data is stored above this in flash memory and is modified whenever a new switch configuration is written. At the top of the flash memory, there is the write-protected boot sector. The boot sector is write-protected to ensure that at least one section of the flash memory always retains its data integrity, allowing the switch to boot up correctly every time, and because the boot sector contains the diagnostic console that is used to recover from a failed upgrade, which can happen in the event of a power failure during the upgrade process, before a complete image gets written to flash memory.

Exam Essentials

Know the major components of the ClearChannel architecture. They are the management interface, embedded control unit (ECU), forwarding engine, shared buffer memory, and packet exchange bus (X-bus).

Remember the bandwidth of the packet exchange bus (X-bus).
It is 53 bits wide, running at 20MHz, for a total bandwidth of 1Gbps.
This is enough to handle all 27 ports in a completely nonblocking
manner.

**Remember that the forwarding engine is the heart of the
switch.** The forwarding engine is an ASIC that makes it possible to
ensure low latency and high throughput while switching frames at
wire speed on all ports.

Remember that the ECU handles everything else. The
embedded control unit subsystem is essentially a 486 with 512KB of
RAM and 1MB of flash memory. It handles everything not taken care
of by the forwarding engine.

**Know the amount of shared buffer memory, the advantage to
using a shared memory architecture, and the maximum alloca-
tion for any one port at a given instant.** The shared buffer
memory is 3MB of RAM divided into 2048 1.5KB packet buffers.
Shared memory architectures don't have receive queues and are therefore not subject to Head-of-Line blocking. No port is allowed to have
more than half the total shared buffer memory at any given instant to
prevent other ports from being starved out.

Key Terms and Concepts

ASIC: Application Specific Integrated Circuit. A highly specialized chip capable of handling identical repetitive operations very
quickly, but unable to perform any function outside of what it was
created for.

ClearChannel architecture: Name given to the overall internal
architecture of the Catalyst 1900 and 2820 series switches.

ECU: Embedded control unit.

X-bus: Packet exchange bus.

Sample Questions

1. What is the bandwidth of the packet exchange bus (X-bus)?

 A. 450Mbps

 B. 20MHz

 C. 1Gbps

 D. 53 bits

 Answer: C.

2. What part of the internal architecture is considered the heart of the switch?

 A. The packet exchange bus (X-bus)

 B. The forwarding engine

 C. The shared buffer memory

 D. The embedded control unit (ECU)

 Answer: B.

CHAPTER

16

Catalyst 1900 and
Catalyst 2820 Features

Cisco Exam Objectives Covered in This Chapter

▶ **Describe the following key features and applications of the Catalyst 1900 and Catalyst 2820 switches:** *(pages 329 – 334)*

- Switching modes
- Virtual LANs
- Multicast packet filtering and registration
- Broadcast storm control
- Management support, CDP, and CGMP

▶ **Trace a frame's progress through a Catalyst 1900 or a Catalyst 2820 switch.** *(pages 334 – 337)*

This chapter will give you an overview of the Catalyst 1900 and 2820 switches. You will receive details of LAN switching methods, VLANs, multicast packet filtering, and management support.

This chapter will finish by discussing the forwarding engine, which determines if a packet needs to be forwarded.

This is an important chapter to read and understand if you work in a switched internetwork and also if you are gathering information for the CLSC exam.

Describe the following key features and applications of the Catalyst 1900 and Catalyst 2820 switches:

- Switching modes
- Virtual LANs
- Multicast packet filtering and registration
- Broadcast storm control
- Management support, CDP, and CGMP

This first objective will give you the features of the Catalyst 1900 and 2820 switches. You will receive details on LAN switch types, VLANs, packet filtering, broadcast control, and management support.

This is an important objective when studying the 1900 and 2820 features.

Critical Information

This section will give you details on the following:

- LAN switching modes
- VLANs
- Multicast packet filtering
- Broadcast control
- Management support

Switching Modes

The Catalyst 1900 and 2820 series switches support three types of switching methods: FastForward, FragmentFree, and store-and-forward.

FastForward (cut-through): This method provides the least amount of latency by immediately forwarding the packet after reading the destination address of the packet. Problems can arise with this type of switching because the packet is not checked for errors, which means that packets with errors are sent. Latency is measured in FastForward by timing first in, first out (FIFO). Fast-Forward is typically used on ports connected to single nodes.

FragmentFree (modified cut-through): This method removes some of the problems associated with FastForward switching by eliminating collision fragments. Essentially, this method waits until the switch has determined that the frame is not fragmented before forwarding the frame, so you might want to try this method if your network is experiencing a significant number of collision fragments. Again, latency is measured by FIFO.

Store-and-forward: This method stores the entire packet before forwarding it to another port. Typically used for forwarding between 10Mbps and 100Mbps segments, this switching configuration is suggested for networks experiencing FCS or alignment errors. The switch controls unwanted errors, providing the most error-free methodology. Latency is measured by last bit received to first bit transmitted (LIFO).

Virtual LANs

The Catalyst 1900 and 2820 series switches each support up to four separate VLANs. This allows you to configure four separate broadcast domains for devices plugged into ports on the switch. You'll gain two benefits from implementing VLANs between broadcast domains: It allows the control of multicast flooding within a VLAN, and traffic does not cross over to other VLANs. It is necessary to have a router present to route traffic between domains when moving between VLANs.

Multicast Packet Filtering and Registration

Multicast address filtering allows the Catalyst switches to handle both IP multicasts and MAC address multicast protocols. You can combine the filtering with source-port filtering to balance the server load across servers. Source-port filtering is the method of filtering traffic based on the destination of the packet and the source port.

Multicast address registration allows you to specify which multicast addresses and their ports are allowed to receive forwarded packets. Beware—the default configuration has the switch forwarding all multicast or broadcast packets to all ports, which will flood your network. Use the switch management to specify which ports will handle which multicast traffic and disable flooding of multicasts across the network.

Broadcast Storm Control

Cisco also has included broadcast storm control. Cisco's IOS allows you to control deployment between routers and switches, thus restricting packets' transmissions to specified ports. Communication with routers is established using Cisco Group Management Protocol (CGMP).

The Catalyst 1900 and 2820 switches have a management option that allows you to set a threshold that controls the number of broadcast packets that can be received from a port before forwarding is disabled at that port. Another management option allows you to configure a packets-per-second (pps) threshold that enables the port once again to forward packets. Broadcast storm control is disabled in the initial startup of the switch.

WARNING   It is important to know that the switch does not eliminate broadcasts; it only prevents a broadcast storm from being forwarded across all ports.

Management Support, CDP, and CGMP

In this section, some of the management options possible once you've deployed one of the switches will be reviewed. Cisco has developed both in-band and out-of-band management capabilities into all of their switches. Besides providing management tools, Cisco has allowed for statistics collection by including an RMON MIB. An implementation of RMON called SPAN allows you to place a traffic analyzer on the switch to monitor traffic across the backplane.

SNMP Management

Any SNMP- or SMT-based management platform can help you manage the Catalyst 1900 and 2820 switches. You can access the menu by connecting a console or modem to the RS-232 port on the rear of the switch. If the switch has been configured with an IP address, you can manage it with a Telnet session. Up to seven sessions can be held simultaneously. A built-in RMON MIB allows a platform that communicates via SNMP to monitor nine groups of information pertaining to the switch's operation.

CDP

Cisco Discovery Protocol (CDP) is a protocol developed and used by Cisco devices to exchange information between themselves and other devices on the network. Cisco IOS employs its CDP to form a "picture" of the surrounding network.

CDP gathers information from other devices concerning their types, configuration information, and the amount of interfaces and their activity within each device. The CDP packet is sent in a Sub-Network Access Protocol (SNAP) frame and is not routable. In other words, no logical layer 3 information is contained in the header. CDP packets are broadcast every 60 seconds by default out all active interfaces.

CGMP

Cisco Group Management Protocol provides a methodology for intelligent routing software that limits multicast flooding to only specific ports interested in receiving the traffic. CGMP is a layer 3 enhancement that bridges the gap between Cisco's switches and the routers' IOS.

Exam Essentials

Remember that the Catalyst 1900 and 2820 series switches support three types of switching methods. The three types are Fast-Forward, FragmentFree, and store-and-forward.

Remember the amount of VLANs supported by the 1900 and 2820 switches. The Catalyst 1900 and 2820 series switches each support up to four separate VLANs.

Key Terms and Concepts

SSE: Silicon Switching Engine. The software component of Cisco's silicon switching technology, hard-coded into the Silicon Switch Processor (SSP).

Switch: In networking, a device responsible for multiple functions such as filtering, flooding, and sending frames. It works using the destination address of individual frames.

Sample Questions

1. Which LAN switching methodology runs a CRC?

   A. Store-and-forward

   B. FastForward

   C. First in, first out

   D. LIFO

   Answer: A.

2. What is the default switching method configured on startup for the Catalyst 1900?

   A. Store-and-forward

   B. Modified cut-through

   C. FastForward

   D. FragmentFree

   Answer: C.

3. How does the Catalyst 2820 handle broadcast storm control? (Choose all that apply.)

   A. Menu configuration

   B. Port closure

   C. Threshold setting

   D. Spanning-Tree Protocol

   Answer: B, C.

Trace a frame's progress through a Catalyst 1900 or a Catalyst 2820 switch.

This objective will provide information on the Catalyst 1900 and 2820 switches and how a frame progresses through the forwarding engine.

This is important information when troubleshooting the Catalyst switches and when gathering information for the CLSC exam.

Critical Information

Figure 16.1 shows how Cisco implements the forwarding engine on an ASIC, providing you with lower latency and higher throughput.

The implementation of the forwarding engine supplies the logic necessary for examining packets, allocating packet buffers, determining destination addresses, and collecting statistics. Statistics collected include packet lengths, throughput, errors, and exceptions that can be relayed to management stations located on the network for review.

F I G U R E 16.1: The forwarding engine

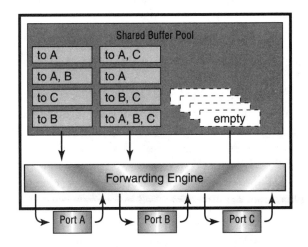

The forwarding engine determines whether a packet needs to be forwarded upon arrival at the bus. If the packet must be forwarded, the forwarding engine pauses and receives the bytes associated with the configured switching mode (FastForward, FragmentFree, or store-and-forward), then the packet is correctly forwarded to the outgoing port.

TIP Catalyst 1900 and 2820 switches use a shared buffer implementation. Most switches have port buffers that cause head-of-line blocking of packets.

The embedded control unit (ECU) is a separated subsystem that handles the components of network management. The ECU subsystem provides diagnostics, error handling, switch configuration, in-band

and out-of-band management, and statistics reporting. This clear separation frees the forwarding engine to use its full processing power for packet forwarding, leaving the ECU to process its own operations.

The ECU consists of an embedded CPU, 512KB of DRAM, and 1MB of flash memory for firmware, configuration data, and statistics. The flash memory is divided into three areas: the software image (768KB), switch configuration data (192KB), and the boot sector (32KB). The ECU also contains an embedded RMON software agent that provides you with enhanced management information.

The shared memory buffer is made up of 3MB of DRAM. The DRAM supports 2048 packet buffers by establishing guidelines for how large each packet buffer may be. This methodology allows the switch to eliminate the problem of head-of-line blocking, a common under-utilization problem associated with switches. To maintain control over a port's utilization of the shared buffer, a median has been established allowing no port to control more than 1.5MB of the packet buffer memory. This means that no more than half of the available memory can be controlled by any one port.

Exam Essentials

Remember what provides packet forwarding. The forwarding engine determines whether a packet needs to be forwarded upon arrival at the bus.

Key Terms and Concepts

SSE: Silicon Switching Engine. The software component of Cisco's silicon switching technology, hard-coded into the Silicon Switch Processor (SSP).

Switch: In networking, a device responsible for multiple functions such as filtering, flooding, and sending frames. It works using the destination address of individual frames.

Sample Questions

1. What does the forwarding engine do? (Choose all that apply.)

   A. Examines packets

   B. Maintains switch statistics

   C. Controls STP

   D. Handles diagnostics and errors

   Answer: A, B.

2. What determines if a packet needs to be forwarded?

   A. ECU

   B. SMU

   C. The forwarding engine

   D. DRAM

   Answer: C.

CHAPTER

17

Configuring Catalyst 1900 and
Catalyst 2820 Switches

Cisco Exam Objectives Covered in This Chapter

▶ **Use the Catalyst 1900 and Catalyst 2820 switch menus for configuration.** *(pages 341 – 344)*

▶ **Configure IP addresses and ports on the Catalyst 1900 and Catalyst 2820 switches.** *(pages 344 – 350)*

▶ **Configure VLANs on the Catalyst 1900 and Catalyst 2820 switches.** *(pages 350 – 355)*

▶ **View the Catalyst 1900 and Catalyst 2820 switch reports and summaries.** *(pages 355 – 360)*

▶ **Configure the ATM LANE module on the Catalyst 2820 switch.** *(pages 361 – 367)*

In this chapter, you will learn how to configure the Catalyst 1900 and 2820 switches. You will see the different switch menus, including how to set an IP address on the 1900 and 2820 switch.

You'll also learn how to configure ports and VLANS, as well as view the Catalyst switch reports and summaries. This chapter will finish by showing you how to configure the ATM LANE module used on the Catalyst 2820 switch.

This is a very important chapter to understand, as it will give you the needed information to configure your switches and to study for your CLSC exam.

Use the Catalyst 1900 and Catalyst 2820 switch menus for configuration.

In this first objective, you will read about the main menu and how to access this menu from a console port. This section will start off by giving you basic key points when connecting to a console port and accessing the main menu.

This objective is important to understand because it will give you the basic information you need to start configuring your Catalyst 1900 and 2820 switches, and will also provide the understanding you need when studying for your CLSC exam.

Critical Information

Configuration on both the Catalyst 1900 and Catalyst 2820 is menu-driven from the management console. There are some key points to understand before configuration may begin:

- To access a menu, press the bracketed letter shown to the left of that command. For example, pressing I opens the menu for IP configuration. Choosing any command will either open a lower-level menu or take you directly to the configuration of the item chosen.

- Always press the Enter key after inputting each parameter.

- In any menu, the X key will take you back to the previous menu.

- Input is not case sensitive. The only time case sensitivity can be an issue is when descriptive strings are entered into the switch.

- The Backspace key works as expected, deleting the previous character in the string. Pressing Backspace when the cursor is over the beginning of the character string will erase the entire parameter.

WARNING A parameter will take effect immediately, but it may take up to 30 seconds before being written to memory. If the switch is rebooted during this time, the change will be lost.

Choose the [M] option to enter the main menu, where you'll do all your other configuration. The menu is shown below:

```
Catalyst 1900 - Main Menu

    [C] Console Settings
    [S] System
    [N] Network Management
    [P] Port Configuration
    [A] Port Addressing
    [D] Port Statistics Detail
    [M] Monitoring
    [V] Virtual LAN
    [R] Multicast Registration
    [F] Firmware
    [I] RS-232 Interface
    [U] Usage Summaries
    [H] Help

    [X] Exit Management Console
```

The main menu of the Catalyst 2820 is shown below:

```
Catalyst 2820 - Main Menu
    [C] Console Settings
    [S] System
    [N] Network Management
    [P] Port Configuration
    [A] Port Addressing
    [D] Port Statistics Detail
    [M] Monitoring
    [B] Bridge Group
```

```
[R] Multicast Registration
[F] Firmware
[I] RS-232 Interface
[U] Usage Summaries
[H] Help
[X] Exit Management Console
Enter Selection:
```

NOTE   The 1900 has a VLAN option, and the 2820 has a Bridge Group option instead of the VLAN option.

Exam Essentials

Remember how to access the main menu on the Catalyst 1900 and 2820 switches.   After connecting to the switch with the console port, choose [M] to access the main menu.

Key Terms and Concepts

Catalyst: Series of switches acquired by Cisco.

Switch: In networking, a device responsible for multiple functions such as filtering, flooding, and sending frames. It works using the destination address of individual frames. Switches operate at the Data Link layer of the OSI model.

Sample Questions

1. Which of the following is true?

    A. The console works only at 9600 baud.

    B. You do not have to press the Enter key after making a selection.

    C. Input is case sensitive.

    D. Input is not case sensitive.

    Answer: D. Input is not case sensitive. The only time case sensitivity can be an issue is when descriptive strings are entered into the switch.

2. Which of the following is true?

    A. The console works only at 9600 baud.

    B. You have to press the Enter key after making a selection.

    C. Input is case sensitive.

    D. You cannot use the Backspace key.

    Answer: B. Always press the Enter key after inputting each parameter.

Configure IP addresses and ports on the Catalyst 1900 and Catalyst 2820 switches.

This objective will demonstrate how to assign an IP address to the switch for in-band management. Configuring an IP address on the switch then allows you to configure the switch from an SNMP-compatible workstation, a Telnet session, or a Web console.

This objective is important because it is important to be able to assign an IP address to a switch to provide in-band management.

Critical Information

As this objective consists mainly of procedures, see the "Necessary Procedures" section just below for the critical information of this objective.

Necessary Procedures

In this section, you will learn how to assign an IP address to the switch.

Configuring IP Addresses

After POST finishes, the Console Logon screen appears. Press the **I** key to enter the IP Configuration menu.

1. The IP Configuration menu will appear on the management console screen as shown below:

```
Catalyst 2820 - IP Configuration
Ethernet Address:    00-D0-1D-7D-D4-40
-------------------Settings-----------------
[I] IP address                        0.0.0.0
[S] Subnet mask                       0.0.0.0
[G] Default gateway                   0.0.0.0
[M] IP address of DNS server 1        0.0.0.0
[N] IP address of DNS server 2        0.0.0.0
[D] Domain name
[R] Use Routing Information Protocol       Enabled
--------------------- Actions ---------------------------
[P] Ping
[X] Exit to previous menu
Enter Selection:
```

2. Press I again to assign an IP address to the switch. Press Enter to accept the address after you have finished typing it in.

3. Press **S** to assign the subnet mask to the switch. Press Enter to accept the address after you have finished typing it in.

4. Press **G** to assign the default gateway to the switch. Press Enter to accept the address after you have finished typing it in.

5. If the network utilizes DNS servers, they may also be assigned from this menu by pressing **M** to assign the first DNS address and **N** to assign the secondary DNS address. A domain name may also be configured for the switch. Typically, this is used in environments with DNS servers so that a name resolution can be made to the switch. To configure the domain name, press **D**, type the domain name on the command line, and press Enter or Return.

6. Press **X** to exit the IP menu. The switch is now configured with an IP address.

TIP Remember that the switch will take 30 seconds before it saves the configuration change to memory. The IP address, however, has already taken effect once you press Enter.

---

7. After waiting at least a minute (to make sure the switch has taken the configuration), reset the switch.

In the next section, you will learn how to configure individual ports on a Catalyst 1900 and 2820 switch.

Configuring Ports

The Port Configuration menu (accessed from the main menu by pressing **P**) allows you to display the operating status of a port or module. You can also configure port descriptions, modify a port's status, and configure STP parameters. Typical Port Configuration menus for a 10BaseT and two different 100BaseT ports are shown below.

10BaseT Port Configuration

```
Port Configuration Menu (10BaseT Ports)
Catalyst 2820 - Port 1 Configuration
Built-in 10Base-T
802.1d STP State:    Blocking    Forward Transitions:    0
-------------------Settings------------------
[D] Description/name of port
[S] Status of port                    Suspended-no-linkbeat
[F] Full duplex                       Disabled
[I] Port priority (spanning tree)     128 (80 hex)
[C] Path cost (spanning tree)         100
[H] Port fast mode (spanning tree)    Enabled
------------------Related Menus--------------
[A] Port addressing         [V] View port statistics
[N] Next port               [G] Goto port
[P] Previous port           [X] Exit to Main Menu
Enter Selection:
```

Switched 100BaseT Port Configuration

```
Port Configuration Menu (Switched 100BaseT Ports)
Catalyst 2820 - Port B1 Configuration (Right Slot)
Module Name:    100Base-TX(1 Port UTP Model), Version 0
Description:    1 Port 100Base-TX
802.1d STP State:    Blocking    Forward Transitions:    0
--------------------- Settings ------------------------
[D] Description/name of port
--------------------- Module Settings -------------------
[M] Module status                      Suspended-no-linkbeat
[I] Port priority (spanning tree)      128 (80 hex)
[C] Path cost (spanning tree)          10
[H] Port fast mode (spanning tree)     Disabled
[E] Enhanced congestion control        Disabled
[F] Full duplex / Flow control         Half duplex
---------------------- Related Menus --------------------
[A] Port addressing         [V] View port statistics
[N] Next port               [G] Goto port
[P] Previous port           [X] Exit to Main Menu
Enter Selection:
```

Shared 100BaseT Port Configuration

```
Port Configuration Menu (Shared 100BaseT Ports)
Catalyst 2820 - Port A1 Configuration (Left Slot)
Module Name:    100Base-TX(8 Port UTP Model), Version 0
Description:    8 Port 100Base-TX Class 2 Repeater
802.1d STP State:    Blocking    Forward Transitions:    0
--------------------- Settings -------------------------
[D] Description/name of port
[S] Status of port                          Suspended-no-linkbeat
------------------- Module Settings --------------------
[M] Module status                    Suspended-no-linkbeat
[I] Port priority (spanning tree)    128 (80 hex)
[C] Path cost (spanning tree)        10
[H] Port fast mode (spanning tree)   Disabled
[E] Enhanced congestion control      Disabled
[F] Full duplex / Flow control       Half duplex
--------------------- Related Menus --------------------
[A] Port addressing         [V] View port statistics
[N] Next port               [G] Goto port
[P] Previous port           [X] Exit to Main Menu
Enter Selection:
```

The functions of the most important menu options above are as follows:

[D] Description/name of port: Allows you to assign a description to an individual port. The field will accept up to 60 characters.

[S] Status of port: Provides an indication of the current status of a port.

[V] View port statistics: Displays a detailed port statistics report.

[N] Next port: Shows the Port Configuration menu for the next numbered port of the switch.

[G] Goto port: Displays the Port Configuration menu for a specified port.

[P] Previous port: Displays the Port Configuration menu for the port whose number is one less than the current port.

[X] Exit to Main Menu: Drops you back one level to the main menu.

Exam Essentials

Remember how to set an IP address on a switch. After POST finishes, the Console Logon screen appears. Press the I key to enter the IP Configuration menu.

Key Terms and Concepts

Catalyst: Series of switches acquired by Cisco.

IP address: Logical address that allows packets to be sent through an internetwork. Assigned to all hosts in an internetwork.

Switch: In networking, a device responsible for multiple functions such as filtering, flooding, and sending frames. It works using the destination address of individual frames. Switches operate at the Data Link layer of the OSI model.

Sample Questions

1. Which option from the main menu lets you enter the IP Configuration menu?

   A. Q

   B. F

   C. I

   D. D

   Answer: C. Press the I key to enter the IP Configuration menu.

2. Which of the following is true? (Choose all that apply.)

A. You must save the configuration after every change.

B. The switch automatically saves each change.

C. The IP address is not saved automatically.

D. The IP address is saved as soon as you press Enter.

Answer: B. Remember that the switch will take 30 seconds before it saves the configuration change to memory. The IP address, however, has already taken effect once you press Enter.

Configure VLANs on the Catalyst 1900 and Catalyst 2820 switches.

In this objective, you will learn how to configure virtual LANs on a Catalyst 1900 and 2820 switch. They differ slightly, but both can configure VLANs. A VLAN is a broadcast domain created in a switched environment.

This is an important objective to understand, because it will show you how to configure broadcast domains in a Catalyst switched environment when using 1900 and 2820 switches.

Critical Information

To display the menu for configuring VLANs, select **V**. The Catalyst 1900 and Catalyst 2820 can be configured with up to four VLANs. The default configuration of a switch has all ports belonging to VLAN 1. The management domain is also contained within VLAN 1. A proper configuration will have at least one port that belongs to VLAN 1.

NOTE The 2820 uses four bridge groups instead of VLANs.

The opening menu for VLAN configuration on a 1900 looks like this:

```
Catalyst 1900 - Virtual LAN Configuration
-------------------Information----------------
VTP version: 1
Configuration revision: 1
Maximum VLANs supported locally: 1005
Number of existing VLANs: 6
Configuration last modified by: 172.16.30.196 at 05-03-1999 18:35:56


------------------Settings-----------------
[N] Domain name
[V] VTP mode control Server
[F] VTP pruning mode Disabled
[O] VTP traps Enabled


------------------Actions-----------------
[L] List VLANs          [A] Add VLAN
[M] Modify VLAN         [D] Delete VLAN
[E] VLAN Membership     [S] VLAN Membership Servers
[T] Trunk Configuration [W] VTP password
[P] VTP Statistics      [X] Exit to Main Menu

Enter Selection:
```

The functions of the most important menu options are as follows:

[N] Domain name: Allows you to assign a management domain to the switch before creating a VLAN. A Catalyst 1900 or Catalyst 2820 switch comes configured in a no-management domain state until a management domain is configured or the switch receives an advertisement for a management domain.

[V] VTP mode control: May be set to either Transparent or Server. A Catalyst 1900 or Catalyst 2820 switch is configured as a VTP server by default, receiving advertisements on a configured trunk port. A switch automatically changes from VTP server mode to VTP client mode when it receives an advertisement with more than 128 VLANs.

[F] VTP pruning mode: Controls whether to restrict the flood traffic of a VLAN to just those switches that have member ports. Each trunk is configured with its own pruning eligible list of VLANs.

[A] **Add VLAN:** Adds a VLAN to the allowed list for the trunk. The default configuration allows all configured VLANs on a single trunk.

[M] **Modify VLAN:** Allows you to modify an existing VLAN.

[D] **Delete VLAN:** Allows you to delete an operating VLAN. The ports assigned to the VLAN will default back to VLAN 1.

[X] **Exit to Main Menu:** Drops you back one level to the main menu.

Necessary Procedures

In this section, you will learn how to define a VLAN, configure VLAN trunks, and configure the VLAN Trunk Protocol.

Defining a VLAN

Defining a VLAN requires setting some attributes, including the VLAN number, name, IEEE 802.10 SAID value, and MTU size.

1. Access the VLAN Configuration menu by selecting **V** from the main menu. Then press **A** to select Add VLAN.

2. You must choose the type of VLAN. For Ethernet, enter **1**.

3. Press **N** to configure the VLAN number, and enter the number of the VLAN to be added.

4. Define the VLAN name by pressing **V** and entering the name of the VLAN to be added.

5. To set the IEEE 802.10 SAID value, press **I** and enter the appropriate value. The SAID value must be within the range shown, and it cannot be the same as another IEEE 802.10 value.

6. To set the MTU size, press **M** and enter the MTU size.

7. Enable the VLAN by pressing **T** to select VLAN State, and select Enabled.

Configuring VLAN Trunks

A VLAN trunk is important because it allows a physical link between two VLAN-capable switches or a VLAN-capable switch and a VLAN-capable router. A VLAN trunk can carry the traffic of multiple VLANs. This allows you to have VLANs extend into multiple Catalyst switches.

1. Access the Virtual LAN menu by selecting **V** from the main menu.

2. Press **T** to access the Trunk Configuration menu. Select the appropriate trunk port by choosing either **A** or **B**, and press Enter.

3. To turn on trunking for the selected port, enter **T**, select **1**, and press Return or Enter.

Configuring the VLAN Trunk Protocol

The VLAN Trunk Protocol (VTP) helps maintain the VLAN uniformity across the network and assists with the alteration of VLANs. VTP allows VLAN changes to be communicated across the network to the other switches.

1. Access the Virtual LAN menu by selecting **V** from the main menu.

2. Confirm that a management domain name has been set.

3. Press **N** to access the Domain Name menu.

4. Confirm that the server has a VTP management domain, which ensures that VTP information can be exchanged with other VTP switches in the management domain.

5. Press Enter to view the Virtual LAN Configuration menu.

6. Open the VTP Mode Control menu by selecting **V**.

7. Choose the server mode by entering **S** at the prompt.

The switch can learn about other VTP-configured switches only by receiving their advertisements across the network. There must also be at least one trunk port configured on a switch.

Exam Essentials

Remember how to access the VLAN menu. To display the menu for configuring VLANs, select V.

Remember how many VLANs can be configured per switch. The Catalyst 1900 and Catalyst 2820 can be configured with up to four VLANs.

Remember the default VLAN. The default configuration of a switch has all ports belonging to VLAN 1.

Key Terms and Concepts

Switch: In networking, a device responsible for multiple functions such as filtering, flooding, and sending frames. It works using the destination address of individual frames. Switches operate at the Data Link layer of the OSI model.

VLAN: Virtual LAN is a way of creating broadcast domains within a switched internetwork.

Sample Questions

1. Which is required when defining a VLAN? (Choose all that apply.)

   A. VLAN name

   B. SAID value

   C. MTU size

   D. VLAN number

   Answer: A, B, C, D. Defining a VLAN requires setting some attributes, including the VLAN number, name, IEEE 802.10 SAID value, and MTU size.

2. Which is true regarding trunk ports?

A. Trunk ports are available only on the 5000 series of switches.

B. You can trunk only 10Mbps ports.

C. A VLAN trunk can carry the traffic of only a single VLAN.

D. A VLAN trunk can carry the traffic of multiple VLANs.

Answer: D.

View the Catalyst 1900 and Catalyst 2820 switch reports and summaries.

In this objective, you will be shown the reports and summaries from the 1900 and 2820 switches. You can view these reports from the main menu of the switch console.

This is an important objective to understand when working in a production environment and when gathering information in your studies for the CLSC exam.

Critical Information

You can reach the general statistics and report information on the 1900/2820 switches by pressing **U** at the main menu.

```
Enter Selection: M
Enter password:  ********
        Catalyst 1900 - Main Menu
   [C] Console Settings
   [S] System
   [N] Network Management
   [P] Port Configuration
   [A] Port Addressing
```

```
[D] Port Statistics Detail
[M] Monitoring
[V] Virtual LAN
[R] Multicast Registration
[F] Firmware
[I] RS-232 Interface
[U] Usage Summaries
[H] Help
[K] Command Line
[X] Exit Management Console
Enter Selection: U
```

By typing U at the Enter Selection prompt, you will get the following menu:

```
Catalyst 1900 - Usage Summaries
[P] Port Status Report
[A] Port Addressing Report
[E] Exception Statistics Report
[U] Utilization Statistics Report
[B] Bandwidth Usage Report
[X] Exit to Main Menu
```

The list below explains each of the submenus:

[P] Port Status Report: This will give you the status of all ports on the switch.

[A] Port Addressing Report: This submenu will display the MAC addresses or the number of MAC addresses of a specific port.

[E] Exception Statistics Report: This screen will show you the different errors received on a port. You can view the receive, transmit, and security violations.

[U] Utilization Statistics Report: This screen will give you the cumulative frame count per port. It will keep track of unicast, multicast, and broadcast frames. The forward column contains the number of frames that were received by a port and then switched out an exit port.

[B] Bandwidth Usage Report: This will give you the peak bandwidth across the switch's backplane during a particular time.

Each of the statistics shown in the various reporting screens is refreshed automatically every 5 seconds. However, if you have the console connection set to 2400 baud or less, the statistics are refreshed every 8 seconds.

Necessary Procedures

In this section, the output of each of the submenus as they appear will be displayed:

- [P] Port Status Report
- [A] Port Addressing Report
- [E] Exception Statistics Report
- [U] Utilization Statistics Report
- [B] Bandwidth Usage Report

[P] Port Status Report

```
Catalyst 1900 - Port Status Report
1  : Enabled                    13 : Suspended-no-linkbeat
2  : Enabled                    14 : Suspended-no-linkbeat
3  : Enabled                    15 : Suspended-no-linkbeat
4  : Enabled                    16 : Suspended-no-linkbeat
5  : Enabled                    17 : Suspended-no-linkbeat
6  : Suspended-no-linkbeat      18 : Suspended-no-linkbeat
7  : Enabled                    19 : Suspended-no-linkbeat
8  : Suspended-no-linkbeat      20 : Enabled
9  : Suspended-no-linkbeat      21 : Enabled
10 : Suspended-no-linkbeat      22 : Enabled
11 : Suspended-no-linkbeat      23 : Enabled
12 : Suspended-no-linkbeat      24 : Enabled
                                AUI: Enabled
A  : Suspended-no-linkbeat
B  : Suspended-no-linkbeat
Monitor port: B, Network port: None, Trunk port: None
Select [X] Exit to previous menu:  X
```

[A] Port Addressing Report

```
Enter Selection: A
         Catalyst 1900 - Port Addressing Report
  Port                 Addresses          Port          Addresses
-------------------------------------- --------------------------------------
  1  :                 Unaddressed        13 :           Unaddressed
  2  :Dynamic          00-A0-C9-E9-15-F7  14 :           Unaddressed
  3  :Dynamic          00-00-86-34-AA-40  15 :           Unaddressed
  4  :                 Unaddressed        16 :           Unaddressed
  5  :Dynamic          00-10-7B-B5-92-E1  17 :           Unaddressed
  6  :                 Unaddressed        18 :           Unaddressed
  7  :Dynamic 2        Static 0           19 :           Unaddressed
  8  :                 Unaddressed        20 :Dynamic     00-00-0C-05-C1-44
  9  :                 Unaddressed        21 :Dynamic     00-10-5A-97-FA-3F
  10 :                 Unaddressed        22 :Dynamic     00-00-0C-47-71-1F
  11 :                 Unaddressed        23 :Dynamic     00-10-7B-3A-D7-D8
  12 :                 Unaddressed        24 :Dynamic     00-10-7B-B5-92-E0
                                          AUI:           Unaddressed
  A  :                 Unaddressed
  B  :                 Unaddressed
Select [X] Exit to previous menu:  X
```

[E] Exception Statistics Report

```
Enter Selection: E
         Catalyst 1900 - Exception Statistics Report (Frame counts)
         Receive   Transmit  Security           Receive   Transmit  Security
         Errors    Errors    Violations         Errors    Errors    Violations
         ------------------------------         ------------------------------
  1  :   0         0         0          13 :    0         0         0
  2  :   0         0         0          14 :    0         0         0
  3  :   0         0         0          15 :    0         0         0
  4  :   0         0         0          16 :    0         0         0
  5  :   0         0         0          17 :    0         0         0
  6  :   0         0         0          18 :    0         0         0
  7  :   0         0         0          19 :    0         0         0
  8  :   0         0         0          20 :    0         0         0
  9  :   0         0         0          21 :    0         0         0
  10 :   0         0         0          22 :    0         0         0
  11 :   0         0         0          23 :    0         0         0
  12 :   0         0         0          24 :    0         0         0
                                        AUI:    0         0         0
  A  :   0         0         0
  B  :   0         0         0
Select [R] Reset all statistics, or [X] Exit to previous menu:  X
```

[U] Utilization Statistics Report

```
Enter Selection: U
        Catalyst 1900 - Utilization Statistics Report (Frame counts)
          Receive   Forward   Transmit         Receive   Forward   Transmit
        -----------------------------          -----------------------------
  1  :   1313      1313      452184    13 :    0         0         0
  2  :   171154    171154    562157    14 :    0         0         0
  3  :   123782    123782    278803    15 :    0         0         0
  4  :   4087      4087      172828    16 :    0         0         0
  5  :   320494    254496    573792    17 :    0         0         0
  6  :   0         0         0         18 :    0         0         0
  7  :   6731      6731      449062    19 :    0         0         0
  8  :   0         0         0         20 :    9770      2027      65010
  9  :   0         0         0         21 :    26109     26109     435644
 10  :   0         0         0         22 :    392024    326027    675674
 11  :   0         0         0         23 :    110317    99364     156232
 12  :   0         0         0         24 :    279933    213935    590901
                                       AUI:    0         0         451206
  A  :   0         0         0
  B  :   0         0         1076462

Select [R] Reset all statistics, or [X] Exit to previous menu:  X
```

[B] Bandwidth Usage Report

```
Enter Selection: B
        Catalyst 1900 - Bandwidth Usage Report
        --------------------- Information ------------------------------------
        Current Bandwidth Usage                      0 Mbps
        Peak Bandwidth Usage during this interval    0 Mbps
        Peak Time recorded since start up            7d 13h 36m 09s
        --------------------- Settings --------------------------------------
        [T] Capture time interval                    24 hour(s)
        [R] Reset capture
        [X] Exit to previous menu
Enter Selection:  X
```

Exam Essentials

Remember that you can reach the general statistics and report information on the 1900/2820 switches by pressing *U* at the main menu.   The following menu will appear:

- [P] Port Status Report

- [A] Port Addressing Report

- [E] Exception Statistics Report

- [U] Utilization Statistics Report

- [B] Bandwidth Usage Report

Key Terms and Concepts

Catalyst: Series of switches acquired by Cisco.

Switch: In networking, a device responsible for multiple functions such as filtering, flooding, and sending frames. It works using the destination address of individual frames. Switches operate at the Data Link layer of the OSI model.

Sample Questions

1. What does the Port Addressing Report provide?

A. Configuration of a port

B. The MAC addresses or the number of MAC addresses of a specific port

C. The different errors received on a port

D. The status of all ports on the switch

Answer: B.

2. What does the Utilization Statistics Report provide?

A. Configuration of a port

B. The MAC addresses or the number of MAC addresses of a specific port

C. The different errors received on a port

D. The frame count per port

Answer: D. The Utilization Statistics Report will give you the cumulative frame count per port. It will keep track of unicast, multicast, and broadcast frames.

Configure the ATM LANE module on the Catalyst 2820 switch.

This section demonstrates the steps necessary for configuring the ATM module as a trunk or nontrunk ATM module. You'll see how to configure the ATM LAN Emulation (LANE) Client (LEC) from the command line interface and verify the configuration.

This is an important chapter to understand when studying for your CLSC exam and when working in a production environment that uses ATM with 2820 switches.

Critical Information

The Catalyst 2820 supports four types of ATM modules: the ATM 155 multimode (MM) Fiber module, the ATM 155 single-mode (SM) medium-reach (MR) Fiber module, the ATM 155 single-mode (SM) long-reach (LR) Fiber module, and the ATM 155 UTP. You can use the ATM module to connect workstations, hubs, and other switches to a range of ATM devices.

The ATM modules include the following features:

- Full-duplex operation

- 155.52Mbps data transfer rate

- Store-and-forward packet relay

- LAN Emulation Client (LEC) for emulated LANs (ELANs)

- ATM Adaptation Layer 5 (AAL5) for LAN Emulation (LANE) data transfer

- Multiple-ELAN support for LANE (Catalyst 2820 switch firmware version 7.02 or later with Cisco IOS 11.3 or later)

- Multiple virtual LAN (VLAN) mappings for RFC 1483 (Catalyst 2820 switch firmware version 7.02 or later with Cisco IOS 11.3 or later)

- User Network Interface (UNI) 3.0 and 3.1 for Switched Virtual Connections (SVCs) and Permanent Virtual Connections (PVCs)

- Support for Catalyst 2820 switch firmware version 5.35 and version 7.02

The ATM modules support the following ATM management features:

- Interim Local Management Interface (ILMI) for ATM UNI 3.0 and 3.1 Management Information Bases (MIBs)

- Operation, Administration, and Maintenance (OAM)

To access the command line interface from the Catalyst 2820 management console, select **P** (Port Configuration) from the Catalyst 2820 main menu. Select the port where the ATM module is installed. For slot A (interface 0), press **A**, or, if the module is installed in slot B (interface 1), press **B**.

Next you'll see the Port Configuration menu either for a nontrunk ATM module or for a trunk ATM module. Select [K] from either menu to access the command line interface. The switch response is shown:

```
Port Configuration Menu for Nontrunk ATM Module
       Catalyst 2820 - Port A Configuration (Left Slot)
       Module Name:  ATM 155 MM Fiber, Version 01
       Description:  Multimode Fiber ATM Network Status: Operational
802.1d STP State:  Forwarding   Forward Transitions: 5
------------------Settings------------------
[D] Description/name of port
-----------------Module Settings-------------
[M] Module status                         Enabled
[I] Port priority (spanning tree)         128 (80 hex)
[C] Path cost (spanning tree)             10
[H] Port fast mode (spanning tree)        Enabled
-------------------Actions------------------
[R] Reset module    [F] Reset module with factory defaults
-----------------Related Menus-------------
[K] Command Line Interface    [L] ATM and LANE status
[A] Port addressing           [V] View port statistics
[N] Next port                 [G] Goto port
[P] Previous port             [X] Exit to Main Menu
```

```
Port Configuration Menu for ATM Trunk Module
        Catalyst 2820 - Port A Configuration (Left Slot)
        Module Name:  ATM 155 MM Fiber, Version 03
        Description:  Multimode Fiber  ATM Network Status: Operational
---------------------- Setting --------------------------
[D] Description/name of port
[S] Status of trunk                          Enabled
---------------------- Module Settings -------------------
[I] Port priority (spanning tree) - option 1    128 (80 hex)
[J] Port priority (spanning tree) - option 2    128 (80 hex)
[C] Path cost (spanning tree)                    10
---------------------- Actions --------------------------
[E] Show VLAN port priorities      [Z] Show VLAN States
[M] Assign VLANs to option 1 port priority
[O] Assign VLANs to option 2 port priority
[R] Reset module      [F] Reset module with factory defaults
---------------------- Related Menus --------------------
[K] Command Line Interface         [L] ATM and LANE status
[A] Port addressing                [V] View port statistics
[N] Next port                      [G] Goto port
[P] Previous port                  [X] Exit to Main Menu
Enter Selection:
```

The ATM module does not forward any frames from the switch until the LANE clients have been defined. After configuring a LANE client with an ELAN mapped to a VLAN, you must configure the ATM module with the VLAN information. The ATM module then forwards the traffic to the appropriate ELAN.

Necessary Procedures

In this section, you will learn how to configure the LEC from the command line interface.

Configuring the LEC from the Command Line Interface

To configure the LEC from the command line interface:

1. To enter the privileged EXEC mode, enter the enable command:

```
ATM> enable
ATM#
```

2. To enter the global configuration mode, enter the `configure terminal` command:

   ATM# **configure terminal**

3. To enter the interface configuration mode, enter the `interface type_number.subif` command:

   ATM(config)# **interface atm0.1**
   ATM(config-if)#

4. To configure the LEC, enter the `lane client ethernet vlan_number elan_name` command:

   ATM(config-if)# **lane client ethernet 1 marketing**
   ATM(config-if)#

5. Exit the interface configuration mode and return to EXEC mode:

   ATM(config-if)# **^Z**
   ATM#

The ATM module is now configured to transmit and receive data between the LAN and the ATM network. The next step is to verify that the configuration is operating correctly.

You can verify the ATM and LANE status by using the `show lane` command, which verifies that the LEC is operational and shows the ATM addresses of the LANE configuration.

```
ATM> show lane
    LE Client ATM1.1 ELAN name: TESTELAN Admin: up State: operational
Client ID: 2 LEC up for 6 minutes 14 seconds
Join Attempt: 2
    HW Address: 00c0.1dfc.a2fc Type: ethernet Max Frame Size: 1516
    VLANID: 1
    ATM Address: 39.000000000000000000000000.00A02DFCA2FC.00 ATM Address
    VCD rxFrames txFrames Type ATM Address
    0 0 0   configure 39.000000000000000000000000.00705C28DA23.00
    4 0 2   direct 39.000000000000000000000000.00604D38DA21.01
    5 0 0   distribute 39.000000000000000000000000.00605C28DA21.01
      0 20send 39.000000000000000000000000.00605C28DA22.01
     13 0  0 forward 39.000000000000000000000000.00605C28DA22.01
      8 58 55 data 39.000000000000000000000000.00605C28DA20.01
ATM>
```

To verify that the ATM module is transmitting and receiving data across the ATM network, you can review the port statistics. The display shows the number of ATM Adaptation Layer 5 (AAL5) frames and ATM cells transmitted and received. To view port statistics on the Catalyst 2820, first press **P** from the main menu to display the Port Configuration menu; then press **V** to choose View Port Statistics. A typical ATM statistical report is shown below:

```
Catalyst 2820 - Port B (Right Slot)
Receive Statistics              Transmit Statistics
--------------------------------------- ---------------------

Good AAL5 frames             0  Good AAL5 frames             1
Good ATM cells               0  Good ATM cells               3
Broadcast/multicast frames   0  Broadcast/multicast frames   0
Good frames forwarded        0  Queue full discards          0
Frames filtered              0
Runt frames                  0
No buffer discards           0
Other discards               0
Errors:
CRC errors                   0
Cell HEC errors              0
Giant frames                 0
Address violations           0
Select [A] Port addressing, [C] Configure port,
       [N] Next port, [P] Previous port, [G] Goto port,
       [R] Reset port statistics, or [X] Exit to Main Menu:
```

Exam Essentials

Remember the configuration parameters for an ATM interface.
To enter the interface configuration mode, enter the interface *type_ number.subif* command. For example:

```
ATM(config)# interface atm0.1
ATM(config-if)#
```

Remember the command to configure an LEC. To configure the LEC, enter the `lane client ethernet` *vlan_number elan_name* command. For example:

```
ATM(config-if)# lane client ethernet 1 marketing
ATM(config-if)#
```

Key Terms and Concepts

ATM: Asynchronous Transfer Mode. The international standard, identified by fixed-length, 53-byte cells, for transmitting cells in multiple-service systems such as voice, video, or data. Transit delays are reduced because the fixed-length cells permit processing to occur in the hardware.

Switch: In networking, a device responsible for multiple functions such as filtering, flooding, and sending frames. It works using the destination address of individual frames. Switches operate at the Data Link layer of the OSI model.

Sample Questions

1. How many different types of ATM modules does the Catalyst 2820 support?

   A. One

   B. Two

   C. Four

   D. Eight

   Answer: C. The Catalyst 2820 supports four types of ATM modules: the ATM 155 multimode (MM) Fiber module, the ATM 155 single-mode (SM) medium-reach (MR) Fiber module, the ATM 155 single-mode (SM) long-reach (LR) Fiber module, and the ATM 155 UTP.

2. How do you configure an LEC?

    A. `lane client` *`elan_name`* `ethernet` *`vlan_number`*

    B. `lane client ethernet` *`vlan_number elan_name`*

    C. *`vlan_number`* `lane client ethernet` *`elan_name`*

    D. `ethernet lane client` *`vlan_number elan_name`*

Answer: B. To configure the LEC, enter the `lane client ethernet` *`vlan_number elan_name`* command.

CHAPTER

18

Catalyst 3000 Series Switches

Cisco Exam Objectives Covered in This Chapter

▶ **Describe Catalyst 3000 series LAN switch products.** *(pages 371 – 374)*

▶ **Describe Catalyst 3000 series LAN switch product differences.** *(pages 375 – 379)*

▶ **Describe the Catalyst Stack System.** *(pages 379 – 383)*

Ethernet switches are wonderful tools to apply to typical congestion problems that arise when you have too many users, or applications and network devices with voracious appetites. For instance, with these switches, you can allot each bandwidth-greedy device (such as a server) its very own 10 or 100Mbps segment.

It's very common for throughput bottlenecks to occur at servers and between other bandwidth-challenging devices such as routers, bridges, and switches in a standard Ethernet network. With the Catalyst 3000, you can address this issue by configuring full-duplex communication for each segment connected to one of its ports. Ethernet usually functions in half-duplex mode, allowing devices to either transmit or receive. Full-duplex technology, however, enables two stations to receive and transmit simultaneously. With that kind of free flow, bandwidth capacity is multiplied from 10Mbps to 20Mbps for 10BaseT ports and increases to a staggering 200Mbps on FastEthernet ports.

The Catalyst 3000 series switches comply with IEEE 802.3 and are designed to increase the throughput on an Ethernet network in the range of 300 to 1000%! And since they're MAC-layer machines, they are versatile, protocol independent, and work in complete harmony with a variety of systems from NetWare, XNS, and AppleTalk to TCP/IP, LAT, and DECnet.

In this chapter, the major features of the Catalyst 3000 switches, the different hardware used, and the functions of the switch's major components will be covered.

Describe Catalyst 3000 series LAN switch products.

There is a variety of configurations where the Catalyst 3000 series switches become stars that will lavish you with greatly enhanced network performance. Each Cisco Catalyst product affords its users the ability to design systems that are highly efficient as well as fluidly scalable. Those qualities, combined with the Catalyst 3000's reliability and its capacity for media flexibility, make these products ideal solutions for both present and future networking requirements in your Ethernet configuration.

There are three different 3000 switches, and they will be discussed in this chapter. This is important information if you need to maintain a 3000 switch in a production network, and when studying for the exam.

Critical Information

You will be shown the different types of LAN switch products available with the Cisco Catalyst 3000 switch.

Catalyst 3000

The Catalyst 3000 switch has 16 10Mbps switch ports; 24 10baseT ports; and 2 100BaseT ATM or 100VG-AnyLAN ports. The standard configuration is 16 10BaseT ports, 8MB of DRAM, 1MB of flash memory, a console port, a SwitchProbe port, an AUI, and two optional slots. You can configure the optional slots in the switch with the following options:

- 4-port 10BaseT
- 1-port 10pBaseT/F

- 2-port 100VG-AnyLAN
- 3-port 10BaseFL
- 1-port 155 MBPS ATM
- 3-port 10Base2 thinnet
- 3-port 100BaseT/ISL
- 2-port 100BaseT/ISL

Catalyst 3100

The Catalyst 3100 provides all the features of the 3000 and more. It comes with 24 switched 10Mbps ports and a FlexSlot that can be used for WAN access or an expansion module. By using the double-wide FlexSlot with the WAN access module, you can create a Catalyst Stack with WAN support.

Catalyst 3200

The Catalyst 3200 is a larger chassis than either the 3000 or the 3100 switch. It can handle seven slots with one slot available for an extra-wide module. Its other features are as follows:

- Up to 21 10BaseFL ports
- Support for the double-wide WAN module
- Redundant power supplies
- 8MB of DRAM
- FastEthernet ISL and LANE support

Four Main Elements

All of the Catalyst 3000 switches have four main elements:

Cross-point switch matrix (AXIS bus): This is used to connect between two network segments. Each connection lasts only as long as packets are being transmitted.

AUI connector: The Attachment Unit Interface is typically used to connect by way of a transceiver (transmitter/receiver) to dissimilar physical media, such as connecting thinnet to 10BaseT or 10BaseFL.

Expansion module: Two expansion slots are included in each Catalyst 3000 switch. You can add up to eight 10Mbps ports or two FastEthernet connections for connecting to servers or backbones. ATM and fiber-based LANs are also supported.

Stack ports: The 3000 switch supports up to eight Catalyst 3000 units connected together, forming one virtual unit.

Exam Essentials

Remember how many switch ports the 3000 switch can support. The 3000 switch has 16 10Mbps switch ports.

Remember how many switch ports the 3100 switch can support. The 3100 switch has 24 10Mbps switch ports.

Remember the amount of slots available for the 3200. It can handle seven slots with one slot available for an extra-wide module.

Remember how many expansion slots are available in the 3000 series of switches. Two expansion slots are included in each Catalyst 3000 switch.

Key Terms and Concepts

AUI: The Attachment User Interface is the IEEE 802.3 interface between a thinnet and an NIC (network interface card) or other media.

Catalyst: Series of switches acquired and designed by Cisco Systems, Inc.

Expansion module: Card that can be put into a Catalyst switch that allows the switch to expand its capabilities.

> **Switch:** Multiple-connection device that works at the Data Link layer of the OSI model and can filter, forward, and flood frames based on the hardware destination address of each frame.

Sample Questions

1. How many switch ports are available on a single Catalyst 3000 switch?

   A. 4

   B. 8

   C. 16

   D. 24

   Answer: C. The Catalyst 3000 switch has 16 10Mbps switch ports and 24 10BaseT ports.

2. How many expansion slots are included in each Catalyst 3000 switch?

   A. One

   B. Two

   C. Four

   D. Eight

   Answer: B.

3. How many switch ports are available on a single Catalyst 3100 switch?

   A. 4

   B. 8

   C. 16

   D. 24

   Answer: D. The 3100 comes with 24 switched 10Mbps ports and a FlexSlot that can be used for WAN access or an expansion module.

Describe Catalyst 3000 series LAN switch product differences.

This objective is not too different from the first one in this chapter. However, you will continue to see some differences between the LAN switch products, and a figure will be provided to illustrate each one.

This is important information when studying for your CLSC exam and if you have to understand the difference between the switches in a production environment.

Critical Information

In this section, you will continue to see the differences among the Cisco Catalyst 3000 LAN switch products.

Catalyst 3000

Figure 18.1 shows the front and back of the 3000 switch. Notice that the back has Reset and Sys Req buttons, console and SwitchProbe ports, and switches for setting full- or half-duplex mode.

The Catalyst 3000 switch can be configured administratively to support half- and full-duplex operation on all ports, cut-through or store-and-forward switching, VLAN support, and demand aging for hardware address tables. Demand aging is used to purge the address table when it reaches capacity.

The 3000 can support up to 1700 addresses per port and up to 10,000 addresses per switch. Also, by using the Catalyst Matrix, you can connect up to eight switches to create a stack system.

FIGURE 18.1: The Cisco Catalyst 3000 switch, front (top) and back (bottom)

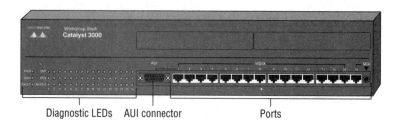

Diagnostic LEDs   AUI connector   Ports

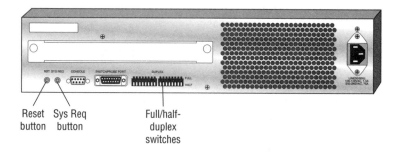

Reset   Sys Req   Full/half-
button   button   duplex
                                switches

Catalyst 3100

The Catalyst 3100 WAN module has two serial ports and a BRI port for ISDN capability. The serial ports can support speeds up to E1 (2.048Mbps) and can run in either asynchronous or synchronous mode. The WAN module also has an auxiliary port that can be used either for console modem support or as a backup asynchronous line.

However, no LAN support is included on the WAN module. All local packets are routed from the Cisco WAN module through the Catalyst 3100 or 3200 AXIS bus. The WAN module supports connectivity to a single VLAN network or network segment. Figure 18.2 shows the Cisco Catalyst 3100 switch.

FIGURE 18.2: The Cisco Catalyst 3100 switch

Catalyst 3200

It is important to not over-subscribe the 3200 switch. Refer to the user guidelines before buying any module, or ask your Cisco reseller for information about the 3200 high-speed modules and their performance. Figure 18.3 shows the Cisco Catalyst 3200 switch.

FIGURE 18.3: The Cisco Catalyst 3200 switch

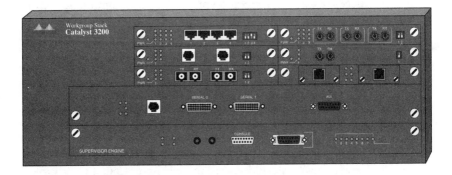

Exam Essentials

Remember how many hardware addresses a 3000 switch can support per port. The 3000 can support up to 1700 addresses per port.

Remember how many hardware addresses a 3000 switch can support per switch. The 3000 can support up to 10,000 addresses per switch.

Remember what the 3100 WAN module supports. The Catalyst 3100 WAN module has two serial ports and a BRI port for ISDN capability.

Remember the speeds a serial port can provide. The serial ports can support speeds up to E1 (2.048Mbps).

Key Terms and Concepts

BRI: Basic Rate Interface is used in ISDN to provide two bearer channels of 64Kb and one D channel of 16Kb for signaling.

Catalyst: Series of switches acquired and designed by Cisco Systems, Inc.

ISDN: Integrated Services Digital Network is a digital network provided by the phone companies for Internet access, with typical speeds of 128Kb. Data and voice can be used simultaneously over the same line.

Switch: Multiple-connection device that works at the Data Link layer of the OSI model and can filter, forward, and flood frames based on the hardware destination address of each frame.

Sample Questions

1. How many MAC addresses can be supported in a Catalyst 3000?

A. 500

B. 1700

C. 24,000

D. 10,000

Answer: D. Each switch can support a total of 10,000 hardware addresses in the filter table.

2. How many hardware addresses are supported per port on a Catalyst 3000 switch?

 A. 500

 B. 1700

 C. 24,000

 D. 10,000

 Answer: B.

3. The serial port on the WAN module can support up to what speed?

 A. 1.544Mbps

 B. 128Kbps

 C. 2.048Mbps

 D. 4Mbps

 Answer: C. The serial cards were designed to support up to E1 speeds (2.048Mbps).

Describe the Catalyst Stack System.

A Catalyst 3000 series Stack is not just a bunch of switches connected together; it virtually combines to form a single unit. There are two ways of configuring Catalyst 3000s, either as single standalone units or as a logical combination of up to eight units. The logical combination of units is called a Catalyst Stack.

If you have multiple 3000 switches, you need to understand the configurations presented in this objective. This objective is also important when studying for the CLSC exam.

Critical Information

The Catalyst 3000 Stacks can be configured in either of the following ways:

- Two Catalyst 3000 series switches cabled directly together in a back-to-back configuration

- A Stack of up to eight Catalyst 3000 series switches connected together via a Catalyst Matrix

Catalyst 3000 series switches were designed with savvy! On power-up, after first running through a prescribed set of self-diagnostics, the Catalyst 3000 runs through a stack-discovery mode, which is used to find out whether the switch is cabled to another Catalyst 3000. If the switch is connected to one or more others, the switches automatically combine to form a Stack. If a Catalyst 3000 is not connected to another, it will function as a stand-alone.

The creation of a Catalyst 3000 Stack gives a port density of up to 192 10BaseT Ethernet, 16 FastEthernet, or 16 ATM interfaces and can provide up to 280Mbps connections between switches.

The Catalyst Matrix is a cross-point matrix switch designed for high throughput that performs a round-robin port arbitration. Each port can operate independently and in parallel.

The connections between the Catalyst 3000 switch and the matrix are SCSI-2 cable with male connectors on both ends. Also, two modules can be placed in the matrix for full redundancy.

The Catalyst Matrix has the following features:

- Eight I/O Stack ports using 50-pin SCSI-2 type connectors (one per port)

- 280Mbps per port (full-duplex)

- 1.12Gbps total Catalyst Matrix capacity

- The ability to move packets between switches

- Round-robin output port arbitration

- Independent, parallel port operation (except for multicast)

- Replication of multicast packets

- No processor (the device is managed by the attached Catalyst 3000 units)

- Optional redundant modules

- Hot-swappable modules

- Front access to field-replaceable modules

Stack Management Software

The Catalyst 3000 Stack is software driven. Connecting two Catalyst switches together (or three or more switches) using the Catalyst Matrix can create a Stack. The Stack software is responsible for the topology and configuration of the Stack.

As you already know, a Catalyst 3000 switch runs in a discovery mode when two or more switches are connected. It does this by sending out a heartbeat broadcast to its neighbors, which includes the stack ID, MAC address of the source box, and box number. If a new switch is inserted into the stack, the switch console will prompt the administrator to push the Sys Req button. This will download the stack parameters to all switches.

When a switch is removed from the stack or a unit fails, all other switches will reconfigure the stack. All switches send out a heartbeat every 2 seconds. If the neighbor units do not hear a heartbeat for five consecutive heartbeats, it will assume the unit has failed or been removed. If a unit has been removed from the stack but is still powered up, it will revert to stand-alone mode.

TIP The Catalyst 3000 must have a different password from the Catalyst Stack. If you have forgotten the password, you can delete it by pressing the Sys Req button on the back panel of the Catalyst 3000 for 5 seconds, releasing it, and then selecting Clear Non-Volatile RAM from the menu that appears. Also, you can change the password only from the console itself. There are no command line interface (CLI) commands available.

Exam Essentials

Understand what the Catalyst Matrix is.   The Catalyst Matrix is a cross-point matrix switch designed for high throughput that performs a round-robin port arbitration.

Understand how the Catalyst Matrix works.   Each switch port can operate independently and in parallel.

Remember how to perform password recovery.   If you have forgotten the password, you can delete it by pressing the Sys Req button on the back panel of the Catalyst 3000 for 5 seconds, releasing it, and then selecting Clear Non-Volatile RAM from the menu that appears.

Remember from where you can configure the switch.   You can change the password only from the console itself.

Remember that you must use different passwords.   The Catalyst 3000 must have a different password from that of the Catalyst Stack.

Key Terms and Concepts

Catalyst: Series of switches acquired and designed by Cisco Systems, Inc.

Catalyst Stack: A logical combination of up to eight switch units.

Heartbeat: A discovery mode when two or more switches are connected.

Switch: Multiple-connection device that works at the Data Link layer of the OSI model and can filter, forward, and flood frames based on the hardware destination address of each frame.

Sample Questions

1. Which of the following is true regarding passwords on a 3000 switch?

   A. You can use Esc+Del to clear the password.

   B. The password must be at least five characters.

   C. You can change the password only from the console.

   D. The password for a 3000 switch must be the same as for the Catalyst Stack.

   Answer: C. Even though this seems to be a weak answer, the other answers are all wrong. The password can be longer and shorter than five characters, and the password for the 3000 switch must be different from that of the Stack. You press the Sys Req button, not the Esc+Del keys, to clear the password.

2. Which of the following is true regarding the Catalyst 3000 switch? (Choose all that apply.)

   A. Each switch in the Stack must have its own unique password.

   B. All passwords throughout the Stack must be the same.

   C. You can delete a Catalyst 3000 switch password by pressing the Sys Req button at boot-up.

   D. You can delete a Catalyst 3000 switch password by pressing Esc+Del at boot-up.

   Answer: A, C. The switch password must be different from that of the stack, and you press the Sys Req button at startup to clear.

CHAPTER

19

Configuring the Catalyst 3000
Series Switches

Cisco Exam Objectives Covered in This Chapter

▶ **Perform initial setup of a Catalyst 3000 series switch.**
  (pages 387 – 392)

▶ **Configure the switch for management.** *(pages 392 – 399)*

▶ **Configure port parameters.** *(pages 399 – 402)*

▶ **Configure VLANs and trunk links.** *(pages 402 – 407)*

▶ **Configure the ATM LANE module.** *(pages 408 – 410)*

▶ **Perform basic router module configuration.** *(pages 411 – 412)*

T his chapter introduces the installation and configuration of the Catalyst 3000 switches. The 3000 switch is configured entirely through a menu-driven system, which is illustrated throughout this chapter. You will learn in this chapter how to configure a switch using this menu system for IP addressing, ATM, VLANs, and port parameters. This chapter demonstrates all of the features of the 3000 switch.

This chapter is important to study and understand. The problem with the Cisco CLSC course and exam is that they still test on products no longer supported. The 3000 series is no longer supported by Cisco. However, the new CLSC course and exam will not be out for quite a while, so understanding the 3000 series of switches and how to perform configurations are essential to success on the exam. If you work in a production environment that is using 3000 series switches, this chapter will give you the knowledge you need to configure and maintain the Catalyst 3000 series of switches.

Perform initial setup of a Catalyst 3000 series switch.

In this first objective, you will learn how to connect a console cable to the switch and perform the initial setup of a Cisco 3000 series switch. After the initial configuration is complete, you can then use the Telnet program to maintain the configuration.

When either working in a production environment or studying for your CLSC exam, you must understand how to connect to a 3000 switch and perform basic configurations. This objective will give you that knowledge.

Critical Information

To install and configure the Cisco Catalyst 3000 switches, you need to connect to the switch, either by physically connecting a stand-alone PC to the console port or, once the initial configuration of the switch is complete, by Telnetting into the switch from a computer on the network.

Cisco describes these different approaches as out-of-band or in-band management.

- *Out-of-band* management is management outside of the network using a console connection. This means you're not using the same physical channels used for network traffic.

- *In-band* management is the management of the Catalyst 3000 through the network using Simple Network Management Protocol (SNMP) or Telnet. This means your connection is through the network cabling, and it therefore uses network software.

Connecting by the Console Port

The first thing you will learn is how to connect the console cable to the 3000 switch. Console interfacing can be established by connecting to the Console serial port on the back panel of the Catalyst 3000. Here are the two steps:

1. Connect the Catalyst 3000 to a PC or other DTE (Data Terminal Equipment) device using a straight, 25-pin-to-9-pin EIA RS-232 cable and a null modem adapter. The male DB-9 connector on the Catalyst 3000 is configured as a DTE device.

2. Set the console configuration parameters on your PC's terminal session as shown in Table 19.1.

T A B L E 19.1: Console Configuration Default Settings

Configuration Item	Setting
Baud rate	2400, 4800, 9600; 19.2Kbps, 38.4Kbps, 57.6Kbps (default: 9600)
Parity	None
Data bits	Eight
Stop bits	One
Handshaking	None
Terminal emulation	VT100
Duplex	Full
Soft flow control (XON/XOFF)	Off (input and output)
Hard flow control (RTS/CTS)	Off

Establishing a Telnet Session

To connect using Telnet, you need to have the switch plugged into a live network with a valid IP address. Your workstation running the

Telnet program must also be on a live network with a valid IP address. You will see the menu where you set an IP address on the switch later in this chapter.

Once your IP addresses are set, you can then use Telnet or an SNMP management program on your workstation to connect to the switch. This will allow you to manage and configure the switch.

Using the Catalyst 3000 Console

Once you've made the physical connection, powered up the switch, and gone through the initial diagnostics, you're ready to work with the management console application. It's a very simple menu-driven program; there are just a couple of basic things to remember before starting with it:

- You choose a menu item by using the arrow keys to highlight it and pressing Return or Enter. You'll be prompted if the program needs additional information for that item.

- Generally, new choices are saved once you select Return to Previous Menu.

- The term *More* indicates that there is more information than can be displayed on one screen. Select More and press Return to view the next screen of information.

- To return to the main menu from any screen, press Ctrl+P. Don't forget that any change made to the screen you were in will not be saved in such an instance. To return to the initial greeting screen, press Ctrl+B.

- If you are using a Catalyst VLAN, remember to set up IP, SNMP, spanning-tree values, and VTP.

- The console automatically returns to the greeting screen after 5 minutes of inactivity. (You can change this default time using the Main ➤ Configuration ➤ Console Configuration menu.)

- You can protect your system against unauthorized access to configuration screens by setting a password that users must enter at the initial greeting screen. If a password is not already configured, press Return or Enter to bring up the main menu. You may set a password using the Main ➤ Configuration ➤ Password menu.

The Main Menu

The main menu (see Figure 19.1) is used for all management operations: configuring the switch, monitoring statistics, and downloading and uploading files. In this chapter, the focus is on configuration, but the other menus available here will also be examined briefly.

F I G U R E 19.1:   The Catalyst 3000 management console's main menu

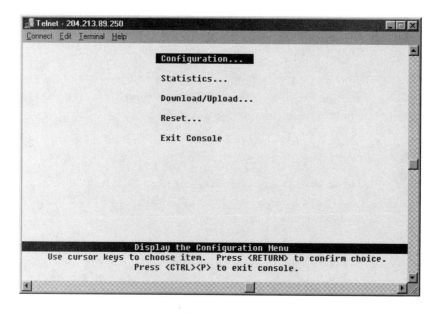

The main menu offers the following options:

Configuration: Displays the Configuration menu, which enables you to view and set the Catalyst 3000 configuration parameters.

Statistics: Displays the Statistics menu for the Catalyst 3000. The statistics can be used to monitor switch and network performance, which is a valuable troubleshooting aid.

Download/Upload: Used to load the flash memory in the Catalyst 3000. The Download menu displays two download options: Trivial File Transfer Protocol (TFTP) and Serial Link download.

Reset: Displays the reset options available through the Catalyst 3000 switch.

Exit Console: Highlighting this selection and pressing the Return or Enter key will return the console to the greeting screen (on a Telnet session, this causes the session to close).

Exam Essentials

Remember what out-of-band management is.   *Out-of-band* management is management outside of the network using a console connection. This means you're not using the same physical channels used for network traffic.

Remember what in-band management is.   *In-band* management is the management of the Catalyst 3000 through the network using Simple Network Management Protocol (SNMP) or Telnet. This means your connection is through the network cabling, and it therefore uses network software.

Key Terms and Concepts

In-band management: The management of the Catalyst 3000 through the network using Simple Network Management Protocol (SNMP) or Telnet. This means your connection is through the network cabling, and it therefore uses network software.

Out-of-band management: Management outside of the network using a console connection. This means you're not using the same physical channels used for network traffic.

Sample Questions

1. Which of the following are examples of in-band management? (Choose all that apply.)

    A. Console

    B. Telnet

    C. Async

    D. SNMP

    Answer: B, D. *In-band* management is the management of the Catalyst 3000 through the network using Simple Network Management Protocol (SNMP) or Telnet. This means your connection is through the network cabling, and it therefore uses network software.

2. Which of the following is an example of out-of-band management?

    A. Console

    B. Telnet

    C. MIB

    D. SNMP

    Answer: A. *Out-of-band* management is management outside of the network using a console connection. This means you're not using the same physical channels used for network traffic.

Configure the switch for management.

When maintaining a Catalyst 3000 switch or switches in a production environment, you must be able to add an IP address, subnet mask, and default gateway. Also, if you are using SNMP, this objective will show you how to configure SNMP in your switch for management through an SNMP management station. Included in this objective is the menu screen for the Spanning-Tree Protocol. The Spanning-Tree Protocol is very important to understand when running Catalyst 3000 switches in your production environment.

This objective is important if you are studying for your CLSC exam or setting up your switch or switches in a production environment and want to manage the switch or switches from a management station.

Critical Information

In this section, the IP configuration screen, the SNMP management screen, and the Spanning Tree menu will be examined.

IP Configuration

Use the IP Configuration menu, shown in Figure 19.2, to configure the IP address and related information for the switch.

NOTE   As an administrator, you must know the values of these options before trying to configure your switch.

Interface MAC Address: This is the hardware address of the switch, assigned by the manufacturer.

IP Address: Shows the configured IP address. The default is 0.0.0.0.

Default Gateway: Shows the current default gateway assigned. The default is 0.0.0.0.

Subnet Mask: Shows the currently assigned mask.

IP State: Can be IP Disabled, BootP When Needed, or BootP Always.

IP Packet Type: Shows the media used.

Send PING: Can be used to ping a device from the switch console.

F I G U R E 19.2: The IP Configuration menu

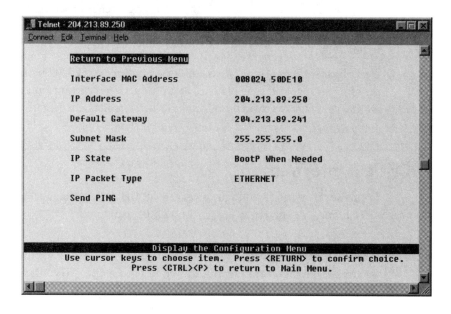

SNMP Configuration

SNMP can be configured through the SNMP Configuration menu, as displayed in Figure 19.3.

Send Authentication Traps: Can be set to either Yes or No— indicates whether SNMP should send trap messages.

Community Strings: Can be set with either Read or Read/Write permissions. The default is Read for public and Read/Write for private. This is shown in Figure 19.4. Notice that the public community string is read-only, and the MISAdmin community string is read/write.

Trap Receivers: Used to tell the switch where to send trap messages.

FIGURE 19.3: SNMP Configuration menu

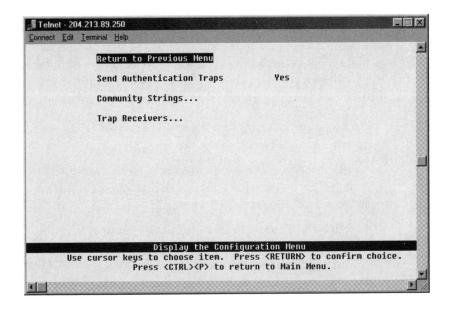

FIGURE 19.4: SNMP community strings

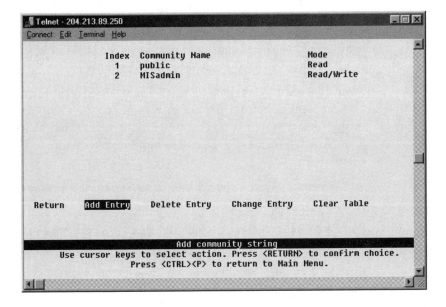

Spanning Tree

The Spanning-Tree Protocol (STP) was developed to stop network loops in bridged environments. STP is a bridge-to-bridge link management protocol that allows multiple paths to the same location without loops occurring in the network. To use STP with Catalyst 3000 switches, you must assign a port cost and a port priority to each network segment. Figure 19.5 shows the Spanning Tree menu.

Participate in Spanning Tree   Selecting Yes enables STP when the screen is exited. The default is No.

Switch Priority: Allows you to enter a priority value for the switch. The lowest value is the switch that becomes the root. The range is 0–65,535, and the default is 32,768.

Switch Hello Time (in Seconds):   Allows you to enter a value for the configuration messages when the switch is configured with the lowest switch priority or root. It cannot be lower than 1, or higher than the lower of 10 or ([Switch Maximum Message Age ÷ 2] – 1). The upper range limit that appears reflects the value currently selected for Switch Maximum Message Age. The default is 2.

Switch Maximum Message Age (in Seconds):   Used when the switch is configured as the root, and sets the maximum message age. The minimum cannot be less than 6 or twice the Switch Hello value plus 1. The maximum may not be more than the lower of 40 or (2 × [Switch Forward Delay – 1]). The default is 20.

Switch Forward Delay (in Seconds):   The time a switch waits between transitions from listening to learning and from learning to forwarding. It cannot be less than 4 or twice the ([Switch Maximum Message Age ÷ 2] + 1), and cannot be higher than 30. The default is 15.

Port Priority: A user-selected value for choosing the topology path to the root.

Port Path Cost: A user-selected value that shows the value of the port in the path to the root.

Current Spanning Tree Information: Shows the switch's current spanning-tree information.

FIGURE 19.5: The Spanning Tree menu

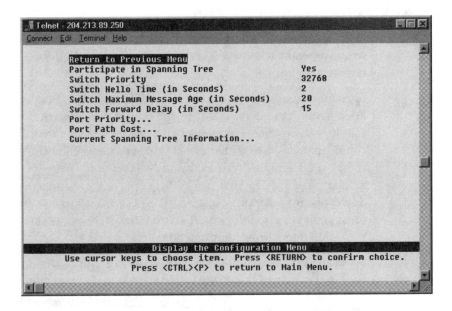

Exam Essentials

Remember the IP configuration options that are available. IP address, subnet mask, and default gateway are parameters that should be filled out if you are going to use in-band management.

Understand what SNMP is used for. Simple Network Management Protocol is used to gather statistics and information from devices on the internetwork running either IP or IPX.

Understand the concept of Spanning Tree. Spanning Tree was developed to stop possible network loops in an internetwork and find redundant paths.

Key Terms and Concepts

Default gateway: Address configured in an IP device that tells IP where to send packets when it receives packets destined for a remote network.

Spanning Tree: The bridge protocol (IEEE 802.1) that enables a learning bridge to dynamically avoid loops in the network topology by creating a spanning tree using the spanning-tree algorithm. Spanning-tree frames called Bridge Protocol Data Units (BPDUs) are sent and received by all switches in the network at regular intervals. The switches participating in the spanning tree don't forward the frames; instead, they're processed to determine the spanning-tree topology itself. Cisco Catalyst series switches use STP 802.1d to perform this function.

Subnet mask: Also simply known as *mask*, a 32-bit address mask used in IP to identify the bits of an IP address that are used for the subnet address. Using a mask, the router does not need to examine all 32 bits, only those selected by the mask.

Sample Questions

1. Which menu lets you send a Ping?

   A. Configuration

   B. Diagnostic

   C. IP Configuration

   D. Console

   Answer: C. One of the features of the IP Configuration menu is that it allows you to send a Ping.

2. What options are available for configuration with SNMP?

 A. Password

 B. Send Authentication Traps

 C. Community Strings

 D. Trap Receivers

 Answer: B, C, D. You can configure Send Authentication Traps to a network management station, Community Strings, and Trap Receivers.

3. What is the default IP address on a 3000 switch?

 A. 10.0.0.0

 B. 172.16.10.1

 C. 0.0.0.0

 D. 192.168.10.1

 Answer: C. By default, all IP configurations are 0.0.0.0.

Configure port parameters.

There is only one menu to choose from when configuring individual ports on your Catalyst 3000 switch. In this objective, the different parameters available when configuring individual ports will be discussed.

This is a small objective, but the information is important when studying for your CLSC exam and configuring a Catalyst 3000 switch.

Critical Information

The Port Configuration screen (see Figure 19.6) allows you to enable or disable individual ports on the switch. For each port, the screen shows the following information:

Port: The port number.

Type: The interface type.

Link: Used to indicate if a valid link is connected.

MDI/MDIX: The setting for 10BaseT.

Speed: The speed of the port.

Mode: Displays the LAN switching type. A-CT is auto/cut-through; F-FS is store-and-forward; and F-CT is cut-through.

Duplex: Displays whether the port is using full- or half-duplex communication.

Enabled/Disabled: The status of the port and the only configurable part of this menu.

Exam Essentials

Remember what the Mode displays. The Mode displays the LAN switching type. A-CT is auto/cut-through; F-FS is store-and-forward; and F-CT is cut-through.

Remember that you can view the duplex from this screen. Displays whether the port is using full- or half-duplex communication.

Understand there is only one configurable part of the menu. Enabled/Disabled is the status of the port.

F I G U R E 19.6:   The Port Configuration menu

```
Telnet - 204.213.89.250
Connect  Edit  Terminal  Help

Port    Type    Link   MDI/MDIX  Speed   Mode   Duplex  Enabled/Disabled
  1     AUI     up       MDIX      10     A-CT    Half     Enabled
  2    10BaseT  down     MDIX      10     A-CT    Half     Enabled
  3    10BaseT   --      MDIX      10     A-CT    Half     Disabled
  4    10BaseT  down     MDIX      10     F-SF    Half     Enabled
  5    10BaseT  down     MDIX      10     F-CT    Half     Enabled
  6    10BaseT  down     MDIX      10     A-CT    Half     Enabled
  7    10BaseT  down     MDIX      10     A-CT    Half     Enabled
  8    10BaseT  down     MDIX      10     A-CT    Half     Enabled
  9    10BaseT  down     MDIX      10     A-CT    Half     Enabled
 10    10BaseT  down     MDIX      10     A-CT    Half     Enabled
 11    10BaseT  down     MDIX      10     A-CT    Half     Enabled
 12    10BaseT  down     MDIX      10     A-CT    Half     Enabled
 13    10BaseT  down     MDIX      10     A-CT    Half     Enabled
 14    10BaseT  down     MDIX      10     A-CT    Half     Enabled
Return      More         Change

                    Return to previous menu
      Use cursor keys to choose item.  Press <RETURN> to confirm choice.
            Press <CTRL><P> to return to Main Menu.
```

Key Terms and Concepts

Full-duplex: The capacity to transmit information between a sending station and a receiving unit at the same time.

Half-duplex: The capacity to transfer data in only one direction at a time between a sending unit and receiving unit.

Switch: In networking, a device responsible for multiple functions such as filtering, flooding, and sending frames. It works using the destination address of individual frames. Switches operate at the Data Link layer of the OSI model.

Sample Questions

1. Which menu allows you to set the duplex mode?

A. Configuration

B. Module

C. Switch

D. Port

Answer: D.

2. Which menu allows you to set the speed of a port?

A. Configuration

B. Module

C. Switch

D. Port

Answer: D.

Configure VLANs and trunk links.

The 3000 switch supports VLANs and trunked links. Virtual LANs allow you to break up a switch into smaller broadcast domains. Remember that each switch port already creates individual collision domains, but, by default, the switch is one large broadcast domain. In addition, trunked links allow you to have more than one switch port in multiple VLANs.

This is an important objective to understand when connecting switches together or adding servers to your network. By creating VLAN and smaller broadcast domains, trunked links become very important. The greatest feature of VLANs is that they allow you to create broadcast domains by function, protocol, or even hardware—not location—which is the way that hubs provide connections.

Critical Information

In this section, you will see the VLAN and VTP Configuration menu, the ISL Port Configuration menu, and the EtherChannel menu.

VLAN and VTP Configuration

This menu is used to set up VLANs. From the Configuration menu, choose VLAN and VTP Configuration. Figure 19.7 displays the VLAN and VTP Configuration screen. It has the following options:

Local VLAN Port Configuration: Shows the current VLAN port assignments. You can change the assignment by using the cursor and then selecting Change. Only 14 ports are displayed at a time. Select the More option to see the other assigned ports.

VTP Administrative Configuration: Displays the domain name and the operation mode of the domain—Server, Client, or Transparent. In Server mode, changes can be made only from the local device. In Client mode, you can make changes only from remote devices. Transparent mode passes VTP packets.

VTP VLAN Configuration: Shows each VLAN administratively assigned and allows you to edit the assignments.

Local Preferred VLANs Configuration: Shows all configured VLANs.

Reassign Ports in Local VLAN: Used for moving a fully configured stack into an existing VTP administrative domain.

ISL Port Configuration

Inter-Switch Link (ISL) can be used to trunk ports on a Catalyst 3000 switch. You want to trunk ports when you need a host in more than one VLAN at the same time; for example, in a server. The ISL menu is used to configure the ISL trunking mode for each ISL port.

FIGURE 19.7: The VLAN and VTP Configuration menu

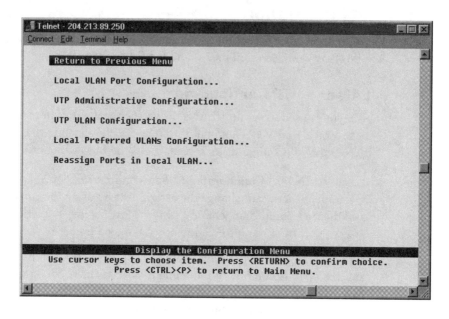

The ISL screen displays four menu headings:

Port: Shows the participating ISL ports on the switch

State: Gives the state of the port, either trunk or static

Note: A diagnostic message about the trunking states

Trunking Mode: Gives the status of the port—On, Off, Auto, or Desirable

EtherChannel

EtherChannel is used to combine multiple FastEthernet links between Cisco switches. Choosing EtherChannel from the Configuration menu displays the screen shown in Figure 19.8, where you can set (or simply view) configuration options:

EtherChannel Configuration: Used to get into the EtherChannel Configuration screen, which has the following options:

EtherChannel: Lists the different EtherChannel setups.

Ports: Refers to ports configured for EtherChannel.

Add Entry: Allows you to select the ports used in EtherChannel.

Delete Entry: After prompting to confirm your selection, deletes the selected EtherChannel.

Change Entry: Prompts you to reenter the port numbers in the selected EtherChannel.

Clear Table: Deletes all EtherChannel information.

Running EtherChannel Information: Shows you the existing configured EtherChannel information.

F I G U R E 19.8: The EtherChannel menu

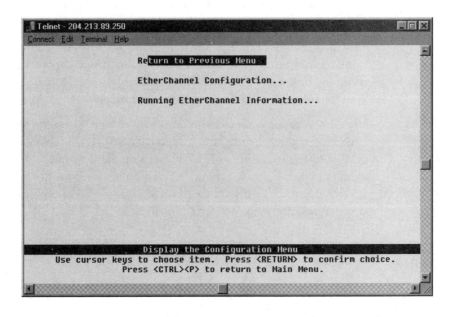

Exam Essentials

Understand the function of a VLAN. Virtual LANs allow you to break up a switch into smaller broadcast domains.

Remember what function a switch port provides. Each switch port already creates individual collision domains, but, by default, the switch is one large broadcast domain.

Remember what a trunked link is. Trunked links allow you to have more than one switch port in multiple VLANs.

Key Terms and Concepts

Broadcast domain: A group of devices receiving broadcast frames initiating from any device within the group. Because they do not forward broadcast frames, broadcast domains are generally surrounded by routers.

Collision domain: The network area in Ethernet over which frames that have collided will spread. Collisions are propagated by hubs and repeaters, but not by LAN switches, routers, or bridges.

Switch: In networking, a device responsible for multiple functions such as filtering, flooding, and sending frames. It works using the destination address of individual frames. Switches operate at the Data Link layer of the OSI model.

VLAN: A group of devices on one or more logically segmented LANs (configured by use of management software), enabling devices to communicate as if attached to the same physical medium, when they are actually located on numerous different LAN segments. VLANs are based on logical instead of physical connections, and thus are tremendously flexible.

Sample Questions

1. Which menu allows you to physically connect more than one port to another switch and combine the bandwidth?

    A. IP Configuration

    B. Console

    C. EtherChannel

    D. VLAN/VTP

    Answer: C. EtherChannel is used to combine multiple FastEthernet links between Cisco switches.

2. Which is true regarding VLANs? (Choose all that apply.)

    A. They can be created by protocol.

    B. They create smaller broadcast domains.

    C. They create smaller collision domains.

    D. They cannot be used on a 3000.

    Answer: A, B. The greatest feature of VLANs is that they allow you to create broadcast domains by function, protocol, or even hardware—not location—which is the way that hubs provide connections.

3. From which menu can you reach the VLAN Configuration menu?

    A. Switch Information

    B. VTP Configuration

    C. Statistics

    D. Download

    Answer: B. The VLAN and VTP Configuration menu is used to set up VLANs.

Configure the ATM LANE module.

ATM (Asynchronous Transfer Mode) LANE (Local Area Network Emulation) is a way to resolve the difference between ATM's connection-oriented, point-to-point protocol and the connectionless, broadcast domains of a LAN medium. Before LANE, a proprietary conversion device was needed to convert from a LAN to ATM.

Since it is possible that upper-layer protocols expect the lower layer to use a connectionless service, LANE is used to allow an upper-layer protocol to make connections to lower-layer ATM connection-oriented services. What this means is that LANE provides a switching service that is transparent to the 802.*x* networks.

If you have a 3000 series switch and need ATM support, you can add an ATM LANE card in the switches. In this objective, you will learn the necessary configuration.

Critical Information

LANE services must provide connectivity among all ATM devices and all LAN devices. This connectivity extends to devices that are attached ATM stations as well as attached LAN devices that are crossing the ATM network. Connectivity among ATM devices and all other LAN devices is done through emulated LANs (ELANs). ELANs are also used to create independent broadcast domains that are similar in concept to Ethernet segments or Token Ring networks. ELANs also allow ATM to work with existing older equipment.

Asynchronous Transfer Mode (ATM) can be used with the Catalyst family of switches, including the 3000 series. Local Area Network Emulation (LANE) is used on the switch to emulate a network broadcast environment such as Ethernet.

The Catalyst 3000 uses the WS-X3006A ATM module for ATM support.

The ATM Configuration menu provides three options:

Operation Mode: Can be set to either client or server.

Configuration Type: Sets the address for registration to the ATM switch.

ATM SNAP Prefix: Sets the ATM prefix, LECS ESI address, and a selector byte value of FF to form the ATM address for the LECS.

Exam Essentials

Understand what LANE is used for. ATM (Asynchronous Transfer Mode) LANE (Local Area Network Emulation) is a way to resolve the difference between ATM's connection-oriented, point-to-point protocol and the connectionless, broadcast domains of a LAN medium. Before LANE, a proprietary conversion device was needed to convert from a LAN to ATM.

Remember that the Catalyst 3000 series of switches supports ATM. Asynchronous Transfer Mode (ATM) can be used with the Catalyst family of switches, including the 3000 series. Local Area Network Emulation (LANE) is used on the switch to emulate a network broadcast environment such as Ethernet.

Key Terms and Concepts

ATM: Asynchronous Transfer Mode. The international standard, identified by fixed-length, 53-byte cells, for transmitting cells in multiple-service systems such as voice, video, or data. Transit delays are reduced because the fixed-length cells permit processing to occur in the hardware. ATM is designed to maximize the benefits of high-speed transmission media such as SONET, E3, and T3.

LANE: LAN Emulation. The technology that allows an ATM network to operate as a LAN backbone. To do so, the ATM network is required to provide multicast and broadcast support, address mapping (MAC to ATM), SVC management, and an operable packet format. Additionally, LANE defines Ethernet and Token Ring ELANs.

Switch: In networking, a device responsible for multiple functions such as filtering, flooding, and sending frames. It works using the destination address of individual frames. Switches operate at the Data Link layer of the OSI model.

Sample Questions

1. What protocol does ATM use to communicate from its native, cell-based network to a broadcast, frame-based network?

   A. Large Area NDIS Evolution

   B. Local Area Network Emulation

   C. Wide Area Network Emulation

   D. LDIS Network Emulation

   Answer: B. LANE is a way to resolve the difference between ATM's connection-oriented, point-to-point protocol and the connectionless, broadcast domains of a LAN medium.

2. What is true about ATM LANE?

   A. It is used on only Token Ring and FDDI.

   B. It is used on only Ethernet.

   C. It is used to allow an upper-layer protocol to make connections to lower-layer ATM connection-oriented services.

   D. It is used to allow a lower-layer protocol to make connections to upper-layer ATM connection-oriented services.

   Answer: C. Since it is possible that upper-layer protocols expect the lower layer to use a connectionless service, LANE is used to allow an upper-layer protocol to make connections to lower-layer ATM connection-oriented services.

Perform basic router module configuration.

You can install a router module in a 3000 switch that will allow you to perform layer 3 routing. This is used when you have VLANs configured and you need them to communicate.

This section is small, and is not tested on. However, it might be important if you ever see a 3000 switch using a router module.

Critical Information

There are some configurable parameters on the 3000 switch for a router module. The parameters that can be configured are the boot-up process, router reset, flow control, and access. This can be done only if a router module is present.

The configuration screen of the router module configuration has only one option:

Enter a Port Number: The port number associated with the router module

Exam Essentials

Remember what the router module accomplishes. The router module allows you to configure the switch to communicate between VLANs without having an external router connected.

Key Terms and Concepts

Router: A Network-layer mechanism, software or hardware, using one or more metrics to decide on the best path to use for transmission of network traffic. Sending packets between networks by routers is based on the information provided on Network layers.

Switch: In networking, a device responsible for multiple functions such as filtering, flooding, and sending frames. It works using the destination address of individual frames. Switches operate at the Data Link layer of the OSI model.

Sample Questions

1. What are the configurable parameters on a router module? (Choose all that apply.)

   A. Boot-up

   B. Reset

   C. Flow control

   D. Access

   Answer: A, B, C, D.

CHAPTER

20

Maintaining the Catalyst 1900 and Catalyst 2820 Switches

Cisco Exam Objectives Covered in This Chapter

▶ **Describe the POST and diagnostic messages on the Catalyst 1900 and Catalyst 2820 switches.** *(pages 414 – 417)*

▶ **Describe the cabling guidelines for the Catalyst 1900 and Catalyst 2820 switches.** *(pages 418 – 421)*

▶ **Use the statistics and reports to maintain the Catalyst 1900 and Catalyst 2820 switches.** *(pages 421 – 424)*

▶ **Describe the firmware upgrade procedures for the Catalyst 1900 and Catalyst 2820 switches.** *(pages 425 – 428)*

In this chapter, the different ways to maintain the Catalyst 1900 and 2820 switches will be described. Maintaining the Catalyst 1900 and 2820 switches involves diagnostic messages, cabling guidelines, gathering statistics and reports, and upgrading the firmware on the switches.

This is an important chapter to understand if you have 1900 or 2820 switches in a production environment or if you are gathering information for the CLSC exam.

▶ Describe the POST and diagnostic messages on the Catalyst 1900 and Catalyst 2820 switches.

In this first objective, you will begin to read about information on maintaining the Catalyst 1900 and 2820 switches. You will see the Power On Self Test (POST) messages, as well as diagnostic information.

This objective is important to understand when troubleshooting Catalyst 1900 and 2820 switches and when studying for your CLSC exam.

Critical Information

When you first power up the switch, the screen should scroll as the switch begins POST (Power On Self Test).

If your switch fails the POST with a fatal error, the switch will not work, and the console will not be available. Your only option is to send the switch to Cisco.

However, if the switch has a nonfatal error during the POST, the system LED will be amber, and a POST failure message will be displayed. The example message displayed below for a Catalyst 1900 switch shows that ports 1x to 8x failed the POST. (The 2820 output is exactly the same.)

```
Catalyst 1900 Management Console
Copyright (c) Cisco Systems, Inc.  1993-1997
All rights reserved.
Ethernet address:      00-C0-1F-3E-A4-21
PCA Number: 72-2249-03
PCA Serial Number: SAD01200021
Model Number: WS-C1924-EN
System Serial Number: FAA01200021
-------------------------------------------------
*** Power On Self Test (POST) failed ***
*** Failed Test(s): 1
*** Failed Port(s): 1 2 3 4 5 6 7 8
1 user(s) now active on Management Console.
Press any key to continue.
```

If the POST is successful, the Management Console Logon screen should appear as shown below:

```
Catalyst 2820 Management Console
Copyright (c) Cisco Systems, Inc.    1993-1998
All rights reserved.
Standard Edition Software
Ethernet address:        00-D0-1D-7D-D4-40
PCA Number: 99-9999-01
PCA Serial Number: ABC1234567
Model Number: WS-C2822-A
System Serial Number: ABC12345678
-----------------------------------------------
        User Interface Menu
          [M] Menus
          [I] IP Configuration
    Enter Selection:
```

If nothing has happened after a few moments, check the connections between the switch and the modem or the management console. If the connections are in order and the terminal is configured correctly according to the guidelines above, begin the troubleshooting sequence for the switch.

Exam Essentials

Remember when the POST runs. The Power On Self Test runs when the equipment is powered on. If it is successful, the operating system will run. If it is not successful because of a fatal error, the operating system will not continue to boot.

Remember what happens if a nonfatal error occurs. If the switch has a nonfatal error during the POST, the system LED will be amber, and a POST failure message will be displayed.

Key Terms and Concepts

POST: Power On Self Test is used to test the hardware of a switch when it is powered on.

Switch: In networking, a device responsible for multiple functions such as filtering, flooding, and sending frames. It works using the destination address of individual frames. Switches operate at the Data Link layer of the OSI model.

Sample Questions

1. What happens if a Catalyst 1900 or 2820 switch fails the POST with a fatal error?

   A. It continues to boot and gives you a warning.

   B. It immediately stops booting and gives you a warning.

   C. It continues to boot and does not give you a warning.

   D. It immediately stops booting, and the console does not work.

   Answer: D. If your switch fails the POST with a fatal error, the switch will not boot and the console will not be available. Your only option is to call Cisco.

2. What happens if a Catalyst 1900 or 2820 switch fails the POST with a nonfatal error?

   A. It continues to boot and gives you a warning.

   B. It immediately stops booting and gives you a warning.

   C. It continues to boot and does not give you a warning.

   D. It immediately stops booting, and the console does not work.

   Answer: A. If the switch has a nonfatal error during the POST, the system LED will be amber, and a POST failure message will be displayed.

Describe the cabling guidelines for the Catalyst 1900 and Catalyst 2820 switches.

In this objective, the different ways to maintain your Catalyst 1900 and 2820 switches will continue to be described. You will read about the cabling guidelines, as well as other important installation information.

This objective is important to understand when installing your Catalyst 1900 and 2820 switches and when gathering information for your CLSC exam.

Critical Information

The first thing to do in preparing for the installation of the switch is to review the placement of the switch. The placement of the switch must take into account several factors:

- Ensure that the cable lengths from the switch to other network equipment are within the guidelines established for Ethernet:

Ethernet Cabling Type	Maximum Number of Nodes per Segment	Maximum Distance per Segment
10Base2	30	185 m
10Base5	100	500 m
10BaseT	1024	100 m
10Base-FL	2	2000 m

- You must also consider the physical environment. Is the table/room/closet too hot? Too cold? What is the humidity? Is altitude a factor? Here are the environmental operating ranges of the Catalyst 1900 and 2820:

Operating temperature	23° to 113°F (–5° to 45°C)
Storage temperature	–13° to 158°F (–25° to 70°C)
Operating humidity	10% to 85% (noncondensing)
Operating altitude	Up to 9842 ft (3000 m)

- Ensure that there is ample clearance around the switch so that air may flow freely. Check to make sure that there will be nothing to block viewing of the front LEDs or hamper air from being pulled into the switch from the rear. The physical dimensions of each switch are shown below:

Catalyst 1900

Weight	7 lb (3.2 kg)
Dimensions (H × W × D)	1.73 × 17.5 × 8.25 in (4.4 × 44.5 × 21 cm)

Catalyst 2820

Weight (no modules)	13 lb (5.9 kg)
Dimensions (H × W × D)	3.5 × 17.5 × 12 in (8.9 × 44.5 × 30.5 cm)

- Check to make sure that there will be ample power for the switch. Here are the guidelines provided by Cisco:

AC input voltage	100 to 127/200 to 240 VAC (auto-ranging) 50 to 60 Hz
DC input voltage	+5 V @ 6 A, +12 V @ 1 A
Power consumption	50 W

- Finally, check to make sure that all cabling meets the Ethernet guidelines and is not placed directly next to any sources of electrical noise.

Exam Essentials

Remember the number of workstations permitted and the distance of a 10Base2 network.   In a 10Base2 network, you can have 30 workstations per segment with a maximum distance of 185 meters.

Remember the number of workstations permitted and the distance of a 10Base5 network.   In a 10Base5 network, you can have 100 workstations per segment with a maximum distance of 500 meters.

Remember the number of workstations permitted and the distance of a 10BaseT network.   In a 10BaseT network, you can have 1024 workstations per segment with a maximum distance of 100 meters.

Remember the number of workstations permitted and the distance of a 10Base-FL network.   In a 10Base-FL network, you can have two workstations per segment with a maximum distance of 2000 meters.

Key Terms and Concepts

10Base2:   10Mbps Ethernet on thinnet coax cable.

10Base5:   10Mbps Ethernet on thicknet coax cable.

10Base-FL: 10Mbps Ethernet on fiber-optic cable.

10BaseT: 10Mbps Ethernet on twisted-pair cable.

Sample Questions

1. What is the maximum distance of a 10BaseT segment?

   A. 50 meters

   B. 100 meters

   C. 185 meters

   D. 500 meters

   Answer: B.

2. What is the maximum distance of a 10Base2 segment?

   A. 50 meters

   B. 100 meters

   C. 185 meters

   D. 500 meters

   Answer: C.

Use the statistics and reports to maintain the Catalyst 1900 and Catalyst 2820 switches.

This objective will continue providing information on maintaining the Catalyst 1900 and 2820 switches. You will learn how to gather statistics and reports, which will help you when troubleshooting and baselining your Catalyst switched internetwork.

Critical Information

You can reach the general statistics and report information on the 1900/2820 switches by pressing U at the main menu.

```
Enter Selection: M
Enter password: ********
        Catalyst 1900 - Main Menu
    [C] Console Settings
    [S] System
    [N] Network Management
    [P] Port Configuration
    [A] Port Addressing
    [D] Port Statistics Detail
    [M] Monitoring
    [V] Virtual LAN
    [R] Multicast Registration
    [F] Firmware
    [I] RS-232 Interface
    [U] Usage Summaries
    [H] Help
    [K] Command Line
    [X] Exit Management Console
Enter Selection: U
```

By typing U at the Enter Selection prompt, you will get the following menu (Catalyst 1900 Usage Summaries):

Port Status Report: This will give you the status of all ports on the switch.

Port Addressing Report: This submenu will display the MAC addresses or the number of MAC addresses of a specific port.

Exception Statistics Report: This screen will show you the different errors received on a port. You can view the receive, transmit, and security violations.

Utilization Statistics Report: This screen will give you the cumulative frame count per port. It will keep track of unicast, multicast, and broadcast frames. The forward column contains the number of frames that were received by a port and then switched out an exit port.

Bandwidth Usage Report: This will give you the peak bandwidth across the switch's backplane during a particular time.

Exam Essentials

Remember what the Port Status Report provides. This will give you the status of all ports on the switch.

Remember what the Port Addressing Report provides. This submenu will display the MAC addresses or the number of MAC addresses of a specific port.

Remember what the Exception Statistics Report provides. This screen will show you the different errors received on a port. You can view the receive, transmit, and security violations.

Remember what the Utilization Statistics Report provides. This screen will give you the cumulative frame count per port. It will keep track of unicast, multicast, and broadcast frames. The forward column contains the number of frames that were received by a port and then switched out an exit port.

Remember what the Bandwidth Usage Report provides. This will give you the peak bandwidth across the switch's backplane during a particular time.

Key Terms and Concepts

Catalyst: Series of switches designed by Cisco.

Switch: In networking, a device responsible for multiple functions such as filtering, flooding, and sending frames. It works using the destination address of individual frames. Switches operate at the Data Link layer of the OSI model.

Sample Questions

1. What does the Port Status Report provide?

   A. Configuration of a port

   B. The MAC addresses or the number of MAC addresses of a specific port

   C. The different errors received on a port

   D. The status of all ports on the switch

   Answer: D.

2. What does the Port Addressing Report provide?

   A. Configuration of a port

   B. The MAC addresses or the number of MAC addresses of a specific port

   C. The different errors received on a port

   D. The status of all ports on the switch

   Answer: B.

3. What does the Exception Statistics Report provide?

   A. Configuration of a switch

   B. The MAC addresses or the number of MAC addresses of a specific port

   C. The different errors received on a port

   D. The status of all ports on the switch

   Answer: C.

Describe the firmware upgrade procedures for the Catalyst 1900 and Catalyst 2820 switches.

In this objective, you will learn how to upgrade the Catalyst 1900 and 2820 switches. To be able to upgrade the firmware, you first need to gather the appropriate file from Cisco. After you have the file, you need to copy it to your TFTP host. You can then use the TFTP host to upgrade the firmware on your Catalyst 1900 and 2820 switches.

This is an important objective to understand because you might have to upgrade or replace the file on a Catalyst 1900 or 2820 switch.

Critical Information

To upgrade Catalyst firmware, copy the new file into a temporary directory or TFTP default directory. When you upgrade, the switch will validate the new file before copying it to flash memory and resetting itself. Be sure you know the filename and the IP address of your TFTP host before proceeding.

To upgrade or replace the switch firmware, choose the [F] option from the console main menu. This will display the firmware version currently in use and the size of the switch flash memory. (The same options work for both the 1900 and 2820 switches.)

```
Catalyst 2820 - Firmware Configuration
----------------System Information------------
FLASH:  1024K bytes
V6.00
Upgrade status:
No upgrade currently in progress.
-------------------Settings-----------------
[S] Server:  IP address of TFTP server        0.0.0.0
[F] Filename for firmware upgrades
[A] Accept upgrade transfer from other hosts    Enabled
-------------------Actions------------------
[U] System XMODEM upgrade     [D] Download test subsystem (XMODEM)
[T] System TFTP upgrade       [X] Exit to Main Menu
Enter Selection:
```

Here is an explanation of the options:

[S] Server: IP address of TFTP server, [F] Filename for firmware upgrades, [T] System TFTP upgrade: Used together, these upgrade the firmware from a TFTP server. You need to first enter the name of the TFTP server and then the name of the file containing the upgrade.

[A] Accept upgrade transfer from other hosts: Use this option to enable [E] or disable [D] the switch from accepting an upgrade of the firmware from another host on the network.

[U] System XMODEM upgrade: Allows an upgrade via the XMODEM protocol through the console port on the switch.

[D] Download test subsystem (XMODEM): Used by Cisco personnel only.

[X] Exit to Main Menu: Displays the console main menu.

WARNING Do not interrupt the download by turning off the switch—it could possibly corrupt the firmware. It is important to remember that the switch might not respond for several minutes during the download.

Exam Essentials

Remember what is needed to upgrade the firmware on a Catalyst 1900 and 2820 switch. You need to add the TFTP server IP address [S], and the filename for the firmware upgrades [F] and for the system TFTP upgrade [T].

Key Terms and Concepts

Firmware: Memory that is not lost when the switch is rebooted and that holds the POST and bootstrap programs.

Switch: In networking, a device responsible for multiple functions such as filtering, flooding, and sending frames. It works using the destination address of individual frames. Switches operate at the Data Link layer of the OSI model.

Sample Questions

1. Which menu options must you configure to upgrade the firmware from a TFTP server? (Choose all that apply.)

    A. [S]

    B. [F]

    C. [A]

    D. [T]

    Answer: A, B, D.

2. Which menu option do you choose from the main menu to upgrade the switch firmware?

   A. [S]

   B. [F]

   C. [A]

   D. [T]

   Answer: B. To upgrade or replace the switch firmware, choose the [F] option from the console main menu.

CHAPTER

21

Troubleshooting the Catalyst
3000 Series Switches

Cisco Exam Objectives Covered in This Chapter

▶ **Troubleshoot the Catalyst 3000 series switch subsystems.**
(pages 430 – 435)

▶ **Troubleshoot network interfaces and connections.**
(pages 435 – 439)

▶ **Use the switch LEDs to isolate problems.** *(pages 439 – 442)*

▶ **Isolate network segment problems.** *(pages 443 – 447)*

In this chapter, troubleshooting the Catalyst 3000 series of switches will be examined. The 3000 series subsystem will be discussed so that you have a fundamental understanding of how these switches work, which will help you find a problem when a troubleshooting opportunity presents itself.

You will also learn how the 3000 series switch can use the Ethernet connections and how to isolate problems with the switch using LEDs of modules. The chapter will finish with a review of how VLANs can create smaller broadcast domains by using routers.

This is an important chapter to understand when gathering information for your CLSC exam, as well as when troubleshooting a switched internetwork.

Troubleshoot the Catalyst 3000 series switch subsystems.

This section discusses the architecture of the Catalyst 3000 switches, describing the AXIS bus, the LAN Module ASIC (LMA), and the Proprietary Fat Pipe ASIC (PFPA).

By understanding the architecture of the 3000 series switch, you will be able to troubleshoot it easier. This information is also needed when studying and gathering information for the CLSC exam.

Critical Information

The 3000 switch uses the AXIS bus to facilitate frame switching. If you have a node at 10Mbps that has a destination node running at 10Mbps, the switch will use the LAN Module ASIC (LMA) to perform the port switching. Any ports running above 10Mbps will use the Proprietary Fat Pipe ASIC (PFPA). Figure 21.1 shows the Catalyst 3000 architecture.

F I G U R E 21.1: Catalyst 3000 architecture

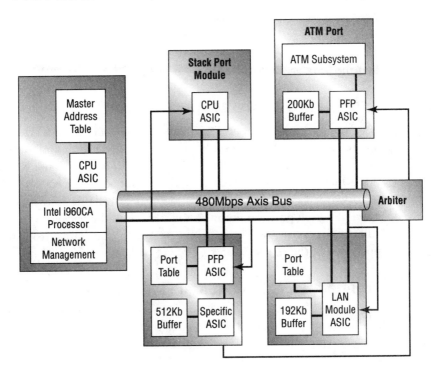

Notice in Figure 21.1 how all switching ASICs connect to the AXIS bus, and each ASIC has its own buffer to prevent congestion. 10Mbps ports have 192KB buffers, and 100Mbps ports have 512KB buffers.

AXIS Bus

The AXIS bus uses a synchronous time-division multiplexed (TDM) bus for 10Mbps-to-10Mbps traffic and an asynchronous TDM bus for all others. The basic purpose of the AXIS bus is to switch packets between heterogeneous LMAs and PFPAs. The central bus arbiter allocates bandwidth for the AXIS in 52 time slots rated at 10Mbps. The AXIS bus supports simultaneous packet transfers of 10 to 170Mbps. This helps prevent packet overflow by supporting over-subscription, or congestion of bandwidth.

ASIC

An Application Specific Integrated Circuit (ASIC) is a chip that is built around a general core and is usually available as a set of different cores brought together to work on the same chip. The different cores that the Catalyst 3000 switch uses are LMA, PFPA, and CPA.

LAN Module ASIC (LMA)

A switch-port LAN Module ASIC will receive a packet from a LAN and request access to the destination port. The LMA at this point will put the packet onto the AXIS bus if the destination port is not busy. If it is busy, the packet is buffered in the output port. The packet will be forwarded as soon as the destination port is available. However, if the destination port is unknown, it will forward the packet to the CPU, which in turn will forward the packet as a broadcast from all ports except the receiving port.

Proprietary Fat Pipe ASIC (PFPA)

The Fat Pipe is used to connect different types of network topologies to the AXIS bus, which allows switching. Any time an expansion module is added to the 3000 switch, the module will implement a PFPA. The PFPA is used in the following modules:

StackPort: Uses a 280Mbps interface to the Matrix.

100BaseX: PFPA is the interface between the standard ASIC and AXIS bus.

ATM: PFPA is the interface between the bus and SAR.

ISL: Allows communication to the AXIS bus from ASIC ISL.

CPU ASIC (CPA)

The 3000 switch uses an Intel i960SA 16.25MHz processor that has four main components:

CPA: The CPU ASIC gives the CPU access to address filtering, aging, and learning.

Main memory: Used to store the system code.

Network memory: This is where the master address is stored. When a packet is received with an unknown destination, the packet will be sent to the network memory, which tells the CPU to begin address learning.

i960SA: The CPU processor.

Exam Essentials

Remember what the LMA does. The LAN Module ASIC will receive a packet from a LAN and request access to the destination port.

Remember the different components used with the CPA. The CPU ASIC uses an Intel i960SA 16.25MHz processor that has four main components:

CPA: The CPU ASIC gives the CPU access to address filtering, aging, and learning.

Main memory: Used to store the system code.

Network memory: This is where the master address is stored. When a packet is received with an unknown destination, the packet will be sent to the network memory, which tells the CPU to begin address learning.

i960SA: The CPU processor.

Key Terms and Concepts

ASIC: An Application Specific Integrated Circuit (ASIC) is a chip that is built around a general core and is usually available as a set of different cores brought together to work on the same chip.

AXIS: The AXIS bus uses a synchronous time-division multiplexed (TDM) bus for 10Mbps-to-10Mbps traffic and an asynchronous TDM bus for all others.

Sample Questions

1. What is an ASIC chip?

   A. A chip that uses a TDM for transmission

   B. A chip that is used to translate from asynchronous to synchronous clocking

   C. A chip that is built around different cores and is usually available as a set of general cores brought together to work on the same chip

   D. A chip that is built around a general core and is usually available as a set of different cores brought together to work on the same chip

   Answer: D.

2. The AXIS uses what type of clocking for 10Mbps-to-10Mbps transmission?

   A. LMA

   B. Sync

   C. ASIC

   D. Async

   Answer: B.

Troubleshoot network interfaces and connections.

One drawback of Ethernet is that it cannot support more than one conversation at a time. The Catalyst 3000 fixes this problem by providing support for multiple simultaneous, full-duplex conversations, which improves throughput. The beauty of the Catalyst 3000 is that it creates multiple data paths that combine fast-packet switching technology with FastEthernet. Switched connections between segments last only as long as necessary for the packet to be processed, so new connections between different segments are made as needed for the next packet.

This objective is important because it will give you information on how the 3000 series works with interfaces, and with connections into a switched internetwork.

Critical Information

Throughput is increased in direct proportion to the number of LAN segments that are connected through the switch, just as more lanes can support a proportional increase of cars on the road.

The Catalyst 3000 will send broadcast and multicast packets on all Catalyst 3000 segments at the same time except for on the port of entry. For example, Figure 21.2 shows Host 1 sending a packet to Host 2. Because it isn't necessary to send packets to all other ports, the Catalyst 3000 connects only lines 1 and 2. Another switching circuit can then connect Host 3 and Host 4 at the same time, resulting in simultaneous conversations.

FIGURE 21.2: Multiple conversations through a Catalyst 3000 switch

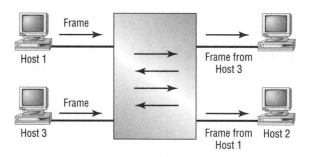

Low Latency

Network devices that use the cut-through switching method enable another great Catalyst 3000 feature—minimized latency—by initiating packet transmission immediately after looking at the first 6 bytes of the packet's destination address. (Remember that latency is the time required to forward a packet from one Ethernet segment to another.) Packets arrive at the output port only 40 microseconds after entering the input port, and if a packet needs to be switched to another LAN segment, its data will begin flowing out the destination port before the entire packet has been received.

Devices that use the store-and-forward method will cause much higher latency, because the entire packet must be received before it can be forwarded.

Address Management

At power-up, the Catalyst 3000 system address table does not hold any information—it's a blank sheet, you might say. As the switch begins processing packets, it records both the source and destination addresses in its table. If a Catalyst 3000 receives a packet with an unknown source or destination address, it learns the new source address by putting its location into memory before it forwards the packet. Once the Catalyst 3000 learns the new source address, it forwards the packet to its destination address. If the destination address is not known, the packet will be sent to all of the Catalyst 3000 output ports. After the response packet comes back, its location is added to the address table.

The system address table holds up to 10,000 entries with 8MB of DRAM. The port address tables maintain up to 1700 active Ethernet addresses.

Address Filtering

The Catalyst 3000 supports MAC-layer filters for source or destination addresses to be configured on a per-port basis. This feature allows you to manage the network and maintain security by designating client access to certain resources, restricting access to servers or MAC addresses, or permitting an end user to communicate with only one server.

On-Board Buffering

The Catalyst 3000 will store a packet in one of its internal buffers if the destination port is receiving a packet from another Catalyst 3000 port or if the output segment is busy. This feature helps control network throughput when the system is near its peak load and more than one packet is sent to the same port at the same time. Each buffer is capable of holding up to 768 packets, 384 in each direction (incoming and outgoing).

Full-Duplex Communication

Catalyst 3000 allows you to select half-duplex or full-duplex communication. You can double the throughput capacity on the segment by using full-duplex communication because packets flow in both directions at the same time. This flexibility is a huge advantage.

Full-duplex communication also eliminates the poor performance that results from packet collisions. Packets are prevented from colliding because each traverses its own designated path.

Exam Essentials

Remember the number of entries that can be stored in the system address table. The system address table holds up to 10,000 entries with 8MB of DRAM.

Remember the number of entries that the port address table maintains. The port address tables maintain up to 1700 active Ethernet addresses.

Key Terms and Concepts

ISL: Inter-Switch Link can be used to trunk ports on a Catalyst switch. You want to trunk ports when you need a host in more than one VLAN at the same time—for example, in a server.

Switch: In networking, a device responsible for multiple functions such as filtering, flooding, and sending frames. It works using the destination address of individual frames.

Virtual LAN: A group of devices on one or more logically segmented LANs (configured by use of management software), enabling devices to communicate as if attached to the same physical medium when they are actually located on numerous different LAN segments.

Sample Questions

1. What is the number of entries that can be stored in the system address table by default?

   A. 1000

   B. 5000

   C. 10,000

   D. 25,000

   Answer: C.

2. How many entries can the port address table maintain?

   A. 700

   B. 900

   C. 1500

   D. 1700

   Answer: D.

Use the switch LEDs to isolate problems.

In this objective, the different modules that you need to know when troubleshooting the Cisco 3000 switch will be examined. The different LEDs on some of the most important modules will be described.

By understanding the different LEDs on the 3000 series switch, you can more easily isolate problems.

Critical Information

This section will describe the switch LEDs of the following modules, to help isolate problems with the 3000 switch modules:

- 100VG module
- WS-X3006 ATM module
- 10Base2 module

100VG Module

When you connect the 3000 series switch to power, it will run a POST test, and all LEDs will turn on. The self-test diagnostics for the Catalyst switch and 100VG module require approximately 5 minutes. The Catalyst switch DIAG LED and all 100VG module LEDs are on during this test. As soon as the diagnostics are finished, all LEDs are off.

If the 100VG module does not work, check the following:

- All cabling and connections to see if the connections to the transceiver are broken or faulty
- Proper cable polarity
- That the connected device is not transmitting the signal
- That the connection is to a 100VG device

WS-X3006 ATM Module

When the link is established on the WS-X3006 ATM module, the LINK LED will be on and should be green. If the LED is not on, or if the LED is an amber color, run through the following list:

1. Check the cable connections.

2. Try swapping the TX/RX fiber connectors at one end.

3. Verify that you are using the correct type of cable.

4. Test whether the cable is bad by trying a different one.

5. Check the power-up diagnostics to see if any problems were reported.

If the above tests do not correct the problem, contact Cisco support.

10Base2 Module

When the link is established on the 10Base2 module, the LINK LED is on. If the LED is not on, try the following tests:

1. Check the cable connections.

2. Try swapping the TX/RX fiber connectors at one end.

3. Verify that you are using the correct type of cable.

4. Test whether the cable is bad by trying a different one.

5. Check the power-up diagnostics to see if any problems were reported.

If the above tests do not correct the problem, contact Cisco support.

Exam Essentials

Remember that the 100VG module does not work with Ethernet.   The 100VG module is a polling media access and is not compatible with Ethernet.

Remember that the LEDs are off after POST on the 100VG module.   After the POST test finishes and everything is fine, the LEDs will be off.

Key Terms and Concepts

ISL: Inter-Switch Link can be used to trunk ports on a Catalyst switch. You want to trunk ports when you need a host in more than one VLAN at the same time—for example, in a server.

LED: A light-emitting diode is an electronic component that will become illuminated when a certain voltage is applied.

Switch: In networking, a device responsible for multiple functions such as filtering, flooding, and sending frames. It works using the destination address of individual frames.

Sample Questions

1. When the link is established on the 10Base2 module and the LED is not on, what should you do?

    A. Send the switch to Cisco.

    B. Open the switch and check the fuses.

    C. Call Cisco.

    D. Run through the suggested steps of troubleshooting.

    Answer: D.

2. The 100VG module LEDs appear to be OK, but the connection is not working. What could the problem be?

    A. The mainframe is down.

    B. The users are not logging in correctly.

    C. The connection is to an Ethernet LAN card.

    D. The connection is to a 100VG hub.

    Answer: C.

Isolate network segment problems.

To place Cisco Catalyst switches in a network for optimal performance and to isolate network segment problems, you should create virtual LANs. A virtual local area network (VLAN) is a logical grouping of network users and resources connected to administratively defined ports on a switch.

By creating VLANs, you are able to create smaller broadcast domains within a switch by assigning different ports in the switch to different subnetworks. A VLAN is treated like its own subnet or broadcast domain. This means that broadcast frames are switched only between ports in the same VLAN.

This is an important objective to understand, because it will give you an understanding of broadcast domains and how you can create broadcast domains within a switched internetwork. How routers are used in this environment will also be discussed.

Critical Information

Using virtual LANs, you're no longer confined to physical locations. VLANs can be organized by location, function, department, or even the application or protocol used, regardless of where the resources or users are located.

Switches read only frames for filtering; they do not look at the Network layer protocol. This can cause a switch to forward all broadcasts. However, by creating VLANs, you are essentially creating broadcast domains. Broadcasts sent out from a node in one VLAN will not be forwarded to ports configured in a different VLAN. By assigning switch ports or users to VLAN groups on a switch or group of connected switches (called a *switch fabric*), you have the flexibility to add only the users you want in the broadcast domain regardless of their physical location. This can stop broadcast storms caused by a faulty network interface card (NIC) or keep an application from propagating throughout the entire internetwork.

When a VLAN gets too big, you can create more VLANs to keep the broadcasts from consuming too much bandwidth. The fewer users in a VLAN, the fewer are affected by broadcasts.

To understand how a VLAN looks to a switch, it's helpful to begin by first looking at a traditional collapsed backbone. Figure 21.3 shows a collapsed backbone created by connecting physical LANs to a router.

F I G U R E 21.3: Physical LANs connected to a router

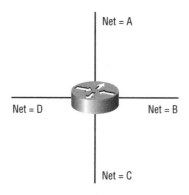

Each network is attached to the router, and each network has its own logical network number. Each node attached to a particular physical network must match that network number to be able to communicate on the internetwork. Now let's look at what a switch accomplishes. Figure 21.4 shows how switches remove the physical boundary.

Switches create greater flexibility and scalability than routers can by themselves. You can group users into communities of interest, which are known as VLAN organizations.

F I G U R E 21.4:   Switches remove the physical boundary.

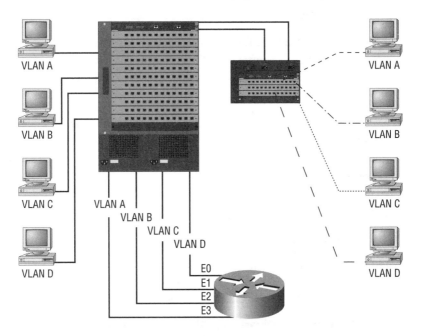

With switches, you don't need routers anymore, right? Wrong. In Figure 21.4, notice that there are four VLANs or broadcast domains. The nodes within each VLAN can communicate with each other, but not with any other VLAN or node in another VLAN. When configured in a VLAN, the nodes think they are actually in a collapsed backbone, as in Figure 21.3. What do these hosts in Figure 21.3 need to do to communicate to a node or host on a different network? They need to go through the router just as when they are configured for VLAN communication, as shown in Figure 21.4. Communication between VLANs, just as in physical networks, must go through the router.

Exam Essentials

Remember that routers are still used in a switched internetwork. Routers break up the broadcast domains and are still used in a switched environment. However, router switch modules (RSMs) can be used in their place.

Understand how broadcast domains are created with switches. Administrators assigning switch ports into a particular VLAN create broadcast domains. A router is used to connect the broadcast domains together.

Key Terms and Concepts

ISL: Inter-Switch Link can be used to trunk ports on a Catalyst switch. You want to trunk ports when you need a host in more than one VLAN at the same time—for example, in a server.

Switch: In networking, a device responsible for multiple functions such as filtering, flooding, and sending frames. It works using the destination addresses of individual frames.

Trunk: Allows a port on a switch to be in one or more VLANs simultaneously. Used for multiple-link connections and allows servers to be in multiple broadcast domains.

Virtual LAN: A group of devices on one or more logically segmented LANs (configured by use of management software), enabling devices to communicate as if attached to the same physical medium when they are actually located on numerous different LAN segments.

Sample Questions

1. To process frames at layer 3, the Catalyst system—including external components—must include what? (Choose all that apply.)

   A. A Supervisor III engine.

   B. Redundant Supervisor engines.

   C. An RSM module.

   D. A connection from each VLAN to a router, via either ISL/802.1q or direct connections to a port in each VLAN.

   E. It is not possible to process layer 3 in the Catalyst system.

   Answer: C, D. Routers break up broadcast domains. Switches work at layer 2 and need a router or RSM to create VLANs.

2. Switching is what kind of process?

   A. Layer 1

   B. Layer 2

   C. Layer 3

   D. Layer 4

   Answer: B. Even though you have heard of layer 3 switches, the CLSC exam is interested only in layer 2 switching.

Index

Note to the Reader: Throughout this index **boldfaced** page numbers indicate primary discussions of a topic. *Italicized* page numbers indicate illustrations.

Boost Your Career with Certification

2nd Edition
Completely revised
and updated for
1999–2000!

Detailed information on all the key computer and network certification programs, including:

- Computer hardware
- Operating systems
- Software
- Networking hardware
- Network operating systems
- Internet
- Instructor and trainer certifications

ISBN: 0-7821-2545-X
640pp • 5 $^{7}/_{8}$ x 8 $^{1}/_{4}$ • Softcover
$19.99

**Learn why to get certified,
when to get certified,
and how to get certified.**

NETWORK®
PRESS
SYBEX®

www.sybex.com

MAKE SURE YOU'RE READY

FOR CISCO® CERTIFICATION WITH EXAM NOTES™ FROM

NETWORK PRESS®

CCNA Exam Notes: Cisco Certified Network Associate	CCNP Exam Notes: Advanced Cisco Routing Configuration	CCNP Exam Notes: Cisco Internetwork Troubleshooting	CCNP Exam Notes: Cisco LAN Switching Configuration
ISBN: 0-7821-2535-2	ISBN: 0-7821-2540-9	ISBN: 0-7821-2541-7	ISBN: 0-7821-2542-
$19.99 U.S.	$19.99 U.S.	$19.99 U.S.	$19.99 U.S.

THE MOST EFFECTIVE REVIEW GUIDES AVAILABLE!

▲ Innovative *Exam Notes* approach reinforces knowledge of key points and identifies your weak spots

▲ Objective-by-objective coverage of the Cisco exams

▲ Essential information arranged for quick learning and review

▲ Exam tips and advice from expert trainers

▲ Perfect complement to Network Press Study Guides

www.sybex.com

SECURE YOUR NETWORK

Network Press® provides the information you need to

- Assess the security of your network
- Devise a workable security plan
- Implement effective security measures

Mastering Network Security
0-7821-2343-0 · US $59.99
704 pages · Hardcover

NT 4 Network Security
0-7821-2425-9 · US $49.99
960 pages · Hardcover

Firewalls 24seven
0-7821-2529-8 · US $34.99
496 pages · Softcover

www.sybex.com

www.24sevenbooks.com

CISCO® STUDY GUIDES

FROM NETWORK PRESS®

- · Prepare for Cisco certification with the experts
- · Full coverage of each exam objective
- · Hands-on labs and hundreds of sample questions

ISBN 0-7821-2381-3
768 pp; 7¹/₂" x 9"; $49.99
Hardcover

ISBN 0-7821-2403-8
832 pp; 7¹/₂" x 9"; $49.99
Hardcover

ISBN 0-7821-2571-9
704 pp; 7¹/₂" x 9"; $49.99
Hardcover

**CCDA™: Cisco® Certified Design
Associate Study Guide**
ISBN: 0-7821-2534-4; 800 pp; 7½" x 9"
$49.99; Hardcover; CD

**CCNP™: Cisco® Internetwork
Troubleshooting Study Guide**
ISBN 0-7821-2536-0; 704 pp; 7½ x 9
$49.99; Hardcover; CD

SYBEX®

www.sybex.com